Seven Games in '62

Seven Games in '62

*The Yankees and Giants Square
Off in a Classic World Series*

John Iamarino

McFarland & Company, Inc., Publishers
Jefferson, North Carolina

ISBN (print) 978-1-4766-8751-3
ISBN (ebook) 978-1-4766-4510-0

LIBRARY OF CONGRESS AND BRITISH LIBRARY
CATALOGUING DATA ARE AVAILABLE

Library of Congress Control Number 2021045559

© 2021 John Iamarino. All rights reserved

No part of this book may be reproduced or transmitted in any form or by any means, electronic or mechanical, including photocopying or recording, or by any information storage and retrieval system, without permission in writing from the publisher.

On the cover: Matty Alou balances on the low Yankee Stadium right field wall watching Tom Tresh's three-run homer in the eighth inning of Game Five. The home run, the only one the Yankees hit at the Stadium in the Series, broke a 2–2 tie and led to a 5–2 New York victory. (National Baseball Hall of Fame and Museum, Cooperstown, N.Y.)

Printed in the United States of America

*McFarland & Company, Inc., Publishers
Box 611, Jefferson, North Carolina 28640
www.mcfarlandpub.com*

To Mary Ann and P.J.,
my championship duo

Table of Contents

Preface … 1
Introduction: Terry's Choice … 3
One. "Ain't It Always So?" … 7
Two. New Locale, Same Rivalry … 20
Three. The Playoff: "This Was More Thrilling!" … 35
Four. Game One: Boyer's Redemption … 49
Five. Game Two: "I Was So Scared" … 56
Six. Game Three: Boos to Cheers for Maris … 66
Seven. Game Four: Haller & Hiller … 75
Eight. Game Five: Dad Couldn't Stop Crying … 87
Nine. The World Series on Hiatus … 103
Ten. Game Six: Return of the Baby Bull … 114
Eleven. Game Seven: High Drama at Candlestick … 126
Twelve. Game Seven: The Aftermath … 139
Thirteen. An Underrated Classic … 146
Fourteen. Today's Paid Attendance—413 … 153
Fifteen. Good, But Not Good Enough … 160
Sixteen. A Yankees and Giants Who's Who … 169

Chapter Notes … 177
Bibliography … 191
Index … 195

Preface

Nineteen sixty-two is the year I became a true baseball fan. I turned seven years old that June and immersed myself in everything I could about the game. Every Friday, when we went grocery shopping as a family, I would take the twenty-five cents my parents gave me as a weekly allowance and buy five packs of Topps baseball cards. Each pack cost a nickel and contained five cards and the ubiquitous flat rectangle stick of pink bubble gum. When we'd get home, I'd unwrap the packs and see what players I'd added to my collection, always hoping there would be as few duplicates as possible.

I'd separate the player cards by team. Once I had at least nine per team (no designated hitter back then), I'd play baseball with them using dice rolls to determine results of each at-bat. With some advice on mathematical probabilities from my father, I'd made up my own game using a pair of dice. Two was a home run, three a double, five a strikeout, seven a groundout (or double play if there was a runner on first), etc. Not caring about preserving the condition of the cards in the days before collectors looked at profit sheets, I'd take a pencil and record the hits, home runs and runs batted in totals for each player on the corners of the back of the card. For the pitchers, I'd simply keep wins and losses.

I also began watching televised ballgames on the two independent stations in the metropolitan New York area. WOR (Channel 9) carried the new, expansion Mets and WPIX (channel 11) televised the Yankees. The bulk of the broadcasts consisted of weekend games, usually Friday night, Saturday afternoon and Sunday afternoon, with the latter often being a doubleheader.

Not every game was televised, so having access to a radio became important. My parents bought me a small black and white transistor radio capable of picking up only AM stations. Now I could hear the Yankees on WCBS-880 or the Mets on WABC-770. I would sometimes listen surreptitiously at night under the covers, barely able to hear the announcer, after I'd been sent to bed relatively early. After all, I had to go to school most days.

I also spent a great deal of free time bouncing a thick red rubber ball, a "Spaldeen" as New York kids called it, off the steps of the front porch or against the shingles on the side of our house. If there were other kids available, then a version of two-on-two or three-on-three baseball in the street was in order. On summer evenings or weekends, my father would hit me an endless string of ground balls and pop flies.

The most dramatic occurrence of that 1962 major league baseball season, the first one I truly followed start to finish, was the World Series between the Yankees and the San Francisco Giants. It lasted the full seven games, with a fitting climactic ending. As the years passed, I never saw what I felt was a worthy review or analysis of that championship, the first between combatants representing both coasts. The retelling of the Series would make an interesting tale, in my opinion. So, with the 60th anniversary rapidly approaching, I decided to wade in and try my hand at bringing the history alive.

In doing the research, I leaned on a number of extensive, reliable sources.

How did baseball researchers ever conduct their business without Sean Forman's amazing interactive website www.baseball-reference.com? In addition to every statistic one can imagine for every player, the game box scores and recaps provide wonderful detail. Want to know where Tom Tresh's three-run homer landed in the fifth game of the 1962 Series? The recap tells you it was hit to right field. Curious as to Billy Pierce's earned run average before and after he shut out the Dodgers in the first game of the National League playoff? It's there if you know where to look (3.72 lowered to 3.51).

The Internet makes finding contemporary articles, columns and commentary easy. Archives hosting such periodicals as *The Sporting News* and *Baseball Digest* are wondrous sources of information and detail. The biography project of the Society for American Baseball Research (SABR)—of which I am a member—provides well-written, painstakingly-documented bios of thousands of major leaguers. All were key ingredients in putting this work together.

It was also a rewarding experience to be able to utilize more than fifty different hardcover books, paperbacks, ebooks and magazines from my personal library of more than five hundred volumes, the majority of which deal with baseball.

My goal here is to provide a lasting record of a tense, exciting World Series played in another era. Young readers may find playing strategies and managers' decisions mind-boggling by today's standards. But the essence of any championship still comes down to two teams battling each other. And the 1962 World Series certainly had that.

Introduction: Terry's Choice

"Do you want to pitch to this guy or walk him?"[1]

Even before New York Yankee manager Ralph Houk walked to the mound and posed that question, pitcher Ralph Terry had begun a set of rapid calculations in his head. There were two men out. Two men on base, both in scoring position. First base was open. A dangerous power hitter stood at the plate. An equally dangerous hitter was swinging a bat on deck. Terry and the Yankees were clinging to a 1–0 lead. A hit would almost certainly score both runners and deliver a championship to the San Francisco Giants.

The string had been pulled about as taut as it could for baseball's 1962 World Series. It was the bottom of the ninth inning of Game Seven with the Yankees and Giants tied at three games apiece. The 43,948 spectators packed into Candlestick Park roared with anticipation as the conference on the mound continued with Houk, Terry and catcher Elston Howard.

Before asking Terry about his options, Houk had tried to reduce the tension for his pitcher. "I really don't know what the hell I'm doing out here, but I thought I better come here and talk to you anyway," he said.[2] Both Houk and Terry grinned at the slight levity, but Howard remained focused on the situation facing them.

"How do you feel?" he asked Terry. "How's your control?"[3]

Terry knew what his catcher was getting at. If he intentionally walked the batter—slugging outfielder Willie McCovey—he'd have to face one of the Giants' best hitters, first baseman Orlando Cepeda, with the bases loaded and no margin of error should he lose the strike zone. A walk would tie the game and put the winning run on third base.

Thus far, Terry's control and command of his pitches had been impeccable. "I warmed up, I had my good stuff and I knew it right away," Terry would later recall. "My slider and all my pitches were working good."[4] He hadn't given up a single base on balls. He'd gone to a three-ball count on just one San Francisco hitter. He'd only thrown 96 pitches to reach this point, one out away from victory.[5]

As Terry processed his options when Houk approached the mound, his thoughts inevitably drifted back two years to the final inning of another Game Seven. Terry had been entrusted with the task of pitching the bottom of the ninth against the Pittsburgh Pirates in the 1960 World Series at Forbes Field. The Yankees had just tied the game, 9–9, with a pair of runs in the top of the ninth, the second coming only after a bit of daring baserunning by Mickey Mantle. Both teams had already seen multi-run leads disappear.

Terry's first pitch to the leadoff hitter in the ninth, Pirate second baseman Bill Mazeroski, was a high fastball for ball one. Noted more for his defensive skills than for his bat, Mazeroski nevertheless had decent power. He'd hit eleven home runs during the season and had nineteen two years earlier. He liked pitches up in the zone. The location of Terry's first offering worried Yankee catcher Johnny Blanchard. After calling for time, he walked to the mound and told the right-hander, "Come on, get it down."[6]

With Blanchard setting his glove for a lower target, Terry delivered a slider that wound up higher than he wanted and without enough break to fool the hitter. Mazeroski swung and powered a fly ball that carried over the wall to the left of the 406-foot sign. It was the first time a World Series ended on a home run and gave Pittsburgh its first championship in thirty-five years. It was arguably one of the two most celebrated home runs in baseball history, right up there with Bobby Thomson's pennant-winning blast off Brooklyn's Ralph Branca in the third game of the 1951 National League playoff.

Now, as he listened to his manager and catcher in the bedlam of Candlestick Park, Terry wondered if his fate would once again be to serve as the foil for another late-inning hero. Would it be, as expressed in a *bon mot* widely attributed (erroneously) to his teammate Yogi Berra, "déjà vu all over again"?[7]

The Series had already been a remarkable competition. It was the first coast-to-coast World Series and featured two teams that as recently as five years ago played in stadiums located roughly one mile apart. Both ballclubs were led by superstar center fielders, neither of whom had been a particularly key contributor in the Series. Dramatic home runs by unlikely sources had resulted in critical victories for both sides. And now it was coming down to the final batter. Terry had to pick his poison and make a choice.

"This place is a madhouse right now!" said George Kell, the former major league infielder now handling the play-by-play duties on the national network radio broadcast for NBC.[8] A memorable climax seemed to be at hand.

Yet, as the years have rushed forward, heaping layer upon layer of sports memories on top, history has not truly appreciated the drama reflected in the seven games played in October of 1962 or Ralph Terry's moment of truth. When considered at all, the '62 Series is normally just a footnote in discussions about the Yankee dynasty of the 1950s and '60s.

Why?

In hindsight, it appears several factors either distracted the attention of casual American sports fans during the Series or served to quickly move it out of the nation's consciousness after it was over. There was a certain tedium in seeing the same team for the thirteenth time in the past sixteen championships. A less glamorous National League opponent than anticipated. Multiple interest-sapping postponements due to uncharacteristically bad weather. Newspaper headlines and television reports trumpeting serious civil rights disturbances. Another achievement by the burgeoning NASA program in the race for domination in outer space. And, ultimately, a national security crisis that would threaten world peace and demand Americans' focus.

In today's world of instant communication, an unprecedented volume of blogs, talk radio and a Twitter-savvy public, the 1962 World Series would be a sports fan's delight. If they occurred today, the games and the managers' decisions would feed social media platforms for an army of second-guessers.

But on October 16, 1962, Ralph Terry was only concerned with how history might treat him. He had an important choice to make. He wasn't aware of it, but he was the first pitcher in thirty-six years to throw a "golden pitch," defined by baseball researchers as one that, depending upon the outcome, could result in a World Series championship for *either* team.[9]

Finally, Terry told Houk and Howard that he did not want to issue an intentional walk and face Cepeda with the bases loaded. He'd pitch to McCovey.

ONE

"Ain't It Always So?"

As spring training camps opened in March, the 1962 baseball season featured a new look.

For the first time, both the American and National Leagues contained ten teams. The '62 NL expansion, coming one year after the AL added franchises in Washington and Los Angeles, would put major league baseball in the state of Texas with the Houston Colt 45s. And it would return the National League to New York after the big city had gone four seasons without a team since the Brooklyn Dodgers and New York Giants both departed. The new franchise would be known as the Metropolitans, or, more commonly, the Mets. A 162-game schedule—a major league staple to this day—would be utilized for the first time by both leagues.

But in the American League, one thing remained constant. The New York Yankees were considered the clear-cut favorite to win the pennant. There was a certain resignation to this among their opponents and the media. Rooting for the Yankees, comedian Joe E. Lewis had famously observed in the late 1950s, "was like rooting for U.S. Steel."[1] But even those who desperately hated the Yankees or just wanted to see a different American League representative in the World Series had a difficult time making a case for it.

The Yankees had captured eleven of the previous thirteen American League pennants. They won eight World Series during that span. The run had begun with stars like Joe DiMaggio, Phil Rizzuto and Allie Reynolds and continued through Mickey Mantle, Yogi Berra and Whitey Ford. The New York franchise had appeared in 63 percent of all World Series played between 1921 and 1961. No other ballclub came close to this sort of domination.

And there didn't appear to be any end in sight. In the early 1960s, a major league draft of high school and college players did not exist. Team scouts could sign as many prospects as they chose in a random fashion, limited only by the amount of bonus money they might offer. A prosperous ballclub like the Yankees could easily outbid hand-to-mouth clubs such as the Kansas City Athletics or Washington Senators for prime talent. Stockpiling young prospects also allowed the Yankees to make late-season trades to plug holes in their roster. The Yanks' acquisition of Roger Maris was a good example.

Maris had shown promise in his first three seasons in Cleveland and Kansas City, averaging almost twenty home runs per year and becoming a solid outfielder with a strong, accurate arm. The Yankees liked his personal maturity and loved his left-handed power stroke that seemed a perfect match for the short right field porch in Yankee Stadium. In December of 1959, Kansas City agreed to trade Maris and two throw-in players, Joe DeMaestri and Kent Hadley, to New York for a four-player package of Hank Bauer, Don Larsen, Norm Siebern and Marv Throneberry.[2] It turned out to be a steal of immense proportions for the Yankees.

Bauer had been the Yankee right fielder through the 1950s, but he was thirty-seven and approaching the end of his career. Larsen was a journeyman pitcher with one moment of glory, his perfect game in the 1956 World Series. He'd never won more than eleven games in a season.

"I hated to see so fine a competitor as Bauer go, and we'll always be indebted to Larsen for his perfect game performance," said George Weiss, Yankee general manager. "However, in Maris we have a young outfielder who should develop into a fine player at the Stadium."[3]

The real incentives for the A's were Siebern and Throneberry. Both were highly rated young prospects who simply could not break into the deep Yankee lineup. Siebern would give Kansas City some value in his four seasons there, twice being named an American League All-Star. But Throneberry, who once hit thirty homers as a New York farmhand, never panned out. After one season in Kansas City, where he hit .250 and struck out once every four at-bats, he was traded again. Eventually, Throneberry found his way to the expansion Mets and became a celebrated cult hero for his insouciance on the field. His biggest claim to fame was being featured in a Miller Lite television ad years after his playing career ended.

Beyond overwhelming tradition and financial advantages, the Yankees boasted a veteran team that had won 109 games in 1961 before routinely dispatching the Cincinnati Reds in five games in the World Series. New York hit a record 240 home runs in '61. Mantle, at the age of thirty, had finished with fifty-four homers, his highest career output. First baseman Bill (Moose) Skowron hit twenty-eight. All three players splitting the catching duties—Yogi Berra, Elston Howard and Johnny Blanchard—hit at least twenty homers.

The leader, of course, had been Maris, the laconic pull-hitting outfielder from North Dakota, who erased Babe Ruth's 1927 mark of sixty homers. Beginning in August and lasting through the end of the season, sports fans were captivated by the so-called "home run derby" of Maris and Mantle pursuing Ruth's record. Mantle's season ended prematurely when he was sidelined by a hip abscess after receiving an injection to treat a heavy cold from a physician with a questionable reputation.[4]

Maris finally overtook Ruth on the final day of the season, rifling a fastball from Boston's Tracy Stallard into the Yankee Stadium right field stands for homer No. 61. His teammates, cheering and applauding, forced Maris out of the dugout to take a curtain call for the crowd of 23,154.

Maris had overcome enormous pressure, a sometimes-unsupportive fan base, and an aggressive, relentless press to break perhaps the most hallowed of all baseball records. Typical of the line of questioning Maris faced on an almost daily basis throughout much of the summer was the reporter who asked him, "What would you rather do, hit sixty home runs or hit .300?" Exasperated, Maris asked the writer, "What would *you* rather do?"

"I'd rather bat .300," the reporter replied. "To each his own," said Maris, shaking his head while turning away.[5]

Even as training camp began for the new season, Maris' critics continued to fire away. Oscar Fraley of United Press International wrote, "If either of my sons has a hero, I hope it's John Glenn. Guys like Roger Maris bat a round zero with me."[6]

An editorial in the March 28 edition of *The Sporting News* ("The Bible of Baseball") stated, "Wonder if Maris realizes that there are a great many things writers would rather do than ask questions of a grumbling, pouting athlete who answers in monosyllables, sneers at questions he thinks are foolish and brushes everybody aside as he hastens to shower."

A reporter for the *Miami News* stated, "If it weren't for sportswriters, Roger Maris would probably be an $18-a-week clerk at the A&P back in Missouri."[7] (Maris made his off-season home in Independence, Missouri.)

In a magazine article titled "Maris in '62: How Many?" former Cleveland Indians general manager Frank Lane said, "He's cold and greedy and he'd cut down his own grandmother to win. But he'll do all right."[8] Rogers Hornsby, an outspoken critic of Maris' skills, stated, "It depends on how much of his publicity he believes and what kind of shape he's in. All this running around to banquets doesn't help a player."[9] During his own Hall of Fame career, the prickly Hornsby was a stickler

Tom Tresh (15) greets Roger Maris after a home run at Yankee Stadium. Tresh earned Rookie of the Year honors in 1962 playing shortstop and then left field in the New York lineup. Maris led the Yankees with thirty-three homers, while Tresh hit twenty (National Baseball Hall of Fame and Museum, Cooperstown, N.Y.).

for all things baseball, notoriously refusing to go to movie theaters out of concern for his batting eye.

Beyond the ability to hit home runs in bunches, the Yankees had a wide number of assets for manager Ralph Houk as he began his second season as skipper. With Howard, Blanchard and Berra, the catching was solid. The outfield consisted of two of the premier players in baseball, Mantle and Maris, along with a left field platoon of Berra, Blanchard and Hector Lopez. Joe Pepitone, a Brooklyn native with a swing made for the short right field fence at Yankee Stadium, was also earmarked for playing time in the outfield and as a backup to Skowron at first base.

The infield, perhaps the best in all of baseball, had become unsettled by the call-up of shortstop Tony Kubek to the U.S. Army reserves the previous autumn, one of approximately thirty professional ballplayers called to service. Because he was a member of a National Guard unit, Kubek's discharge could not be pinpointed by the Army. "This club has no information from the Pentagon or Fort Lewis, Washington, where Kubek is stationed," said publicity director Bob Fishel. "We are not making any inquiries and we are not counting on Kubek for this season. If he is released in August or any other time during the baseball season, Ralph Houk will be delighted."[10]

Two rookies, Tom Tresh and Phil Linz, would fill the position according to Houk, "unless they both break their legs."[11]

The remainder of the infield was solid. Skowron gave the Yanks a power hitter from the right side of the plate and a reliable glove at first base. Second baseman Bobby Richardson and third baseman Clete Boyer were outstanding fielders with the ability to hit in the clutch. Richardson was normally Houk's favorite leadoff hitter despite his low walk count and only slightly above-average speed on the bases. Boyer showed flashes of power, sometimes offset by a propensity to strike out.

Asked about his pitching staff at the Yankees' new spring training camp in Ft. Lauderdale, Florida, Houk quickly identified his top three starting pitchers. Ace left-hander Whitey Ford, coming off twenty-five wins and the majors' Cy Young Award, would continue to anchor the staff as he had for years. Young but experienced right-handers Bill Stafford and Ralph Terry would be heavily counted on as well. Initially, Houk declined to name his fourth starter. The group of contenders included Roland Sheldon, who made the team as a surprise in '61 and won eleven games; veteran left-hander Bud Daley, who could also work in long relief; and rookie fireballer Jim Bouton, who threw with such force that his cap sometimes flew off his head as he followed through.

If the Yankees appeared to have an Achilles heel, it might be the bullpen. Observers wondered if veteran screwball artist Luis Arroyo could approximate his spectacular 1961 performance when he won fifteen games in relief and saved twenty-nine others. Hal Reniff was a largely untried commodity who was battling arm troubles. Jim Coates and Tex Clevenger were old pros who succeeded on guile as much as their fastballs.

Coates was a nasty right-hander who wouldn't hesitate to deck a hitter he felt was digging in against him. The year before, Coates had thrown at Cleveland's Jimmy Piersall *while taking his warmups* because Piersall, standing outside the batter's box, was trying to gauge the break on Coates' curveball. After picking himself up off the ground, the volatile Piersall grabbed the three bats he'd been swinging and fired them toward Coates. Piersall had suffered a well-chronicled mental breakdown earlier in his career and the umpires quickly gathered to restrain him from charging Coates.

"One said, 'Look in his eyes,'" Piersall later wrote. "Suddenly they were all psychiatrists. I said, 'I'm okay. He threw the ball at me, you dumb bastards. Go look in his eyes.'"[12]

The unknown X factor was Marshall Bridges. Nicknamed "The Sheriff" by his teammates, the native of Jackson, Mississippi, had toiled for six years in the minors before getting his chance in the major leagues. The Yankees needed a southpaw out of the pen who could throw hard, and Bridges met both criteria, averaging nearly a strikeout per inning in four years in the National League. He was obtained in December from Cincinnati for light-hitting catcher Jesse Gonder.

When the annual predictions for the season were published in the spring, the Yankees were chosen to win the American League by most of the experts. A preview article by the sports department at NBC-TV stated, "Frantically and sometimes ridiculously, American Leaguers spent the off-season drumming up reasons why the Yankees won't win this year's pennant ... in all, the Yankees of 1962 shape up to be a well-rounded, well-equipped team capable of delivering the goods. Ain't it always so?"[13]

Gabe Paul, the Cleveland Indians' general manager, told reporters he thought complacency would settle in and doom the New Yorkers, who had caught lightning in a bottle with the performances of Maris, Mantle, Ford and others in 1961. The Yankee reaction? "I don't know what he's thinking about," commented general manager Roy Hamey, "but he's way off base."

"Wishful thinking," said Houk. "A bunch of stuff," dismissed Mantle, who very likely used a more colorful term than his quote indicated.[14]

"We've got a good ballclub, a young ballclub," Houk went on. "And what's more important, we know the price you have to pay for winning. Complacency on this club? Not if I've got anything to say about it."[15] And Houk was not a man to challenge or act complacent around.

Ralph George Houk was born on a farm near Lawrence, Kansas, on

August 9, 1919. In addition to performing his daily chores, Houk played football and basketball at Lawrence High School and was good enough to be offered scholarships to play football at the University of Kansas and the University of Oklahoma. Legendary coach Phog Allen wanted him to come play basketball at Kansas.[16] But his favorite sport was baseball, which he played in a semi-pro local league since his high school did not have a team. Famed Yankee scout Bill Essick, who'd signed Joe DiMaggio, Lefty Gomez, Joe Gordon and Frank Crosetti, among others, offered him a $200 bonus and a monthly salary of $75. To the 20-year-old Houk, "I thought, Jesus, that's unbelievable."[17] With his parents' permission, he signed the contract and was sent to a Class D minor league team in Neosho, Missouri.

A right-handed-hitting catcher, Houk slowly progressed up the professional baseball ladder before the Japanese attack on Pearl Harbor led him to enlist in the U.S. Army as a private. After serving as a clerk and enrolling in Officers Candidate School in Fort Knox, Kentucky, Houk was promoted to lieutenant. That was his rank when he was shipped to Normandy shortly after D-Day, leading the 9th Armored Division in the fighting that took place in the hedgerows as the Allies made their way into occupied France. While riding in a jeep one day, Houk had a German bullet pierce the back of his helmet and exit out the front without touching him. He later suffered a shrapnel wound in his upper leg, earning a Purple Heart.[18]

By the time of the German offensive known as the Battle of the Bulge, Houk was a major. As described in Mickey Mantle's book *The Quality of Courage*, "Houk had to take a patrol through the German lines to Bastogne to get information on the number of men there, their equipment and so forth. Then he had to go back through the German lines to the American headquarters with that information.... He made it safely both ways. He won the Silver Star."[19]

Houk's military achievements earned him a nickname that followed him throughout his baseball career—"the Major." But like many other Yankee catching prospects of the time, he had the misfortune to be stuck behind Berra. In parts of eight seasons in New York, Houk played in only ninety-one games and finished his career with just forty-three hits. But he learned about running a ballclub from Casey Stengel and quickly leaped at the opportunity to manage in 1955 when offered the reins of the Yankees' Triple-A club in Denver. After three seasons in Denver, and three as a coach for Stengel, the New York brass deemed him ready. On October 18, 1960, the Yankees held a press conference to announce that Stengel's contract was terminated and Houk would become the manager in 1961.

"I'll never make the mistake of being seventy again," said Stengel, who told the press that he was let go simply because of his age.[20] In truth, the Yankees worried that another team would offer a managerial job to Houk and they'd lose him completely. Stengel's handling of the pitching assignments in the World Series loss to the Pirates just cemented management's decision to make the switch.

Houk immediately won over his troops, many of whom had played for him in the minor leagues and were tired of Stengel's constant lineup shuffling and platooning. He reduced the anxiety Boyer always felt by telling him he was the starting third baseman no matter what he hit. He told Ford that he'd pitch every fourth day instead of every fifth day as he had under Stengel.[21] He talked privately with Mantle about becoming more of a leader in the clubhouse. "I took that seriously," Mantle later wrote. "It meant that Ralph was relying on me and I felt the responsibility ... and I feel that Ralph Houk made a man out of me."[22]

Houk developed a strong reputation as an old school baseball man who supported his players, refusing to criticize them publicly. The Yankees rarely questioned his actions. "I liked playing for Stengel," said Ford, "but I liked Ralph too. I respected his baseball knowledge."[23]

"Ralph's secret was to figure out who were the big guys on the team and get them on his side," said Moose Skowron. "With the Yankees, it was Mickey and Whitey. Ralph won them over and everyone else fell into line."[24] Complacency among the Yankee players was never going to be an issue with Houk.

Like his counterparts with the other nineteen major league franchises, Houk managed his team during the final few spring training games in 1962 in a starkly different way than is seen today. An example was the April 6 contest (commonly called an "exhibition" in that era of limited marketing) between the Yanks and the Kansas City Athletics. With the season opener just four days away, Houk started Mantle in center field despite the Yankee star recovering from a twisted knee and fighting a head cold. As he always did, Mantle played all out—an AP wire service photo showed him sliding into third after advancing two bases on a teammate's single.[25] It would be a safe bet that in 2021, under similar circumstances, Mike Trout or Aaron Judge would not be in a spring training lineup.

The season began with the Yankees scoring two runs in the bottom of the eighth inning to defeat the Baltimore Orioles, 7–6, in a crisp two hours and twenty-eight minutes. Opening day as a prestigious, *gotta-be-there* event was also quite different in the '60s. The paid attendance at Yankee Stadium was 22,978 in a ballpark that officially held more than 67,000. Ironically, the opening day attendance would be exactly the team's average at the Stadium that season for 65 dates (which included fifteen doubleheaders)—22,978.[26]

The club split its first ten games as Houk fiddled with playing time for rookies Pepitone, Tresh and Linz, and platooned Berra and Lopez in left field. The search for a reliable fourth starter to pair with the trio of Ford, Terry and Stafford continued as well. In late April, the Yanks looked very much like the famed Bronx Bombers, scoring thirty-four runs and collecting fifty-two hits in a four-game sweep against the Senators in Washington.

But the team scuffled along as May began, basically playing slightly better than .500 baseball. In the middle of the month, the Yanks dropped three out of four in a series at Cleveland, including a doubleheader sweep to the surprising Indians who moved into first place. There was more bad news when the team announced that Arroyo would be lost indefinitely due to an ailing left elbow. Houk remained confident that his pitching staff would improve once the schedule became more consistent with fewer off days and rainouts. "I'm satisfied with my pitching," he told *The Sporting News*. "Some of my men need more work, but I'm sure the pitching will get straightened out before too long."[27]

Five days after the doubleheader loss at Cleveland, the Yanks hosted the Minnesota Twins on a Friday night. With two out in the bottom of the ninth, Mantle came to bat with Minnesota holding a 4–3 lead and Tresh on second base as the potential tying run. Batting right-handed, Mantle hit a wicked one-hopper that caromed off shortstop Zoilo Versalles' shoulder. Sensing a possible base hit to extend the game, Mantle dug hard down the baseline. As he got within a few feet of the bag, he suddenly fell, going down as if he were shot. The Twins' Bernie Allen later said he could hear the muscle pop from his position at second base.

"I thought I broke my left leg then," Mantle would recall years later. "It wouldn't come back down. It just stuck up and when I fell, I tore the knee up."[28]

He had badly torn a muscle in his right thigh and compounded that by severely straining ligaments in his left knee when he landed awkwardly. "The pain practically turned my brain blue," Mantle wrote.[29] He was expected to be sidelined at least a month. Roland Sheldon recalled the feeling in the clubhouse when Mantle went down. "All we could think was, 'Wow, there goes the pennant,'" he said. "How are we going to go on without Mickey?"[30]

Lacking their best player and inspirational leader, the Yanks did just enough to stay near the top of the American League. From May 13 through June 8, New York was never more than a single game ahead or behind at the top of the AL standings, jockeying for position with the

Twins, Tigers and Indians. Another team within striking distance was the Los Angeles Angels, a club in only its second year of existence after being part of the 1961 expansion. The surprising Angels, managed by ex-Giant skipper Bill Rigney, would move into first place after a July 4 doubleheader sweep at Washington.

The Angels' roster was a combination of prized young talent such as catcher Bob Rodgers, first baseman Lee Thomas and infielder Billy Moran; revitalized veterans like outfielders Leon Wagner and Albie Pearson; and hard-throwing young pitchers Dean Chance, Ken McBride and notorious left-hander Robert (Bo) Belinsky. Born on the lower east side of Manhattan to a Polish father and Jewish mother, Belinsky had already become nationally recognized. A rookie, he began the year winning five straight games. The fourth victory was a 2–0 no-hitter against Baltimore on May 5. As the Angels rushed out of the dugout to congratulate him, Belinsky found his catcher, Rodgers, pointed toward the stands and said, "Hey, look at the blonde with the big tits."[31] Later in the clubhouse, the triumphant southpaw told reporters, "If music be the food of love, by all means let the band play on."[32]

Belinsky had a burning desire to enjoy all that greater Los Angeles and Hollywood could offer. His name began appearing in Walter Winchell's syndicated newspaper column, detailing his relationships with movie actresses Ann-Margret, Connie Stevens, Tina Louise and, most notably, Mamie Van Doren. "Winchell turned him into a partygoer. He then started dating more movie stars. He liked the ladies, but I didn't think he was disruptive," recalled Moran, who earned an invitation to the All-Star game that season. "Bo was just a kid from New Jersey who didn't mind saying what he thought. He wasn't a great pitcher, just a good lefthander."[33]

His star ultimately flamed out early. After the 5–0 start, he lost six of his next eight decisions and wound up the year with a 10–11 record to go with a 3.56 earned run average. He made three starts vs. the Yankees in '62, losing twice and receiving one no-decision. Years later, Belinsky married and divorced both a *Playboy* Playmate of the Year and an heiress to the Weyerhaeser timberland company. He was featured in an episode of the sitcom *My Favorite Martian*, battled through alcoholism, and became a born-again Christian in Las Vegas, of all places.[34]

The Angels shared the same ballpark with the Dodgers in 1962 and would do so until their move to Anaheim Stadium in 1966. The Angels referred to the ballpark as Chavez Ravine, not Dodger Stadium. Regardless of what they called it, being tenants to the landlord Dodgers meant the Angels seldom had prime scheduling arrangements. As an example, immediately after moving into first place on July 4, the

Angels came home for a nineteen-game homestand. (Today's scheduling patterns seldom commit a team to more than nine-to-twelve consecutive games home or away.) The long homestand was followed by a sixteen-game road trip to Detroit, Cleveland, Baltimore, Boston and Chicago. By the time they returned home in early August, the Angels were five games behind the Yankees and never seriously threatened the rest of the way.

On June 24, the Yankees were in Detroit to play the fourth of a five-game wraparound weekend series with one of their leading contenders, the Tigers. The series marked Mantle's return to the Yankee starting lineup after his leg injuries. The Sunday game started at 1:30 in the afternoon, and before two o'clock the Yanks had tallied six runs in the first inning. But New York starter Bob Turley couldn't survive the first inning and the Tigers cut the gap to 6–3.

Eventually, the score was tied at 7–7 after six innings and it remained that way for the next fifteen innings, becoming the longest game in Yankee history and the longest in actual time elapsed—exactly seven hours—in American League history. Finally, in the top of the twenty-second inning, with night descending on Tiger Stadium, Yankee reserve outfielder Jack Reed hit a two-run homer to deep left and the Yanks held on for a 9–7 victory. Reed finished the game in right field after Mantle had started there. The winning pitcher was Bouton, who tossed seven shutout innings in relief. Berra, at thirty-seven years of age, caught all twenty-two innings and came to the plate eleven times.

Whether coincidence or not, the marathon victory triggered the Yanks' best run of the season. They won twenty-one of their next twenty-seven games, and when the surge ended on July 21 they led the AL by three-and-a-half games. Despite lacking the offensive firepower of the previous season, and without a bullpen stopper to match Arroyo's '61 performance, New York never relinquished its lead the rest of the way. But the Yankees could never quite feel comfortable until a 5–2 complete-game victory by Ford at Cleveland on September 12 pushed the margin to five games over Minnesota with roughly two weeks to play. The Twins had become New York's primary challenger beginning in late August. Minnesota boasted a robust offense with Harmon Killebrew (48 HRs, 126 RBIs), Bob Allison (29 HRs, 102 RBIs) and ex-Yankee farmhand Vic Power (.290 average, 16 HRs). But the Twins' pitching couldn't match New York's beyond starters Camilo Pascual (20–11) and Jim Kaat (18–14).

The Yankees had also been boosted by the long-awaited return on August 7 of Kubek from his stint in the Army. Initially, Houk plugged him into starting assignments in left field, but soon decided to put him back at his customary shortstop position. Kubek wound up hitting .314 in forty-five games.

Kubek's return to shortstop solved another problem. Tresh, who had shown good range and a strong arm at shortstop, became the regular left fielder so that his switch hitting could facilitate his playing every day whether the opposing pitcher was left-handed or right-handed. That lengthened Houk's bench, with available reserves in Berra, Blanchard, Lopez, Linz and first baseman Dale Long, a veteran hitter with occasional power whom the Yanks had acquired in a July trade with Washington. The addition of Long meant even less playing time for Pepitone. He was subsequently returned to Triple-A Richmond and would be left off the Yanks' World Series roster.

"How lucky we were to come up with a youngster like Tresh, fine at shortstop and, after Kubek's return, fine in left field," said Houk about the rookie who wore No. 15 and was not quite 24 years old. "Could we do it [win the pennant] without Tresh? That has to be doubted."[35] Tresh would finish the year hitting .286 with 26 doubles, 20 home runs and 93 runs batted in. American League writers voted him the Rookie of the Year award, the first Yankee so honored since Kubek in 1957.

Another positive for Houk had been the relief pitching of the newcomer, Bridges. Primarily used in the eighth and ninth innings, in an era when relievers were expected to come in with men on base as often as not, the left-hander became a reliable resource in the New York bullpen. From mid–June to early July he recorded eight consecutive saves in as many opportunities. He finished the season 8–4 with a team-leading eighteen saves. Perhaps foreshadowing what was to come in October, however, Bridges struggled during the last month of the season, losing two decisions and blowing three save opportunities in September. He yielded six earned runs in his last two innings and saw his ERA go from 2.45 to a final 3.14. There were concerns that his fifty-two appearances had overly taxed him. In his ten-year professional career, he'd never pitched in more than forty games in a season.

But Houk hesitated to trust his other relievers in a clutch spot. Daley was clearly his second-best option. The 29-year-old lefty from California pitched in 105 innings, mostly working out of the pen. He didn't own a blazing fastball, but his best attribute was his control. Daley seldom walked a batter. Applying the modern WAR metric (Wins Above Replacement), Daley rated as the top reliever in the New York bullpen.[36]

Bouton was used as both a starter and reliever and showed promise, but he was still just a 23-year-old rookie. Houk stopped using Arroyo in critical spots after the southpaw went on the disabled list in May and didn't return until almost July. "Little Looie," who registered twenty-nine saves the year before, earned none after July 19. He finished the season 1–3 with an earned run average of 4.81. Opponents also tagged him for five home runs in only thirty-three innings of work, a worse ratio than even Terry, who surrendered more homers than any other American League hurler.

Coates went 7–6 with an unsightly 4.44 ERA. In what turned out to be his final big-league season, Clevenger threw only thirty-eight innings, mostly in mop-up roles. Reniff was plagued all summer with an arm injured during a six-month military commitment and appeared in only two games for the Yankees. The bottom line for Houk was this— his best bet was still to call on either the fatigued Bridges or the steady, soft-tossing Daley, with Coates the only logical right-handed option.

On September 25, the Yanks knocked off the Senators, 8–3, to clinch their twenty-seventh American League pennant in front of an intimate gathering of 11,702 at Yankee Stadium (the following night's crowd would be 4,140). "It's always nice to win 'em," deadpanned Yogi Berra, about to participate in his thirteenth World Series since 1947.[37]

In the clubhouse, most of the veterans dutifully sprayed champagne on the excited newcomers and rookies, and quickly toasted each other before assembling in a back room to watch the world heavyweight championship fight between the champ, Floyd Patterson, and challenger Sonny Liston.[38] That bout proved about as exciting as the Yanks' muted clubhouse celebration—Liston knocked out Patterson in the first round.

The last bit of drama from the regular season dealt with Mantle's late bid to win his second American League batting crown. After sufficiently recovering from his injuries, Mantle had enjoyed a productive season (30 homers, 89 RBIs) and had raised his average from .290 on August 26 to .320 when he went four-for-four in the pennant clincher against Washington. But after missing more than a month it looked like Mantle would finish short of the minimum 502 plate appearances needed to qualify for the batting title.

To give him a chance, Houk inserted No. 7 into the leadoff position in the batting order for the final four games of the season. The move worked—Mantle wound up with exactly 502 plate appearances to qualify. The title, however, went to Boston first baseman Pete Runnels, who hit .326 compared to Mantle's .321. Red Sox manager Mike Higgins told *The Sporting News* he thought Houk's tactic was "un–Yankee-like."

What *was* Yankee-like was the Bronx Bombers preparing to play in another World Series. This time, however, it would take longer than usual to learn who their opponent would be.

Two

New Locale, Same Rivalry

The novelty was beginning to wear off for San Francisco Giants fans.

The pride and recognition of having a major league baseball franchise in San Francisco was still a source of enormous joy for residents of the "City by the Bay," just as it had been since the announcement in August of 1957 that the Giants were pulling up roots in Manhattan and coming to northern California. West Coast fans and media alike were eager to watch one of baseball's fiercest rivalries reemerge after the long-rumored move of the Dodgers from Brooklyn to Los Angeles also become a reality.

The National League schedule-maker wasted no time in renewing a series that began in 1890. Opening day of the 1958 season featured San Francisco hosting Los Angeles on April 15. Instead of the Polo Grounds or Ebbets Field, the Giants and Dodgers met at quaint, intimate Seals Stadium. The opener was a rousing success for San Francisco fans. The Giants hammered Dodger right-hander Don Drysdale for six runs in the first four innings and coasted to an 8–0 victory before a sellout crowd of 23,448. The first hit by a San Francisco Giant came from pitcher Ruben Gomez, who singled in the third inning on his way to pitching a complete game six-hit shutout.

Built during the Great Depression for the Pacific Coast League's San Francisco Seals, Seals Stadium, with an original seating capacity of 18,000, was situated in the Northeast section of San Francisco's Mission District. The cozy ballpark at 16th and Bryant streets featured playing dimensions that were quite different from those the Giants left behind at the Polo Grounds. While the distance down the foul lines was far greater at Seals Stadium—361 feet to left, 350 to right compared to 279 and 257 at the Polo Grounds—the center field fence was 400 feet, a drastic reduction from the mammoth 483-foot slog to dead center field in New York.[1] Joe Adcock, Hank Aaron and Lou Brock were the only players to ever hit a ball into the center field bleachers at the Polo Grounds.[2]

While its bathtub shape permitted easy home runs on lazy fly balls hit down the foul lines, the Polo Grounds robbed sluggers who hit the ball to the power alleys and straightaway center. Sportswriters began wondering how many more home runs Willie Mays might hit in Seals Stadium. But after hitting twenty-two, twenty and seventeen homers at home in his final three years in New York, Mays hit only sixteen in both 1958 and '59 at Seals Stadium.

Despite the ballpark's seating capacity (lowest in the major leagues), the Giants drew 1,272,625 spectators to Seals Stadium in 1958, a whopping 95 percent increase over their 1957 attendance in New York. It was their highest total in four years and registered keenly with the front office. When asked how youthful Giants fans might react to the franchise leaving Manhattan, owner Horace Stoneham had famously replied, "I feel bad for the kids, but I haven't seen many of their fathers lately."[3]

The city had expanded Seals Stadium's capacity to 23,000 to accommodate the Giants' move. But the park had always been considered a stopgap. Stoneham had insisted upon a new stadium in his negotiations with the city to bring the Giants west. As those talks were proceeding, Stoneham had openly flirted with Minneapolis, which promised a new ballpark as well. Stoneham, who inherited the franchise from his father, Charles, would not agree to any move without the promise of a new ballpark. He'd had enough of playing in an aging facility like the Polo Grounds.

Two years after the Giants-Dodgers '58 opener, the newly-built stadium opened near Candlestick Point, adjacent to San Francisco Bay. Christened Candlestick Park following a contest sponsored by the City Recreation and Parks Commission,[4] the ballpark had a seating capacity of 42,000 and was initially a source of immense pride among San Francisco baseball fans. The sellout crowd on opening day, April 12, 1960, included vice-president Richard Nixon, California governor Edmund Brown and San Francisco mayor George Christopher. Nixon told a group of reporters that Candlestick was "the finest ballpark in America."[5] As they had done in their Seals Stadium debut two years earlier, the Giants sent the fans home happy, defeating the St. Louis Cardinals, 3–1. Like the sunny weather that greeted the opener, the new park looked shiny and bright.

It did not take long, however, for the stadium to become a frequent target of player criticism and a national punch line for the media.

"There were a lot of design problems," recalled Giants pitcher Mike McCormick years later. "When it opened, things were leaking, things weren't working. Some of the bathrooms didn't work. They had put thermal heating in the concrete under the box seats and that didn't work."[6]

There were even issues with the playing dimensions themselves. National League umpires would soon alert the league office that the foul poles were incorrectly located entirely in fair territory, rather than on the foul line. Temporary ground rules were instituted until management could fix the problem. "Everybody loved Seals Stadium," said pitcher Stu Miller. "It was a nice, cozy ballpark. But here comes the new ballpark. We said, 'Wait a minute, it's a little windy here.' We thought maybe the first windy day was an aberration."[7]

Ah yes, the wind.

One afternoon while Candlestick Park was being built, Charles (Chub) Feeney, the Giants' general manager and nephew of Horace Stoneham, paid a visit to the construction site. Thinking of the heavy diet of day games the Giants normally played, he stopped a worker and asked, "Does the wind always blow like this?" The construction worker shrugged. "Only between the hours of one and five," he said.[8] One wonders what a thought bubble over Feeney's head might have said at that moment.

Candlestick Park was consistently maligned for its abundance of cold weather, distant sightlines and—most notoriously—its relentless, wicked wind currents that would regularly accelerate in the late afternoon and evening coming off adjacent Bayview Hill. Players quickly discovered that the wind blew in from left field toward right field with a jet stream–like force. Right-handed hitters became frustrated when their well-hit drives to left were held up for outs. Pitchers shared their frustrations when left-handed hitters would hit soft fly balls to right that would carry and carry and disappear over the fence.

Soon after Candlestick's opening, a report was commissioned to study the matter and seek corrections. There were no practical solutions offered. Changing the direction of the playing field would only alter the direction the wind blew, not diminish it. The report did, however, take dead aim at architect John Bolles. "If the winds had been checked before construction," the report scolded, "the stadium might have been shifted a few hundred yards to a more comfortable site."[9] The Giants would have to make the best of the situation.

It didn't take long for the rest of the National League to know what playing in Candlestick meant. "You start thinking about that terrible wind, and that's what the Giants will be doing," commented Cincinnati Reds manager Fred Hutchinson prior to the start of the 1962 season. "We just go into Candlestick for a few days and leave. But the poor Giants are stuck there."[10]

No major league ballpark endured such an overwhelming reputation for chilling, game-affecting wind as did Candlestick Park. To offset the cold conditions, the city had invested in a thermal heating system embedded in the concrete below the box seats. But a construction error buried the natural gas pipes too deep in the concrete. The heating system never worked correctly.[11]

Eventually, Giants management would embrace, in a manner of speaking, the cruel conditions suffered by their fans. In the park's latter years, the *Croix de Candlestick* pin was awarded to all fans remaining to the end of any night game that went extra innings. The pin carried the inscription *Veni, Vidi, Vixi*—"I came, I saw, I survived."[12]

Miller was the leading figure in the most notorious example of the ballpark's fierce wind. Urban legend claimed that while pitching in the 1961 All-Star game at Candlestick, Miller was called for a balk in the ninth inning when he was—as one headline claimed the next day—"blown off the mound."

"I had never seen the wind blow that hard," Miller said, recalling the incident. "By the time I came in, it had gotten worse. There was a man on first and second with one out. Before I threw a pitch, I went into a stretch position and then there was an extra gust of wind and I just wavered a bit like a tree."[13]

The umpires called a balk on Miller.

"I don't think any of the fans knew what happened," Miller said. "They were probably wondering 'why the hell did those runners move up?' I didn't move a helluva lot. The papers made it sound like I was pinned against the center field fence."[14]

Player criticism of Candlestick Park would seldom abate during the stadium's forty years as the home of the Giants. In the 1970s, during the height of the intrigue surrounding the whereabouts of kidnapped newspaper heiress Patty Hearst, Giants outfielder Bobby Murcer once pointed toward Candlestick's upper deck during batting practice. "They've been looking all over for her, but where they ought to check is up there in Section 61," Murcer said. "It's the perfect place to hide."[15]

In the 1980s, the Giants' star outfielder Jack Clark routinely criticized his home stadium and its playing conditions. *Sports Illustrated* once titled a piece on Clark "Jack Jumps All Over Candlestick."[16]

In the early spring of 1962, Giants fans were beyond the thrill of having a new team to root for and a new stadium to watch them in. They wanted a pennant winner. It didn't help matters that the rival Dodgers had already won a World Series since they moved west. Or that L.A.'s new Dodger Stadium, built overlooking downtown Los Angeles in a region known as Chavez Ravine, was receiving glowing testimonials even though it hadn't yet officially opened. San Franciscans *always* compared their city, their quality of life and their sports teams to Los Angeles. They wanted a baseball champion of their own.

Since moving west, the Giants had been consistently better than average, but nowhere near good enough to win it all. They finished third in the eight-team National League in both 1958 and '59, before dropping to fifth place the following season with a nondescript 79–75 record. In 1961, under new manager Alvin Dark, the Giants began to show potential. Although their 85–69 mark was still only good for third place, a corps of solid young players began to emerge, giving Giants fans the promise of better things to come.

The new group was led by Orlando Cepeda. A native of Ponce, Puerto Rico, where his father was a legendary player sometimes referred to as the "Babe Ruth of Puerto Rico,"[17] the six-foot-two, 210-pound Cepeda possessed the talent and ability to hit for power and average, reminding some of a young Willie Mays without the same flair. Nicknamed the "Baby Bull," Cepeda was entering his fifth season with the Giants. He'd already clouted 122 home runs, including forty-six in 1961, to go with 142 RBIs, both figures leading the National League. Writing in the April 1962 issue of *Baseball Digest*, Murray Robinson of the *New York Journal-American* listed Cepeda as the "best bet to eclipse Roger Maris' brand-new record of 61 homers." Signed as a first baseman, Cepeda had somewhat reluctantly agreed to play the outfield when called upon, especially after the arrival of Willie McCovey.

A native of Mobile, Alabama, the six-foot-four, lefty-swinging McCovey had impressively burst upon the scene in 1959. Despite playing only fifty-two games after being called up in late July, McCovey won the National League's Rookie of the Year award by hitting .354 with thirteen homers and thirty-eight runs batted in. His debut with the Giants on July 30 had been storybook material—four hits in four at-bats, including a pair of triples and two RBIs.

Both Cepeda and McCovey were better defensively at first base than in the outfield. Each was an acceptable outfielder, but neither would ever be known for his glove work. Which one would be the primary starting first baseman in 1962 remained a mystery.

Giant fans were also excited by the prospect of watching the Dominican Republic–born Alou brothers, Felipe and Mateo. Felipe was considered the better overall ballplayer, a regal, smooth-hitting corner outfielder with better-than-average power at the plate. He'd swatted eighteen homers in 1961 and hit .289 as a semi-regular in the lineup. The Giants were counting on him as their starting right fielder. The younger Mateo—quickly Anglicized by the media as "Matty"—was a diminutive

Nicknamed "Stretch," Willie McCovey played in six All-Star games primarily as a first baseman. But early in McCovey's career, manager Alvin Dark used him in the outfield to accommodate Orlando Cepeda playing first base for the Giants (© 1963 S.F. Giants).

slap hitter with good speed on the bases and an average throwing arm in the outfield.

Of course, any Giants success rested heavily on the shoulders of No. 24, Willie Mays, the one superstar who had accompanied the franchise from New York to San Francisco. Entering the 1962 season, Mays was a month shy of his 31st birthday and recognized as perhaps the best player in all of baseball. Since his debut in 1951, Mays had proven himself to be the ultimate five-tool player. He could hit, hit for power, run, field his position, and possessed a strong and accurate throwing arm.

As a rookie, Mays had helped the Giants make their heralded run to the National League pennant and the famous playoff series with the Brooklyn Dodgers. Three years later, the Giants won their final championship in New York, with Mays making a potentially game-saving play in Game One of the World Series at the Polo Grounds. Soon dubbed simply "The Catch," Mays had snuffed out a Cleveland Indian rally by pulling down Vic Wertz's towering fly ball to dead center field with an improbable over-the-shoulder catch in front of the 483-foot sign.

In the 1959 All-Star game, Mays knocked in the winning run for the National League by slamming a triple deep into the immense reaches of right-center at Forbes Field. Wrote Bob Stevens of the *San Francisco Chronicle*, "The only man who could have caught it, hit it."[18]

In 1961, Mays batted .308 with 40 home runs, 123 runs batted in and 18 stolen bases. He had already appeared in eleven consecutive All-Star Games, won the Most Valuable Player award in 1954 and, like Cepeda and McCovey, had been a National League Rookie of the Year.

But Cepeda, McCovey and the Alou brothers all made their major league debuts with the *San Francisco* Giants. Mays broke in while the Giants were playing in New York. Despite his tremendous ability and charisma, Mays was not thoroughly accepted by San Francisco fans in his early years out west. "It was as if I had done something wrong by doing well in New York," he wrote in his 1988 autobiography. He attributed some of the coolness to unrealistically high expectations announced by his first San Francisco manager, Bill Rigney, who told California reporters that Mays would hit 61 home runs and drive in 150 runs one of these years. When neither happened, the fans felt let down. And they were sometimes vocal over such failures. "The boos for me were hard to understand," Mays wrote. "I never let on that they hurt me."[19]

One New York writer said of the situation, "San Francisco is the damndest city I ever saw in my life. They cheer Khrushchev and boo Mays."[20]

Most pre-season evaluations for 1962 described the Giants as one of baseball's best-hitting teams with significant question marks around their pitching and defense. One national magazine stated, "Cepeda can whack 60 home runs and Mays can do likewise ... but the Giants won't do anything about the National League pennant if someone doesn't do some pitching."[21] Still, there was no clear-cut favorite in the National League. The previous four seasons had produced four different champions. "All indications are that this will be a wide-open race," declared *The Sporting News*, "which could be won by any of at least six clubs."[22]

The focus for manager Dark at the Giants' spring training camp in Phoenix, Arizona, was the starting rotation. A year earlier, San Francisco's biggest winner had been Miller, who won fourteen games, all in relief. Dark needed more productivity and more success from his starters. When the Giants broke camp in April, the rotation was established as Juan Marichal, Jack Sanford, Billy Pierce and Billy O'Dell, a mixture of two hard-throwing right-handers and a pair of crafty left-handers.

Marichal was considered by most observers to be the ace of the staff. He delighted in deceiving hitters with a long windup and motion that often featured a dramatic high left leg kick. He normally deployed a straight overhand delivery, but sometimes dipped down to throw sidearm against a right-handed hitter. Sanford was a veteran who'd had some success for the lowly Philadelphia Phillies in the late 1950s. Since coming to the Giants in 1959, he had been a workhorse, averaging 219 innings per season, but had a middling 40–35 overall record to show for his three years in San Francisco.

As southpaws, Pierce and O'Dell could benefit by pitching in the stiff winds of Candlestick Park, which normally negated right-handed hitters' power. Pierce had been a top-flight pitcher for the Chicago White Sox for thirteen years, twice winning twenty games. But he was about to turn thirty-five years of age and appeared to be on the downward slope of a long career.

O'Dell didn't strike out many hitters, but he didn't walk many either. The Giants had used him as both a starter and reliever. Dark valued his ability to get out of trouble without relying on the strikeout. Indeed, O'Dell would more than justify his manager's confidence, leading the Giants' staff in innings pitched and complete games while registering the highest strikeout total of his thirteen-year career.

Dark and his pitching coach, Larry Jansen, had concerns about their bullpen beyond the veteran Miller. Jim Duffalo could be used as a spot starter and long man in relief. Young fireballer Bobby Bolin had averaged a strikeout an inning in his rookie season, but also had fits of wildness. Lefty Mike McCormick had been a huge disappointment in '61 after winning fifteen games and leading the National League in earned run average the year before. McCormick did not show enough consistency in the spring and was soon dropped from the potential four-man starting rotation. "He hasn't, in the opinion of Dark, been throwing as smoothly and easily as he did a couple of campaigns ago," wrote Bob Stevens in *The Sporting News*.[23]

The Giants hoped McCormick would bounce back, but to protect themselves, they had acquired right-hander Don Larsen in the same trade with the White Sox that brought Pierce. Larsen's addition would prove a wise move by San Francisco general manager Feeney.

The Alou brothers were solid options in right field and could be easily platooned since Felipe hit right-handed and Matty left-handed. With Mays patrolling center, the defensive liability of a left field platoon of McCovey and 32-year-old Harvey Kuenn could be somewhat negated. Neither McCovey nor Kuenn possessed great speed or a powerful arm. Dark eventually determined that Cepeda would be his first baseman, pushing McCovey to the outfield. "He has proved to me he can catch the routine fly balls and he's also proved that he wants to play very much," said Dark of McCovey. "Nobody worked harder this spring."[24]

The inner defense needed to improve. The Giants ranked next-to-last in the league in double plays in 1961. Shortstop Jose Pagan had an undistinguished .964 fielding percentage and committed 21 errors, as did the second base combination of Joe Amalfitano and Chuck Hiller. Amalfitano was left off the Giants' protected list in the expansion draft and was selected by the Houston Colt 45s. The quiet, intense Hiller would be the starter in '62.

"Hiller has been trying so hard to win and keep the job that sometimes he appears to get so mad he'd like to go ten rounds with himself to a bloody draw," wrote Stevens in his preseason analysis of the San Francisco lineup.[25]

Jim Davenport was a reliable hitter and skilled fielder who led all National League third basemen in fielding percentage in 1961. Dark would pencil his name in at third regardless of the opposing pitcher. Tom Haller and Ed Bailey, both left-handed hitters with home run power, would share the catching duties.

The season began at home in Candlestick and the Giants jumped off on the right note, blanking the Milwaukee Braves, 6–0, behind a three-hit shutout by Marichal. Mays homered off Warren Spahn in the bottom of the first inning, the 320th home run of his career. San Francisco won its next four games, scoring thirty-one runs, to start out 5–0. The month of April ended on another high note as the Giants reeled off ten consecutive victories against the Pirates and Cubs.

On June 1, the Giants made their first trip back to their old home in the Polo Grounds to play the expansion New York Mets, managed by Casey Stengel. McCovey, in his first official game ever in New York, homered twice in a 9–6 victory. Mays, who received a nearly two-minute standing ovation before his first time at bat, celebrated his return with two hits, including a homer. The Mets' second largest crowd of the season, 43,742, mostly rooted for Mays and the Giants, their first chance to do so in person in five years. The four-game San Francisco sweep drew 118,845 fans over three days.

The Giants then struggled through a June swoon, losing 12 of 16 games to fall out of first place. Following a 4th of July doubleheader sweep of the Mets at Candlestick, San Francisco was sitting in second place with a mark of 55–29, one-half game behind the Dodgers.

One of the key ingredients in the Giants' success had been the play of Hiller, the young second baseman. Much to his distress, Hiller was on the way to being nicknamed "Iron Hands," a label used by opposing players and the media to reflect an individual's sub-par defensive skills. But in early July, Hiller and shortstop Pagan were ranked among the National League's leaders in double plays, a pleasant departure from the prior year.

"I was standing straight up and my hands and body were too high," Hiller reflected on his improved defense. "I wasn't getting a good look at ground balls. The ball was playing me instead of me playing it. And Pagan has been making me look good on double plays."[26]

Near the halfway point of the season, Mays was leading the National League with twenty-five home runs and had driven in eighty runs. Writers had him listed as one of the clear favorites for the Most Valuable Player award. Felipe Alou was among the top hitters in the league and both McCovey and Kuenn were above .300. The Giants led the NL in runs scored by a wide margin.

While the bullpen continued to be an adventurous option for Dark, his starting rotation had settled down nicely. Marichal and O'Dell were in double digits in victories, with Sanford and Pierce right behind. One particular silver lining in the relief corps was the work of the hard-throwing Bolin, who continued to average one strikeout per inning in his first nineteen appearances. (Such a statistic is commonplace today, but midway through the '62 season only Sandy Koufax and Bolin were averaging a strikeout per inning in the NL.)

On August 10, the Giants prepared for a crucial three-game series at home with the first-place Dodgers. Trailing Los Angeles by five and a half games, the Giants needed to turn the tide and they were angry about a stinging article from a local bay area writer proclaiming the club the "choke artists of the National League."[27]

On Friday night, San Francisco exploded for six runs in the sixth inning to snap a 2–2 tie and win convincingly, 11–2. The next day, another big sixth inning triggered a San Francisco victory. Trailing 3–2, McCovey launched a three-run homer off Don Drysdale and Miller earned his 15th save in relief as the Giants held on for a 5–4 win. On Sunday, before a near-capacity crowd of 41,812, San Francisco completed the series sweep with a 5–1 win behind three hits by Felipe Alou and a brilliant four-hitter from Marichal.

"There will be more big games to win," wrote reporter Joe King, "but for the first time Marichal proved he was the leader the Giants needed.... Marichal, to this critic at least, proved he could be the man who will win a pennant."[28]

By the beginning of September, the National League had become a two-horse race between the Giants and the Dodgers. The Giants caught fire early in the month, winning nine of ten in one stretch, including three of four from the Dodgers in Los Angeles. The Dodgers also had a September streak of their own, winning seven in a row vs. Pittsburgh, Chicago and Houston. Halfway through the month, however, the Giants dropped six in a row on the road. And both teams saw star players disabled through frightening occurrences.

Shortly before the first All-Star game in Washington (the major leagues played two All-Star games from 1959 to 1962), Koufax had begun experiencing serious pain in his left index finger. He noticed that the finger was sometimes raw to the touch and would turn white after he pitched. On July 12, he threw seven shutout innings against the Mets but had to leave when a blister on the finger burst. Instead of bright red blood coming forth, trainers noticed a pale red color.[29]

Examined in Los Angeles after a difficult outing vs. Cincinnati his next time out (three hits and two runs in one inning), doctors found the circulation in Koufax's index finger was at only 15 percent of normal range. They ruled out Raynaud's Phenomenon, a rare blood disease, and pumped medication into the arteries near the finger. They also told him and manager Walter Alston that Koufax should not pitch until he felt no pain to the touch.

In all, Koufax would miss two months of the season. He was 14–5 with a 2.15 ERA when he was sidelined. It was a huge loss for a team predicated on stout pitching, defense and a light-hitting offense that relied on the stolen base as a primary weapon. Meanwhile, the Giants were about to deal with a strange loss of their own.

Mays, who had played in every game thus far, became the victim of extreme exhaustion and passed out cold on the bench during the Giants game at Cincinnati on September 12. Trainers quickly rushed him to a local hospital. The doctors could not find any specific clinical problem. "I was sitting on the bench when the inning began," remembered Mays. "I felt hot and dizzy. The next thing I remember was [trainer] Doc Bowman looking down at me with a box of smelling salts in his hand."[30]

Mays sat out the next three games, the only ones he missed all season. Returning four days later, he belted a game-tying three-run homer in the top of the eighth inning at Pittsburgh, but the Giants lost on a two-out homer by Smoky Burgess off Miller in the bottom of the tenth. The next day, San Francisco lost again, the big blow being a three-run homer by Pittsburgh's Elmo Plaskett, the only major league home run he'd ever hit.

The Giants were just not a strong road team. They finished the season barely above .500 (42–41) away from Candlestick Park. Conversely, they had the best record in the majors at home, a blistering 61–21.[31] Trailing the Dodgers by four full games, San Francisco managed to win three of five against the Cardinals and Colt 45s to complete the long road trip and pick up one game in the standings. The Giants came home and began the final week of the season by grabbing two of three vs. St. Louis.

The Dodgers continued to struggle mightily and couldn't wrap things up. After dropping three consecutive series to the Braves, Cardinals and Colt 45s, their lead had shriveled to just two games. Entering the final weekend, Los Angeles had lost seven of its last ten. In four of those losses, the vaunted Dodger pitching staff had allowed eight or more runs. The team's psyche was in a precarious position as well. Maury Wills had been insulted after breaking Ty Cobb's stolen base record in September when general manager Buzzie Bavasi told him, "Now that you have the record, maybe we can concentrate on winning a game or two and win the National League pennant."[32]

Duke Snider recounted another conversation that showed confidence was ebbing, at least at the management level.

> There was an ominous development with one week to go in the season. We were in St. Louis for a series with the Cardinals. Mr. O'Malley [Dodger owner Walter] made the trip with us and called a meeting that included Alston, his coaches, our PR man Red Patterson, and me as team captain.
>
> O'Malley laid things right on the table for all of us. "Gentlemen, if we don't win this thing, some heads are going to roll."
>
> I didn't understand why he was so uptight about our chances. The players certainly expected to win. Why wouldn't the rest of the organization, especially our president, feel the same way?[33]

On Friday, September 28, the Dodgers were in L.A. to play the first of a three-game series against St. Louis to close out the regular season. Their magic number to clinch the pennant was two. The Giants were scheduled to host Houston for three games beginning that night, but rain in San Francisco washed out the Friday night game. The Giants and Colt 45s would play a makeup doubleheader on Saturday.

At Dodger Stadium before 51,064, an RBI single in the seventh inning by L.A. shortstop Maury Wills tied the score at 2–2. It remained deadlocked until the tenth inning. The Cardinals then grabbed the lead on a two-out single by Charlie James. The Dodgers were held in check in the bottom of the tenth. Final score—St. Louis 3, Los Angeles 2. The lead was down to a game and a half.

On Saturday in the opener of their doubleheader, the Giants used three hits, two walks and an error to score five runs in the first inning on the way to an 11–5 rout that became Jack Sanford's twenty-fourth victory of the season. The Dodger lead was down to one game as the Giants began the nightcap of the afternoon twin bill. But strong pitching by Houston's Bob Bruce and a costly error by Pagan, one of three by San Francisco, led to a 4–2 Houston victory. That meant a Dodger win in either of the two games remaining vs. St. Louis—or a Giant loss on Sunday—would give the pennant to the Dodgers.

But they couldn't close the deal.

On Saturday evening, St. Louis scored twice off Drysdale in the second inning and held on against the punchless Dodgers, 2–0. Los Angeles managed only two hits off Cardinal starter Ernie Broglio. The next afternoon was more of the same. Veteran Curt Simmons held the Dodgers scoreless through seven innings. Dodger starter Johnny Podres matched Simmons' effort.

While the scoreless match continued in Los Angeles, some 385 miles to the north the Giants came to bat in the bottom of the eighth inning tied 1–1 in their own drama. The Houston pitcher was Dick Farrell, nicknamed "Turk," a hard-nosed competitor with a short fuse. Farrell had joined Drysdale, Koufax and Bob Gibson in striking out 200 batters that season.

"When he loses, his temper is quick and he's moody," a teammate described Farrell, who once shattered a mirror in a bar because "I looked in the mirror and didn't like what I saw, so I threw a punch."[34] Farrell wanted nothing to do with giving the Giants an opening to catch the Dodgers. Sitting at his locker before the game, the Turk told reporters, "I don't intend to lose."[35]

Ed Bailey's home run in the fourth inning had given the Giants a 1–0 lead behind O'Dell. But Houston's Jim Pendleton—a former Dodger—singled in the tying run in the sixth inning. The leadoff hitter in the bottom of the eighth against Farrell was Mays. Despite his

10–19 record, Farrell was the most effective pitcher in the Houston rotation. His earned run average when Mays stepped in was 2.99 in more than 240 innings of work for an expansion team that won only sixty-four games all season.

Farrell fired an inside fastball and Mays turned on it, sending it soaring into the left field bleachers. It was home run number forty-seven for Mays. More importantly, it gave the Giants a 2–1 lead. When Miller struck out Houston pinch-hitter Billy Goodman with two out in the top of the ninth—Goodman's last at-bat of a sixteen-year major league career—the Giants had pulled to within half a game of first place.

The final score was posted on the Dodger Stadium scoreboard. It only ratcheted up the tension felt by the home fans—and the home team. "Golly, they were tight," said Houston manager Harry Craft of the Dodgers. "Tight and tired."[36]

As the eighth inning began in Los Angeles, Podres retired James on a fly ball to center, bringing up St. Louis catcher Gene Oliver. With the count 1–2, Oliver drilled a hanging curveball deep over the left field fence and St. Louis led, 1–0. The Dodger Stadium crowd was stunned, but the blast was met by wild cheering throughout the city of San Francisco where fans listened on their transistor radios. Podres got the final two outs without further damage, but the Dodgers were now desperate and it showed. They were retired one-two-three in both the eighth and ninth innings. Los Angeles had not scored a run in 21 consecutive innings. When Dodger second baseman Jim Gilliam popped out to short right field for the final out, the regular season was over. The Dodgers and Giants were tied with records of 101–61.

In the jubilant San Francisco locker room, Harvey Kuenn said his teammates were certainly tired from the strain of the pennant race, "but we can't be any more pooped than they [the Dodgers] are."[37] Dark, as managers do, was already looking ahead rather than celebrating what had just occurred.

"Sure, we want to win that first game," he commented on the upcoming playoff. "As for pressure, we've played too many games now to worry about that. No matter what happens in the next three days, the fellows have played great."[38]

The next day's bay area newspapers would recap the unlikely circumstances that led to a playoff and discuss which team would have the advantage. But readers couldn't miss the front-page news outside the sports section. "Troops Fire Over Heads of Rioters" blared one headline of a newspaper article describing the death of two persons amid the seething hatred expressed by thousands of demonstrators in Oxford, Mississippi.[39] Under the protection of federalized state troopers,

29-year-old James Meredith was set to enroll as the first black student at the University of Mississippi. He would do so on October 1, attending a class on American History.[40] "Life in the usually sleepy Southern town was at a standstill," the Associated Press reported. "The streets were practically deserted except for rioters, soldiers and newsmen."[41]

President John F. Kennedy initially ordered in 4,000 National Guardsmen to quell the protesters. "I deeply regret the fact that any action by the executive branch was necessary in this case, but all other avenues and alternatives, including persuasion and conciliation, had been tried and exhausted," said the president.[42] By the end of the week, he would deploy additional military police battalions and Guardsmen to head off more violence.

There were also articles discussing the upcoming flight of astronaut Walter Schirra who was scheduled to orbit the Earth six times in the latest step by the United States to regain the lead in the "space race" with the Soviet Union. Fears were circulating that tropical storm Daisy, an Atlantic Ocean disturbance, might delay the flight.[43]

For baseball fans, six months and 162 games had not been enough. It would take a best-of-three playoff to determine a National League champion. League president Warren Giles conducted a September 27 coin flip to prepare for the possibility of a first-place tie. Giants owner Stoneham lost the coin flip. The Dodgers chose to host games two and three (if necessary) and start out on the road. The opening playoff game would begin at one o'clock in San Francisco on Monday afternoon. The playoff winner would then host Game One of the World Series on Thursday, October 4. The playoff games would be nationally televised by the NBC network. Like the rest of the baseball world, the Yankees would be watching.

Three

The Playoff:
"This Was More Thrilling!"

The two teams had already met eighteen times, each winning nine. They were part of the National League's fiercest, most competitive rivalry. There were few, if any, secrets left between the two.

So it really wasn't surprising that on the morning of the first playoff game Dodger management asked the umpiring crew to inspect the dirt area between first and second base at Candlestick Park. Dodger publicity director Red Patterson claimed the Giants' grounds crew had dumped extra sand on the base path to slow down the speedy Dodgers.[1]

Led by shortstop Wills, who had broken Ty Cobb's major league record of 96 stolen bases and would be voted the league's Most Valuable Player, Los Angeles was approaching 200 steals as a team. The next highest total was eighty-six by the Cardinals. The running game was a huge part of the Dodger offense and the team was convinced the Giants were deliberately trying to sabotage them. Patterson lodged a complaint with the plate umpire, the veteran Jocko Conlan, stating that after the extra sand, "they'll turn on the sprinklers and wet it down like it was for water follies." When Conlan ordered the grounds crew to address the excess sand, Alvin Dark bristled. "This is our park and we'll do whatever we want with it," he told Conlan.[2]

A no-nonsense umpire with more than twenty years of big-league experience, Conlan had worked the 1951 playoff and countless games between the two rivals. He was not easily intimidated. He ignored Dark and ordered longtime Giants head groundskeeper Matty Schwab to remove the infield's excess sand and tamp down the rest. Ultimately, multiple wheelbarrows of sand were taken away. Conlan also told Schwab not to wet down the infield prior to the first pitch, a most unusual directive. Schwab, who once lived in an apartment under the stands at the Polo Grounds,[3] later denied that extra sand had been applied, but the tactic became part of the playoff legend.[4]

A crowd of 32,660 were treated to temperatures in the low seventies with much less wind than normal. Some of the male patrons removed their shirts to enjoy the warm California sun. The turnout, almost 10,000 below capacity, was considered satisfactory, given that it was the start of the work week and the contest had been scheduled less than twenty-four hours ahead of the first pitch. The fans settled in to watch a matchup of two very different lefthanders, Pierce, the control artist for the Giants, versus the overpowering Koufax for the Dodgers.

From the Dodger perspective, the loss of Koufax for two months might have been the single biggest reason L.A. found itself in a playoff. Having overcome the severe wildness that plagued him since his debut in Brooklyn in 1955, Koufax won eighteen games in 1961 and had fourteen victories in twenty-four starts before being shut down this season. His powerful fastball and knee-buckling curveball made him the most dominant pitcher in baseball—when healthy. But Koufax didn't seem to be fully recovered from the mysterious circulation problem in his left index finger.

When he returned for three appearances in late September, the results were not promising. In seven and two-thirds innings, Koufax gave up six hits, walked eight and pitched to an unsightly 6.39 ERA. Nevertheless, Dodger manager Alston went to him the night before the first game against the free-swinging Giants. "How do you feel," asked Alston. Koufax later said he knew right then that, while not forcing him into any decision, his manager wanted him to pitch. "I can try," Koufax told him.[5]

After Pierce disposed of the Dodgers in the top of the first inning, Koufax retired Harvey Kuenn and Chuck Hiller before Felipe Alou laced a double to left, bringing up Willie Mays. On a 2–1 pitch, Mays connected with a Koufax fastball and drove it deep over the fence in right-center field to give the Giants a 2–0 lead. In the bottom of the second, San Francisco's Jim Davenport, not normally a slugger, smacked a long fly ball to left. Under normal conditions at Candlestick the ball would have been held up by the wind, but now it carried over the fence to make it 3–0. When Ed Bailey followed with a hard single to right, Alston decided his gamble with Koufax was over and brought in right-hander Ed Roebuck.

Meanwhile, Pierce was keeping the visitors in their miserable batting funk. The Dodgers entered the day having failed to score a run in their last 21 innings versus St. Louis. They had not advanced a runner as far as third base in the past 17 innings. Pierce mixed a fastball, slider and just enough curveballs to keep the anxious Los Angeles hitters off balance all afternoon. "It's the most satisfying game I've ever pitched," he

Three. The Playoff: "This Was More Thrilling!"

Billy Pierce delivers a pitch on the way to a 5–2 Giants win over the Yankees in Game Six. Pierce was undefeated at home in 1962, including an 8–0 shutout in the first game of the NL playoff with the Dodgers. He won 211 games over eighteen seasons (© 1962 S.F. Giants).

later told reporters.[6] That was noteworthy since Pierce once retired the first twenty-six batters he faced while with the White Sox, losing a perfect game with two out in the ninth. But this was his most pressure-filled outing ever and he came through brilliantly.

The Giants piled on the runs against the Dodger bullpen, getting back-to-back solo home runs by Mays and Orlando Cepeda in the sixth and a two-run double by shortstop Jose Pagan in the eighth. The two homers gave Mays forty-nine on the season. The result was a dominant 8–0 victory for the Giants. They seemed to have all the momentum.

Jack Sanford, who had won his last sixteen decisions, would pitch Game Two for the Giants. Alston initially selected Stan Williams to start for the Dodgers but changed his mind on the morning of the game and went with Drysdale, his twenty-five-game winner. The late switch irritated both pitchers. Miffed at not originally being named to start either of the first two games, Drysdale had said, "What the hell are they saving me for, the first spring exhibition game?"[7]

For his part, Williams later admitted, "I was really disappointed when they told me Drysdale was starting instead. I had been building up for the game and I really believed I could beat them."[8]

Before the game, Alston tried to boost his team's sagging confidence, ignoring what was now a thirty-inning scoreless streak. "We're sure as hell overdue," he told reporters. "Our pressing days are over. Now the other team is ahead and we're behind. We've got everything to gain and nothing to lose."[9] He also decided to adjust his lineup, inserting veterans Duke Snider and Wally Moon and moving Tommy Davis from the outfield to third base.

The Dodgers also hoped being back home would cure their anemic offensive attack. A modest paid crowd of 25,321 indicated that many Angelenos did not share Alston's optimism. Spirits were dampened further when Cepeda singled with one out in the top of the second and Felipe Alou doubled him in. San Francisco nursed its 1–0 lead through five innings. Then the roof collapsed on Drysdale.

In the top of the sixth, he walked catcher Tom Haller with one out. Haller went to third on Pagan's double down the third base line. Sanford then hit a slow roller that Drysdale picked up and threw wildly to first, pulling first baseman Moon off the bag. Hiller dropped a single into right to score Pagan, and Davenport followed with a line drive base hit to bring in Sanford. It was 4–0 and Alston again summoned Roebuck from the bullpen. After Mays grounded into a force play, McCovey got the Giants' fourth hit of the inning, a single that scored Hiller.

As they came to bat in the bottom of the sixth, the Dodgers trailed 5–0. They had not touched home plate in the past thirty-five innings. They had only twelve outs left to work with. After having led the National League most of the year, it seemed as if their season was drawing to a rapid, depressing ending.

The bottom of the sixth started with a walk to Jim Gilliam. Dark, perhaps sensing the law of averages working against him, decided to lift Sanford. The workhorse right-hander had given up only two hits, had walked three and had thrown seventy-nine pitches. But Sanford candidly told Dark in the dugout that he was running out of gas. "He's had a cold since he pitched on Saturday," Dark would say later in the locker room. "He didn't have anything left. Jack was exhausted."[10]

Dark's two starting pitchers had shut out the Dodgers through fourteen innings on five hits. For the first time in the playoff, he'd have to rely on his hot-and-cold bullpen. He signaled for Stu Miller, his most trusted relief pitcher. Miller was appearing in his fifty-ninth game of the season. He would wind up leading the Giants with nineteen saves. He'd already worked more than 100 innings in relief.

And then the dam burst.

Snider, the reliable "Duke of Flatbush" during his Brooklyn days, smashed a double to right sending Gilliam to third. Tommy Davis then

Three. The Playoff: "This Was More Thrilling!"

drove a long fly to Mays in center. Both runners advanced and the Dodgers' scoreless streak was over. But L.A. was not done. A walk, three more hits and a hit batsman against two more San Francisco relievers put the Dodgers ahead, 7–5. The inning's big blow was a three-run double to left-center by pinch-hitter Lee Walls.

The Giants put two men on in the seventh inning but failed to score against lefty Ron Perranoski. When Davenport stepped in to face Perranoski in the top of the eighth, it was still 7–5 in favor of the Dodgers. Davenport promptly singled. Mays followed with a single, and Alston replaced Perranoski with Jack Smith. Bailey drilled a single to center to score Davenport, but Mays was out trying to reach third, cut down by a laser throw from Davis, who had moved from third base to center field one inning earlier. This became a crucial out when Cepeda reached on a muffed fly ball by Frank Howard and Felipe Alou walked to load the bases. Johnny Orsino's sacrifice fly tied matters at 7–7.

It stayed that way until the bottom of the ninth. Wills led off and drew a walk against reliever Bob Bolin, who was immediately pulled out of the game by Dark in favor of Dick LeMay. With his attention diverted by Wills, LeMay walked Gilliam on a 3–1 pitch. Once again, Dark changed pitchers, bringing in right-hander Gaylord Perry. A future Hall of Famer, Perry was a 24-year-old rookie pitching in a huge spot. He managed to record an out, but he didn't satisfy his manager.

Facing Perry, ex-Giant Daryl Spencer laid down a bunt that rolled straight toward the mound. Perry fielded it cleanly but didn't think he could get the speedy Wills at third base and threw to first instead, allowing the winning run to move to third. "The play was to third," Dark would state later in the clubhouse. "I think he could have made the putout."[11]

For the seventh and final time, Dark decided to go to his bullpen. Pitcher number eight for San Francisco was the erratic southpaw Mike McCormick, a former ace of the staff. His job was to get out of a one-out jam with runners on second and third.

McCormick began by intentionally walking Davis, the NL batting champion, to load the bases and set up a force at any base and keep the double play in order. He'd have the advantage of pitching to a dangerous, but slow, left-handed hitter in Ron Fairly, who batted just .248 against left-handers that season. A double play would get the Giants out of the inning. Throwing hard stuff, McCormick quickly got ahead in the count, 0–2. Rather than waste one, he threw a breaking pitch in the zone to upset Fairly's timing.

"The third pitch was a curve. I thought it was a strike and I swung," Fairly told a large group of reporters after the game. "I was just trying to get it out of the infield."[12] Expecting hard stuff, Fairly was slightly off-balance and reached out across the plate without taking a hard swing. He got enough wood on it to send a fly ball to medium center field where the Giants' best outfielder was ready. Mays caught it and fired a strong one-hop throw home, but the fleet Wills slid safely past the tag of catcher Orsino to score the winning run.

The hard fought 8–7 Dodger comeback victory set up a winner-take-all third playoff game. It was an exhausting day for two already tired teams. The Giants used twenty-three of their twenty-five eligible players (everyone except pitchers Marichal and Pierce). The Dodgers used nineteen players, including four pinch-hitters and one pinch-runner. The game clocked in at four hours and eighteen minutes, at the time the longest nine-inning game in major league history.[13]

In a relieved Los Angeles locker room, Alston soon grew agitated by a reporter asking him when he thought his club "had stopped choking up."

"They haven't *started* choking up yet," said a stern Alston, his voice slowly rising with emotion. "They were disgusted, they were discouraged. But nobody gave up. This is a team that believes in itself. Choking is kind of a nasty term. The players are tired, they're overworked, especially the pitchers. But so are the Giants."[14]

Alston's third base coach was Leo (The Lip) Durocher one of baseball's most notorious characters and a former manager of both clubs. Durocher piloted the New York Giants to the 1951 pennant on the strength of the "Shot Heard Round the World," Bobby Thomson's game-winning homer in the third playoff game. He'd also been the Dodger skipper when Brooklyn lost the 1946 league playoff in two games to St. Louis. He had become the only member of a team roster participating in every NL pennant playoff in history.

"We'll win it now," he told the Associated Press. "A game like this perks up the whole club. I haven't seen the guys so relaxed in a long time. You know when we really began to relax? When we were behind 5–0 in the sixth inning."[15]

Durocher's former shortstop, Dark, didn't dwell on the missed opportunity of Game Two, or having to face the Dodgers at their home park. "It's fifty-fifty," he asserted. "In no game of baseball do you have an advantage before it starts." Mays was asked what the outlook for the third game might be. "We'll be here," was all he said.[16]

Perry, who failed to try for the lead runner on Spencer's bunt in the ninth, later recalled that Dark ripped a phone off the wall and threw it in anger. "Alvin didn't really speak to me again until two years later, when he was on his way out as manager. He liked to make instant judgments about people, and from that day on I was a loser in his eyes. I wasn't eligible for the Series because I had rejoined the club in September. Dark must have been grateful for that."[17]

Both teams had reason for optimism when naming their starting pitchers for the third game. Juan Marichal was Dark's choice. He had won eighteen, thrown more than 250 innings and had eighteen complete games. Still only twenty-four years old in his third season in San Francisco, the "Dominican Dandy" was building a reputation as a big-game pitcher.

Los Angeles starter Johnny Podres would always own a special place in any Dodger fan's heart—particularly Dodger fans living in Brooklyn. Podres won two games in the 1955 World Series, including the most important game in Dodger history. His 2–0 shutout of the Yankees in the seventh game brought the Dodgers their only World Series championship representing Brooklyn. Overall, he was 3–1 in postseason play. Podres would be making his fortieth start of the year. He was 15–13 with five shutouts. His strikeout to walk ratio was an excellent 2.51-to-1, and he'd pitched in the '62 All-Star game. He was neither a flamethrower like Koufax, nor an intimidating presence like Drysdale, but his experience and knowledge of hitters inspired his teammates.

On the morning of the third playoff game, West Coast residents rose early to watch the 5:15 (PDT) launch of astronaut Walter (Wally) Schirra's Atlas rocket from Florida's Cape Canaveral on a mission to orbit the Earth six times. Nine hours and thirteen minutes later, Schirra's capsule floated down in the Pacific Ocean. The mission had been a huge success and captivated proud U.S. citizens across the country. Americans saw it as a tribute to the nation's technology, resources and willpower. "You did a wonderful job and we are very, very pleased," Schirra was told via a phone call from President Kennedy.[18]

The following morning, directly opposite one newspaper's report detailing Schirra's success, was a photo of James Meredith being hung in effigy from a dorm room on the campus of Ole Miss. A sign on the effigy read, "Go back to where you belong!" Meredith, who served nine years in the U.S. Air Force and rose to the rank of sergeant, was born in central Mississippi.[19]

A larger crowd of 45,693 filled Dodger Stadium on a typical sunny early-autumn afternoon for Game Three. San Francisco leadoff hitter Kuenn hit Podres' third pitch for a single to left, advanced to second on a sacrifice bunt, but couldn't come around as Felipe Alou and Mays both bounced back to the pitcher to end the inning. Likewise, Marichal yielded an infield single to Wills, who took second on Marichal's errant throw to first. But the next three Dodgers popped out to end the threat.

Still scoreless in the top of the third, it was the Giants who drew first blood. Pagan singled to left. Continuing a trend that saw both teams play sloppy baseball, Podres fielded Marichal's sacrifice bunt and threw it into center field trying to nail Pagan at second base. Kuenn's second hit of the game drove in Pagan and moved Marichal to second—where he proceeded to stray too far from the bag, only to see catcher Johnny Roseboro's throw elude the Dodger infield. Marichal ran to third while Kuenn remained at first.

Hiller tried to make the Dodgers pay for Roseboro's error, but instead hit a short fly ball to Duke Snider in left field. Snider's throw to second baseman Jim Gilliam held Marichal at third, but when Gilliam saw Kuenn still retreating to first base, he fired wildly there. The ball got past first baseman Moon and Marichal raced home to give the Giants a 2–0 lead. The Dodgers had committed three errors and basically allowed the opposing pitcher to reach base and score by "tossing the ball around wildly like a bunch of eager kids in a sandlot game," according to the next day's *San Bernardino Sun*.

Back safely on the mound after his baserunning adventures, Marichal held the Dodgers in check in the third, but gave up a run-scoring groundout to Frank Howard in the fourth inning after hits by Snider and Davis.

In the top of the sixth, leading 2–1, the Giants missed a golden opportunity to get some breathing room. Cepeda led off with an opposite-field single to right. Bailey, one of the Giants' slowest runners, hit a grounder in the hole between short and third that Wills couldn't make a play on. When Davenport bunted for a base hit on a sacrifice attempt down the third-base line, the Giants were set up with bases loaded and nobody out.

For the third straight game, Alston decided he wanted Roebuck to replace his starting pitcher in a high-pressure situation. Like Koufax, Roebuck had joined the Dodgers in 1955. He'd pitched almost exclusively in relief. The '62 season had been his busiest ever. When summoned to the mound in the third playoff game, Roebuck was making his 64th appearance of the season. His record stood at 10–2 with nine saves and an ERA slightly above 3.00. He had a lively fastball and could strike out a batter when needed.

Pitching carefully, Roebuck threw a low fastball that Pagan beat in the dirt to Wills at shortstop. Wills threw home to Roseboro for the force-out. Marichal was the next scheduled hitter. Even with the bases loaded, Dark did not want to remove Marichal and play the roulette wheel that was his shaky bullpen. So Marichal strode to the plate. He swung at a 1–0 pitch and chopped it to Wills near second base. Maury stepped on the bag, fired to first and the threat was over. The L.A. crowd exploded with cheers, sensing a shift in the game's momentum.

Now the fans were alive. Snider led off the bottom of the sixth and collected his second hit of the game, a sharp single to left. Marichal fell behind in the count to Davis, then delivered a fastball up in the strike zone. Davis swung and sent a long drive five rows deep over the left-center field wall near the 390-foot sign. The two-run homer, Davis' 27th of the season, gave the Dodgers a 3–2 lead and the atmosphere in Dodger Stadium was electric. Marichal managed to escape further damage that inning, but in the seventh he fell victim to the baserunning wizardry of Wills.

With the Dodgers still ahead by one, Wills reached on a one-out single to left. On Marichal's first pitch to Gilliam, Wills set out for second and easily beat Bailey's throw. He stayed there when Gilliam flied out. On the first pitch to Larry Burright, Wills took off for third despite there being two out. Bailey's throw was low and skipped off the infield and over the left shoulder of Davenport, who had gone to one knee to take the throw and apply a tag. With third-base coach Durocher wildly waving him home, Wills got up and sprinted home to make it 4–2. He had manufactured the run all by himself.

The man of the hour for the Dodgers was now Roebuck.

The right-hander from the small town of East Millsboro, Pennsylvania, about forty-five miles directly south of Pittsburgh, had already hurled three scoreless innings as he took the mound in the top of the ninth with a 4–2 lead. Roebuck used only four pitches to retire the Giants in the eighth inning. The Dodgers were just three outs away from their first World Series meeting with the Yankees since 1956.

Looking to bolster his defense and nail down the pennant, Alston made two moves. He replaced the lumbering Howard in right field by moving Fairly from first base to right, and inserted Tim Harkness to play first. Dark also made a move. He sent Matty Alou up to hit for pitcher Don Larsen. Alou, who had walked only 14 times in 213 plate appearances, was up there to swing the bat. He cut on Roebuck's first delivery and roped a line single to right. Pitching from the stretch, Roebuck then induced Kuenn to hit a sharp grounder to shortstop.

"I got Kuenn to hit a perfect two-hopper to Wills," Roebuck would recall years later, "but someone on the bench had moved [second baseman Larry] Burright into the hole toward first, which you never do when a double play is in order, and he didn't get there in time to turn a double play."[20] Instead Burright took Wills' delayed throw and settled for erasing Alou for the first out of the inning.

Dark again went to his bench, this time selecting Willie McCovey.

Representing the tying run, McCovey had homered twenty times in only 229 at-bats in 1962. Roebuck did not want to give him anything he could drive to right field. He worked the outside part of the plate and walked McCovey on four pitches. Utility infielder Ernie Bowman came in to run for McCovey as the potential tying run.

The next hitter was Felipe Alou. Roebuck's 3–2 delivery missed ("a very close pitch," according to Roebuck), leaving the bases loaded. As the fans buzzed nervously, Alston walked to the mound to speak to Roebuck with Mays the hitter. Satisfied with his pitcher's condition, Alston decided to make no change. Looking for something he could drive, Mays swung at the first pitch and hit a liner to Roebuck's right, about waist high. Roebuck reacted as if he were fooled by the ball's speed. "It was not hit too hard, and I closed my glove a bit too soon and it squirted out," Roebuck said. "That would have been a double play, too."[21]

The official 1962 World Series film produced by Major League Baseball includes highlights from the Giants-Dodgers playoff. It appears that Roebuck, indeed, might have doubled one of the runners if the ball had stuck in his glove. But he had to reach across his body with his glove hand. If Roebuck were a left-hander, the Dodgers might have had a better outcome. However, it was not an easy chance and Roebuck's description ("not hit too hard") seems a bit self-serving.

The play was viewed differently by the Giants. In his book *Say Hey*, Mays wrote, "It was hit so hard it knocked off his glove [this was not verified by the film]. He had no play, the bases were still loaded and our comeback was underway."[22] Durocher said Mays "hit a bullet back at Roebuck."[23] Other contemporary accounts described Mays' hit as having been "rifled," and "slammed."

Regardless of its velocity, Mays' RBI infield single left the bases loaded with the Dodgers up, 4–3. Alston now opened himself up to second guessing that would follow him for the rest of his managerial career. He sent Durocher to the mound to bring in Stan Williams from the bullpen.

Williams was an aggressive veteran with a well-earned reputation for working all parts of the plate and showing hitters no mercy. Primarily a starting pitcher, he was also used to pitching in relief—he'd done that eleven times during the season, most recently as the winning pitcher in Game Two. Williams threw hard. He recorded 205 strikeouts in 235-and-one-third innings in 1961. But he periodically had problems with his command. He'd walked 108 in 1961 and 98 in '62.

Roseboro, the Dodger catcher, remembered the moment. "We all worried about Williams," Roseboro said. "He was wild and inconsistent."[24] Said Roebuck, "He brought in Stanley and all hell broke loose."[25]

Three. The Playoff: "This Was More Thrilling!"

In his autobiography *Nice Guys Finish Last*, Durocher wrote, "Stan Williams was a big, wild right-hander. He had pitched very well toward the end of the season, but in a spot like this? Williams? I went out and I brought in Williams and then I said to the boys on the bench, 'We may as well go in. If I had ten pitchers, this would be the tenth one I'd bring into a spot like this. He'll walk the ballpark.'"

Williams's first pitch to Cepeda was a strike. Cepeda then swung and hit a fly ball deep enough in right field to score Bowman from third and move Felipe Alou from second to third. The game was tied at 4–4 with two out and runners on first and third. The next batter was Bailey. Again, Williams poured in a strike to get ahead in the count. But his next pitch was in the dirt and rolled a few feet away. Roseboro had made a fine play to get his glove on the ball, thereby preventing Alou from scoring, but Mays alertly advanced to second. With first base open, Alston ordered Williams to intentionally walk Bailey.

Most of the Dodgers expected another pitcher to come in at this point, maybe Perranoski, perhaps Larry Sherry. Even Drysdale, the Game Two starter, was an option. But Alston wanted to stay with Williams. He made no move. "Nobody on the bench said a word," wrote Durocher. "Nobody had to. The same thought was on everyone's mind. He's loading the bases with Williams pitching, right after Williams has shown that he hasn't got his control."

On a 3–1 pitch to Davenport, Williams missed outside for ball four. Alou skipped home, happily jumping on home plate. The Giants had taken a 5–4 lead. "It never bothered me that much because I gave it all I had and it didn't work out," Williams said many years later. "Had I let up and thrown a half-assed fastball and the guy got a base hit I never would have forgiven myself. But I walked him at 100 mph, giving it my best shot."[26]

Following the walk to Davenport, Alston finally made a move to his bullpen, sending for Perranoski. The lefty got Pagan to hit a ground ball to second, but the rookie Burright fumbled it, picked it up and threw late to first. Mays scored to make it 6–4. It was the Dodgers' fourth error of the game and the seventh by both teams, an amazingly poor display of baseball with a pennant on the line. The nightmare inning ended for the Dodgers when Perranoski fanned Bob Nieman, the third Giant pinch-hitter of the inning.

Dark went right to a trusted source to close out the game. He bypassed the rest of his bullpen and brought in Pierce, who had tossed the three-hit shutout in Game One. Pierce picked up where he left off, retiring Wills on a grounder to third, Gilliam on a fly ball to center and pinch-hitter Walls on an easy fly ball to Mays, who immediately hurled the ball toward the seats in right field in jubilation.

Eleven years to the day—October 3, 1951, to October 3, 1962—the Giants had overcome another two-run playoff deficit to beat the Dodgers in the ninth inning. This time may not have been as shocking or as memorable as watching Thomson run around the bases while announcer Russ Hodges screamed, *"The Giants win the pennant! The Giants win the pennant!"* But the outcome was just as satisfying to Giant fans in San Francisco as it had been for those in New York eleven years earlier.

While Dark, captain of the '51 Giants, sloughed off comparisons between the two triumphs, his first base coach, Wes Westrum, gladly volunteered his thoughts. "This was more thrilling," said Westrum, a former Giant catcher. "This was more thrilling!"[27]

Williams always felt the Dodgers made him a scapegoat for their failure to win the 1962 pennant. He carried bitter feelings toward his former team into his eighties. "I eventually got over it [the loss], but they never did," Williams told columnist Bill Plaschke of the *Los Angeles Times* in the summer of 2018. "I don't like the Dodgers and they don't like me. They have completely divorced me over the years and I pull against them every night."[28]

"They've never really invited me for anything, and I think originally they held it against me for that walk. Somewhere along the line it must have been passed along that I'm blackballed." Dodger officials told Plaschke they had no bias toward Williams, but their former pitcher wasn't buying it. He even sold his 1959 Dodger World Series ring.[29]

Reporters had a field day mocking the poor defense by the losers. "The Dodgers comported themselves as though they were fighting for last place in the little league," wrote Lou Hatter in the *Baltimore Sun*. The *New York Times*, referencing the historically bad expansion team in New York, stated, "In the third inning, the Dodgers suddenly took to tossing the ball around in a manner that would have had the Mets green with envy."[30]

(Ironically, three members of the Dodgers would *become* New York Mets one year later—Burright, Snider and Harkness.)

Having lived through the excruciating loss in 1951, Snider worried in the Dodger locker room about what might be said by some of the players, angered as they were by their manager's pitching decisions. "I said to my teammates, I'm not going to let the press in for a few minutes, fellows," Snider wrote in his autobiography. "I opened the door slightly and told the reporters waiting on the other side, 'Let's wait a few minutes before you come in. It's pretty grim in there.'"[31]

According to Durocher, while Alston walked over to the Giant locker room to congratulate Dark, several Dodger players were handed bottles of whiskey and proceeded to drink and commiserate for almost an hour while still in their uniforms. "Where they [the bottles] came from I will never know," he said.³² Durocher, a superstitious type, had worn a T-shirt under his uniform that he claimed to have worn in the 1951 playoff. Alas, it brought him no luck. A writer asked Dark if he'd brought any kind of good luck memorabilia from '51. "Yeah, Willie Mays," he said.³³

The Giants' celebration, the typical champagne-soaked spectacle, featured lots of spraying and pouring, but very little drinking. The players were keenly aware that the tight schedule ordered by Commissioner Ford Frick meant the World Series would open tomorrow afternoon in Candlestick Park.

By the time the Giants' charter plane made its initial approach to land at San Francisco International Airport after the brief flight from L.A., approximately 50,000 cheering supporters were on hand. The crowd was so large, it spilled over onto the airfield near the runways. Pilot Orville Schmitt announced to the weary Giants that the plane would be forced to circle until the crowd was put under control. Becoming increasingly irritated by the delay, anxious to get home and unwind for a few hours before having to face the Yankees the next afternoon, the Giants could do nothing but wait. At one point, flying to Sacramento and busing to San Francisco was considered.³⁴

After an extra eighty minutes circling the airport ("We just completed our seventh orbit," yelled one of the players),³⁵ the Giants' flight landed about a mile from the crowd at an old, abandoned depot. The team was then bused to the main terminal, but not before fans mobbed the bus, rocking it back and forth and even cracking a few windows.

Unbeknownst to the cheering throng, Mays had walked off the bus into a waiting taxicab on the tarmac before the bus pulled up to the terminal. Shouts of "We want Willie! We want Willie!" grew louder. On the bus was seldom-used Giant outfielder Carl Boles, who bore a faint facial and physical similarity to Mays. Reserve outfielder Bob Nieman cried out, "Let's throw 'em Boles and get the hell outta here!"³⁶

Fortunately, no one was injured in what Captain Jack O'Brien of the San Mateo County sheriff's office called "by far the largest crowd ever seen at the airport."³⁷

Headquartered in Del Webb's Town House hotel on Market Street, a property belonging to team co-owner Del Webb, the Yankees heard fans yelling and occasionally breaking lobby furniture well into the night before police finally calmed the scene. "We knew there was a World Series in town," said Ralph Houk, tongue in cheek. "We could tell by the noise, bedlam and pandemonium."³⁸

Frank Jordan, later to be elected Mayor of San Francisco, but at the time a young police officer, was assigned to protect several of the Yankees who had received anonymous threats of physical harm. "I never left their sides while traveling to and from the Town House to Candlestick Park," Jordan recalled.[39]

The Yanks were not fazed by the commotion. As they relaxed in their hotel rooms, the players watched evening news updates of the successful Schirra flight. The astronaut would later attribute his success in completing his targeted number of orbits to his careful consumption of fuel.

"I fired my thrusters sparingly, in small bursts that I liked to call micro-mouse farts," Schirra wrote in his 2000 autobiography, *Schirra's Space*. "At the end of my flight, I had over half my fuel left and had to dump it."

Schirra's flight had attracted enormous worldwide attention. Manned space flights were still unique and exciting to the American public. A World Series featuring the New York Yankees, by comparison, seemed almost routine.

Four

Game One: Boyer's Redemption

One of sports' hoariest arguments was center stage as baseball fans and members of the media discussed the prospects of the Giants taking on the Yankees.

Specifically, which team would have the advantage—the one that had all the momentum by winning a dramatic come-from-behind game to get there, or the team that was rested and had its pitching arranged in a precise manner? Would the Giants be emotionally drained from the gauntlet they'd just run in getting into, and winning, a three-game play-off? Would the Yankees be rusty after not having played a game with serious implications for more than a week?

The National League playoff had essentially eliminated much of the opportunity for the media's usual pre–World Series predictions. The first pitch would occur less than twenty-four hours after the Giants' 6–4 win over the Dodgers, providing a far smaller window for prognostications than the usual two or three days at the conclusion of the regular season. Of course, the bookmakers didn't worry about how much time they had to set the betting lines. Nothing would delay the public getting its bets down, legally or otherwise. A 44-year-old Las Vegas sports handicapper named Jimmy (the Greek) Snyder established the Yankees as 3-to-2 favorites to capture the Fall Classic. Conventional wisdom said the Giants had absorbed too much strain down the pennant race and the Yankees were rested. Bookmakers on Broadway in New York listed the Bronx Bombers at 7-to-5 favorites.[1]

Facing its printing deadline with the playoff result still undecided, *Sports Illustrated* hypothetically analyzed the Yankees vs. both the Dodgers and the Giants. In a piece primarily built around the importance of rookie Tom Tresh in the New York lineup, *SI*'s Huston Horn opined that San Francisco had the most balanced pitching of the three teams, particularly given Koufax's injured finger. "Behind [Whitey]

Ford, the Yankee staff is shaky. Twenty-three game winner Ralph Terry has a history of yielding big hits at bad times and Bill Stafford has not blossomed. Yankee relief has been a headache for Ralph Houk all season." SI summed up its preview by stating that a Yankee-Giant matchup "might well turn into a wild, free-swinging affair."[2]

A *Sporting News* editorial was critical of the Commissioner's scheduling, declaring, "Without a question of doubt, the National League went into the World's Series at a disadvantage. The San Francisco Giants were bone-tired, their pitching staff used up. By contrast, the Yankees had clinched the pennant a week before the season ended. They received additional rest during the National League playoff."[3]

In the next few lines, however, the editorial justified the need for the "show to go on as quickly as possible," and pointed out that three of the four teams that had won league playoffs had gone on to win the World Series. The only one that did not was the 1951 New York Giants.

Unable to spend much time analyzing the participants, some members of the press focused on another unique facet of the upcoming Series. It would be the first played between teams from the East and West Coast. In 1959, travel rotated between Los Angeles and Chicago when the Dodgers beat the White Sox in six games. But a New York–San Francisco combination would be an additional thousand miles of travel each way, and feature two of the most expensive cities in America. The required travel would significantly expand airfares and expense accounts for members of the media.

"Many of the smaller newspapers can't cope with the expenses and have contented themselves with covering only one phase of the Series," wrote national columnist Bob Addie. "It robs these men of a chance to see the whole thing."[4]

Some East Coast newspapers addressed the problem by sending writers to the West Coast to cover the Giants-Dodgers playoff, the first two games of the Series in San Francisco, and then simply remain put until possibly needed to cover the sixth and seventh games, if necessary. The bills for hotels and meals figured to offset the steep cost of additional flights back and forth from San Francisco to New York. Listening to the radio in their hotels or restaurants, these media members were likely to hear the new Top 40 song by Tony Bennett that was getting considerable airplay in the bay area. It was called "I Left My Heart in San Francisco."

Whitey Ford would pitch Game One for the Yankees. There really seemed no other logical choice for Houk. Ford had a World Series record of 9–4 and was working on a record consecutive scoreless innings streak that had previously been established by Babe Ruth in

Four. Game One: Boyer's Redemption

1918. The Yankees and their fans would always recall how in 1960 Casey Stengel had bypassed Ford in the opening game of the World Series at Pittsburgh's Forbes Field and held him back for the third game at Yankee Stadium. Instead of possibly pitching three times in a seven-game series, Ford only worked twice—and both times hurled a shutout. With journeyman Art Ditmar starting the decisive seventh game, the Yankees fell behind, rallied, but ultimately lost on Mazeroski's homer off Terry.

"It was the only time I ever got mad at Casey," Ford said in *Slick*, his 1987 autobiography. "I was so annoyed at Stengel I wouldn't talk to him on the plane ride back to New York."

Alvin Dark's pitcher was pretty much a process of elimination. Pierce had thrown nine innings two days earlier, as well as pitching the ninth inning the day before. Sanford, the staff's biggest winner, had pitched on Tuesday and was still battling a cold. Marichal was not available since he'd thrown seven hard innings the day before. That left Billy O'Dell.

One of those rare major leaguers who never played in the minors, William Oliver O'Dell was signed by the Baltimore Orioles in 1954 after his junior year at Clemson University.[5] By offering him a bonus of $12,500 the Orioles triggered the major league rule (in effect from 1953 to 1957) that mandated teams carry a player receiving a bonus of more than $4,000 for at least two years on the big-league roster before he could be sent to the minors.[6]

A native of tiny Whitmire, South Carolina, O'Dell pitched briefly for the Orioles in '54, then served in the Army until being discharged in August of 1956. He worked his way into the Orioles' starting rotation before being traded to the Giants in November of 1959. With San Francisco, he became both a starter and reliever, used wherever the team needed him. In an era when the bullpen primarily consisted of pitchers deemed incapable of succeeding as starters, O'Dell desperately wanted to be part of the four-man rotation. "If the Giants don't let me pitch any more than last season," he told a reporter after the '61 campaign, "I hope they let me go somewhere else."[7]

Dark heard O'Dell and gave him the chance he wanted after the left-hander's solid spring. O'Dell rewarded his skipper with his best season. He made thirty-nine starts in 1962 and threw a career-high 280 and two-thirds innings. He finished 19–14 with 195 strikeouts and twenty complete games. Plus, he'd pitched effectively against New York while with Baltimore, compiling a 2.95 ERA in 17 total appearances. "Dark knew I had success against the Yankees while in the American League," O'Dell would later say.[8] Now he'd pitch the most important game of his career.

With a sellout crowd basking in the excitement of the first World Series game played in San Francisco, O'Dell had the fans roaring as he struck out Tony Kubek to begin the game. Subsequent singles by Bobby Richardson and Tresh, however, put O'Dell in a jam. He fanned Mickey Mantle for the second out to bring up Roger Maris. Booed lustily by Giant fans remembering his comments on the wind and Candlestick Park after the 1961 All-Star game ("If I had to play here, I'd quit baseball"),[9] Maris drove a long fly to deep right-center field. Mays and Felipe Alou chased it before Alou stretched out his glove and tried to backhand it. But his arm banged into the fence and the ball popped loose on the warning track. Both runners scored and Maris reached second with a double. The Yankees had taken a quick 2–0 lead.

In the bottom of the first, Ford retired the Giants in order, extending his Series mark to thirty-two and one-third consecutive scoreless innings, but in the second, after O'Dell stranded two Yankees without a run, the Giants finally ended the streak.

Mays, who had great success against Ford in five All-Star games (6-for-7 with a triple and two home runs), led off with a base hit to left. After Orlando Cepeda took a called third strike, Jim Davenport singled to move Mays to third. When Ford got Ed Bailey on a foul pop fly to Richardson behind the first base line, it seemed the Yanks' ace might escape. But Jose Pagan surprised everyone with a well-executed bunt toward third that Ford picked up, then bobbled. Pagan was safe on the base hit, Mays scored and Ford's historic streak was history at thirty-three consecutive scoreless innings. O'Dell grounded out, but the Giants were on the board.

In the third inning, O'Dell again ran into trouble. Walks to Mantle and Elston Howard brought Moose Skowron to the plate with two out. But O'Dell struck him out swinging to end the threat as the crowd roared. The Giants drew even in their half of the third. After Chuck Hiller doubled to left center and Alou singled to left, Mays came up with one out and runners on first and third. Once again, Ford could not handle the Giants' star who rifled a single to center, scoring Hiller to tie the game at 2–2. Alou stopped at second, but the Giants were in business with two men on and Cepeda coming up. Pitching deliberately, Ford threw a low fastball that Cepeda hit on the ground to Richardson, who started an inning-ending 4–6–3 double play.

After three innings both starting pitchers had been in and out of hot water, but in 1962 starting pitchers rarely were pulled early unless they really were performing poorly. Neither team was panicked at this point. Perhaps getting past some early nervousness, O'Dell settled down. He breezed through the fourth and fifth innings. In the sixth,

Four. Game One: Boyer's Redemption

Howard singled with one out but was erased when Davenport started an around-the-horn double play on a ground ball from Skowron.

The Giants continued to peck at Ford, but the Yankee hurler, nicknamed the "Chairman of the Board" for his commanding presence on the mound, refused to yield. He survived a leadoff walk to Kuenn in the fourth, a third straight single by Mays in the fifth, and left a runner on base in the sixth. The game remained deadlocked as Yankee third baseman Clete Boyer led off against O'Dell in the top of the seventh.

The third Boyer to play major league baseball and one of thirteen children in the family of marble cutter Vern Boyer and his wife, Mabel, Boyer had struggled mightily to become recognized as one of the finest fielding third basemen in the game. A native of Alba, Missouri, Boyer was thrilled to sign a major league contract with the nearby Kansas City Athletics in 1955. After bits of three seasons in Kansas City, he was traded to the Yankees and spent the '58 season as a starting infielder for their Class AA team in Binghamton. He split the following year between Triple-A Richmond and the Yankees, playing both third and shortstop.[10]

By 1960, Boyer was the Yankees' primary third baseman, alternating occasionally with veteran Gil McDougald. He showed a terrific glove, a strong arm and some power at the plate, hitting fourteen homers in less than 400 at-bats. But in the eyes of manager Stengel, Boyer's offense was still a liability. Boyer still dreaded hearing Stengel cry out, "Hold that gun!" his code for calling the hitter back to the dugout because a substitute was on the way.[11] This infuriated the young infielder, who grew to resent the aging Stengel's moves. It all came to a head in Game One of the World Series vs. the Pirates.

Boyer was in the starting lineup as the third baseman batting seventh against Pittsburgh's Vern Law. The Pirates knocked out New York starting pitcher Ditmar with three runs in the first inning. After the first two Yankee batters singled to open the top of the second, Boyer was pulled from the lineup as Stengel called on Dale Long to pinch-hit. "It was one of the biggest thrills in my life, starting in a World Series, and the first time up in the first game the old bastard took me out for a pinch-hitter," Boyer recalled. "I wanted to hit him over the head with the fucking bat."[12] When Long flied out and the Yanks failed to score in the inning, Stengel was widely criticized for making too many moves and dashing the confidence of his young infielder. Boyer admitted he did not mind seeing the Yankees relieve Stengel of his duties at the end of the Series.[13]

Ralph Houk re-instilled confidence in Boyer, telling him he was the Yanks' regular third baseman regardless of his offensive production. Boyer responded by becoming a superb defensive player who could also contribute at the plate. Like Brooks Robinson in 1970 and Graig Nettles in 1978, Boyer made several outstanding plays at third base in the 1961 World Series against the Reds that cemented his reputation with the glove. That year, he'd hit only .224 with eleven homers and fifty-five RBIs. But in '62, Boyer had enjoyed a solid season offensively. Normally hitting out of the number eight slot in the order, he batted .272 with eighteen home runs and sixty-two runs batted in.

Now with a 2–2 count, Boyer swung at O'Dell's pitch and drove it on a line toward deep left center. He would tell writers after the game he thought he had a double. Instead, the ball cleared the fence to give New York a 3–2 lead. "I'll never forget that homer," Boyer would say with a grin in the clubhouse. "I never got a hit off that guy [O'Dell] when he was with the Orioles."[14]

In the eighth, the Yankees added to their lead on an RBI single by Long, batting for Skowron, and Boyer's popup to short left field that became a sacrifice fly when left fielder Kuenn and shortstop Pagan collided, with the latter making the catch. When he finally turned around, Pagan could not get enough steam behind his throw to the plate and Howard scored to make it 5–2. In the ninth, the Yanks added a final run when Howard's base hit off Stu Miller brought in Tresh, who had singled and stolen second base.

Ford, meanwhile, had thrown another typical Whitey Ford game. He walked two, scattered ten hits and struck out six (including Mays looking in the eighth, the only time he retired Willie in four trips). The Yankee

Clete Boyer's solo home run in the seventh inning put the Yankees ahead to stay in the first game of the Series. Boyer hit .318 with four RBIs against the Giants, capping off his best offensive season in New York (National Baseball Hall of Fame and Museum, Cooperstown, N.Y.).

Four. Game One: Boyer's Redemption 55

infield helped him out with a pair of double plays. New York had eleven hits off three San Francisco pitchers. The only starters without a hit were Skowron, who left in the seventh inning with a stiff back, and Mantle, who went zero-for-four and struck out twice. "I got too eager," Mantle said. "I went after some bad pitches."[15]

In the quiet Giant locker room, Dark was asked if his team's lack of offense was a result of being tired. "Ford just pitched a great game, that's all," he said. "Tomorrow is another day and we can't expect anyone as good as he is."[16]

Told that Mays was now nine-for-eleven lifetime against him, Ford laughed. "He's one of the greatest hitters in baseball. There's a lot of National League left-handers who don't get him out either."[17] Houk didn't seem too concerned about the Mays vs. Ford matchup. "His three hits were all singles, weren't they?"[18]

The front page of the next day's *Santa Cruz Sentinel* showed a photo of the Game Two starting pitchers shaking hands. It would be Jack Sanford for the Giants and Ralph Terry for the Yankees. Prominently featured on the front page was a news article updating readers on James Meredith's progress at Ole Miss. Accompanied by three U.S. federal marshals, Meredith had eaten his first meal in the student cafeteria. "People stared," the article noted, "but nothing more."[19]

Still, to be on the safe side, the Department of Defense ordered the weekend's Ole Miss football game vs. the University of Houston to be moved from the Oxford campus to Jackson, some 170 miles to the south. It would be a precaution against any further violence.[20]

Five

Game Two: "I Was So Scared"

Friday dawned fair in the bay area of northern California. Some morning cloudiness gave way to blue skies with temperatures slated to reach the upper sixties by the afternoon. The forecast for Game Two's 12 noon start called for a more robust wind—and a colder one at that—than the ballplayers and spectators experienced the day before.[1]

The Giants certainly understood the importance of gaining a split at home. A second loss would leave them with the prospect of having to win four of the next five games, with three coming in Yankee Stadium. But there was no panic or dire urgency in the Giants' clubhouse. Dark pointed out that his team had been under constant pressure for more than a month trying to catch the Dodgers, surviving a three-game playoff, and now playing the defending world champions. They'd just play their game and take their chances, especially with Jack Sanford on the mound.

Sanford's journey from a barely above-average high school prospect to a twenty-four-game winner for the National League champions was an unlikely one. Born in Wellesley Hills, Massachusetts, a western suburb of Boston, he grew up as Johnny Sanford, a child who seldom showed much passion in his activities. He was an average student in school. At the request of his mother, he agreed to take violin lessons. To motivate him, the violin teacher told him he could keep the violin supplied him for lessons if he completed twenty lessons. Sanford quit after the nineteenth session. He played high school baseball, but other than once hurling a no-hitter, did not attract much attention from major league scouts. It took insistent prodding by his older sister, Nancy, to convince the 18-year-old Sanford—by this time calling himself the more grownup-sounding "Jack"—to attend a Red Sox tryout camp in 1947.[2]

The Boston scouts were not impressed. The young right-hander threw hard, but his physical makeup did not match the pitcher profile the Red Sox sought in that era. Sanford stood not quite five-foot-ten and weighed only 160 pounds. "When I was through," remembered Sanford, "I went over to a group of Red Sox officials and they told me I was too little."[3] Boston scouts were instructed to sign pitchers with more imposing size. By the mid–1950s, the Boston staff featured mostly tall, physical pitchers. Frank Sullivan (six-foot-six, 215 pounds) and Dave Sisler (six-foot-four, 200) were good examples of the "Red Sox type." Later in the decade, the Sox added prospects like Gene Conley (six-foot-eight, 225 pounds), Dick Radatz (six-foot-six, 240) and Earl Wilson (six-foot-three, 215). By 1962, half of the Boston pitching staff featured players standing at least six feet tall.[4]

But Sanford showed enough promise to interest a bird-dog scout for the Phillies. He signed a basic contract with Philadelphia scout Joe LaBate that called for no bonus money. His salary would be $125 a month as a member of the Class D Dover Phillies of the Eastern Shore League, just about the lowest rung on the professional baseball ladder. To earn enough money to survive, Sanford was paid a few extra dollars to drive the team bus on road trips.[5]

He came close to being released after compiling a 2–9 record with a terrible 7.28 earned run average at Dover. But he managed to win fifteen games the following year in the Class D Georgia-Florida League and was promoted. Told repeatedly that he really wasn't a major league prospect, Sanford finally developed the kind of passion he lacked as a young boy. He vowed to become a success no matter how long it took.

After eight long years of making little money and riding the bus on long, uncomfortable road trips, Sanford finally earned a trip to the majors at the tail end of the 1956 season and pitched effectively in thirteen innings for the Phillies. Manager Mayo Smith made it clear he would be counting on Sanford as someone who could help a Philadelphia pitching staff that had the worst earned run average in the National League.[6]

The following season, Sanford not only established himself as a big-league pitcher, but he also became an All-Star, leading the majors in strikeouts and winning nineteen games for a Philadelphia team that played .500 ball. Despite having a losing season in '58, Sanford was recognized around the league for his steadiness and workhorse qualities. The Giants traded for him that December, sending the Phils catcher Valmy Thomas and Ruben Gomez, the winning pitcher of the Giants' very first game in San Francisco.

After three modest seasons with the Giants, Sanford had become an ace. He tossed 265 and one-third innings in 1962 and strung together sixteen consecutive victories to close out the season. The weight of a World Series assignment would not be too much for a man who'd worked for fifteen years to reach this spot. And Sanford knew he had an advantage he could exploit. He'd be almost a complete stranger to New York's starting lineup. Only Long, who would get the start at first base because of Skowron's ailing back, had ever faced Sanford on multiple occasions. Long was the lone Yankee starter who'd ever played in the National League.

New York countered with its big winner, Ralph Terry. The tall, rangy Oklahoman had won twenty-three games while leading the American League in games started (thirty-seven), complete games (eighteen) and innings pitched (298 and two-thirds). Nobody faced more batters in the American League than Terry. And nobody in *either* league gave up as many home runs. Terry's total of forty was an enormous figure. He was only the second pitcher in American League history to yield forty or more homers in a season.[7] The only redeeming factor was his tendency to limit the damage done by the long ball. Twenty-eight of the forty homers came with no one on base.

Behind Terry, the Yanks would have an altered lineup necessitated by minor injuries. Skowron's recurring back ailment, coupled with the right-handed Sanford for the Giants, made Houk's decision to use Long an easy one. But he also decided to sit Howard after the hard-hitting catcher had trouble gripping the bat with his left hand during batting practice. He had slightly sprained his wrist while sliding into third base the day before. Fortunately, Houk had the luxury of inserting Yogi Berra to replace Howard.

By this stage in his career, Berra was recognized as having been one of baseball's premier players, a three-time Most Valuable Player recipient who'd backstopped his team to nine World Series titles. His unique use of the English language amused his teammates and occasionally the media, although it would be many years before boyhood buddy Joe Garagiola would use his platform as a television announcer/personality to truly promote the cult of Yogi, the inscrutable quote-maker.

In this, his thirteenth Fall Classic, Berra was little more than a 37-year-old left-handed bat off the bench who could occasionally play in the field. During the just-concluded season, Berra caught in thirty-one games, played the outfield in twenty-eight, and pinch-hit in twenty-three others. His .224 batting average was the lowest of his career, but he still had occasional power as evidenced by his ten home runs. Undoubtedly, Houk would have had more concerns with the aging Berra behind the plate against a running team like the Dodgers, but the Giants seldom tried to steal a base. Mays was the team leader with eighteen.

Berra's insertion into the lineup also served as an opportunity to extend the many World Series records he already owned. They included most games played, most at-bats, most hits, most runs batted in, and most winning Series as an active player. He wasn't likely to reach Babe Ruth's record of fifteen homers (Berra had twelve), but otherwise, Yogi's name was all over the record book.

Facing the right-handed Terry, Dark decided to shuffle his lineup. He picked Matty Alou to play left field instead of Harvey Kuenn. Tom Haller would catch in place of Ed Bailey. But his most unusual move was to sit Orlando Cepeda and insert Willie McCovey at first base. It was not surprising at all to see McCovey in the lineup against a right-hander, but essentially the Giants were using Matty Alou instead of Cepeda. This would bolster the outfield defense at a significant reduction in the lineup's power.

"Cepeda has played in about 260 games this year and he's worn out as far as I'm concerned," said Dark in a pre-game conversation with reporters. "I'm not in favor of winter ball for fellows who play regularly in the majors." Cepeda had played the prior winter for Santurce, champions of the Puerto Rican winter league, and was named the league's MVP. Dark's assessment of "260 games" was an exaggeration, but his distaste for his players competing in winter ball was genuine.[8]

Dark made it clear that he intended to change the practice of some of his Hispanic players competing in the off-season. "I don't want Cepeda and Pagan to play winter baseball," Dark said. "I would like to see Matty Alou play, but Felipe Alou and Marichal, no."[9]

Alvin Dark grew up a product of the deep South during the Great Depression. He was born in Comanche, Oklahoma, on January 7, 1922, but his father, who worked in the oil drilling business, soon moved the family to Lake Charles, Louisiana, to work in the plentiful refineries in that part of the country. Young Alvin became an accomplished athlete in high school and earned a football scholarship to Louisiana State University where he lettered in baseball, football and basketball. Dark was an outstanding tailback at LSU, averaging more than seven yards per rush in 1942.[10]

After joining the Marines during World War II, Dark returned home to sign a baseball contract with the Boston Braves. He went on to enjoy a prominent fourteen-year career as a shortstop and third baseman. His most notable success came as a member of the New York Giants for whom he batted .417 and .412 in a pair of World Series. Upon his retirement in 1960, he was cited by many baseball observers as a potential manager for his heady play and knowledge of the game. Giant owner Horace Stoneham wasted no time offering Dark the managerial job for 1961.

Dark's first season at the helm saw the Giants improve, moving from fifth to third place in the standings. A year later, he'd steered his club to a come-from-behind National League pennant and a chance to win a world championship. But Dark's relationship with some of his players in San Francisco was already starting to splinter. In time, it would break apart completely.

He would never have a good rapport with Cepeda. In addition to opposing Cepeda's desire to play winter ball in his native Puerto Rico, Dark began to think of his first baseman as a malignant force in the San Francisco clubhouse. "You don't know how hard we've tried to make a team player, a hustling ballplayer, out of Orlando," Dark once stated. "But nothing has worked for so long.... I'd have to say he's giving out only 70 percent."[11] By 1964, Dark was telling Stan Isaacs of Long Island's *Newsday*, "We have trouble because we have so many Negro and Spanish-speaking players on this team. They are just not able to perform up to the white ballplayers when it comes to mental alertness. You can't make most Negro and Spanish-speaking players have the pride in their team that you get from the white players."[12]

Mays, whom Dark had made captain of the team, later wrote, "After that column ran, I had to put down an uprising. Practically every one of the black and Latin players came to my room for a meeting. I could see the anger in their eyes."[13] Dark would be relieved of his duties at the end of the season. He would later claim that his quote was taken out of context.

It's true that in 1962 Dark's inner feelings on the subject of race had not yet been publicly explored. But it's fair to wonder how some of the Giants' stars got along with a manager harboring those opinions—key players such as Mays, Cepeda, Marichal, McCovey, Pagan and the Alou brothers. On the surface, it had not been a divisive issue. But the little shot at Cepeda being "worn out" didn't help his first baseman's frame of mind. Cepeda's subsequent performance in the Series would seem to bear that out.

Writing about Dark at the time of his death in 2014, sportswriter Jeff Neuman stated, "Had he been born twenty years earlier, he would likely be in the Hall of Fame; twenty years later, he might never have believed or said the things that caused him so much trouble."[14]

With the capacity crowd cheering him on, Sanford disposed of the Yankees rather easily to begin Game Two. He walked Tresh with two out before getting Mantle on a weak popup to Pagan at short. In the bottom of the inning, the Giants' new leadoff hitter, Hiller, got his club off to a quick start, hitting a liner down the right field line. Running hard, Maris reached down and gloved it at his shoetop. But as right field umpire

Five. Game Two: "I Was So Scared"

Hank Soar began to signal an out, the ball came loose as Maris' momentum carried him near the foul line. Soar immediately gave the safe sign with outstretched arms.

"I knew I had caught the ball and then I heard Soar change his call," said Maris, "so I looked down in my glove and the ball wasn't there. I must have kicked it loose while trying to regain my stride. The ball was curving away from me all the way."[15]

In a first-inning strategy that would likely never be seen in today's game, Felipe Alou laid down a sacrifice bunt to move Hiller to third. Did Dark want to relieve a bit of pressure on his team and simply try to grab an early lead? No, the manager claimed it was not his call. Alou bunted on his own, Dark said, "because he knows that everyone on our club is expected to move a runner from second to third when there is none out."[16]

Alou's bunt immediately paid off when brother Matty bounced a grounder to Richardson's right at second base. Richardson could do nothing but throw to first as Hiller scored to give the Giants a 1–0 advantage.

Both pitchers dominated the early innings as the Giants held their lead. In the New York half of the fourth, Tresh bunted for a base hit with one out. For the second straight time, Sanford forced Mantle to pop up on the infield for the second out. After Tresh stole second base, Maris fouled out to Haller and the mild threat was over.

The Giants were having no success with Terry either. The big right-hander struck out five through the first six innings and, after Hiller's leadoff double, had only given up a harmless single by Felipe Alou in the sixth inning. He faced McCovey to lead off the bottom of the seventh. Terry tried to come inside with a slider, but McCovey swung his hips out of the way and got the barrel part of the bat on the pitch. "It was right where I wanted to put it," Terry said later.[17]

McCovey made solid contact, bringing the fans to their feet. There was no question of the distance, it was just a matter of whether the ball would stay fair as Maris raced over to get a good look. It landed fair, among the dozens of fans who had leaped out of their seats hoping to retrieve a souvenir ball in the gap between the permanent bleachers and the outfield fence. Newspapers estimated that McCovey's homer went about 420 feet. Terry was asked by a San Francisco reporter, perhaps teasing him about his proclivity to give up the home run ball, if it was the longest one he'd seen recently. "It was a good shot," said Terry. "But if you think that was long, wait until you see Mantle hit one."[18] Few could have imagined that Mantle's next home run would come six months later in Kansas City.

The Giants, sensing a chance to put the 2–0 game away, immediately threatened to score again. Haller reached on an infield hit. Davenport then smacked what should have been a double play ball to Kubek, but the New York shortstop misplayed it and both runners were safe. Pagan bunted to Boyer at third to move the runners up. The Giants had second and third, only one out in the seventh and the pitcher due up. Dark never considered pinch-hitting for Sanford. "I was looking for signs that he was getting tired, but he never did," said Dark.[19] Besides, Sanford was a pretty good hitting pitcher. In 1961, he'd hit three home runs and in '62 he ranked second only to Marichal among San Francisco pitchers with fifteen hits.

Instead of relying on Sanford's ability to swing the bat, Dark gave third base coach Whitey Lockman the sign for the suicide squeeze bunt. Starting from third on Terry's delivery, Haller was trapped when Sanford missed Terry's fastball. Berra and Boyer executed a quick rundown, thereby preventing Davenport from moving to third. Sanford then smacked one of Terry's sliders to the opposite field for a base hit. Running on contact with two out, Davenport ran through Lockman's stop sign—both arms upraised—and barreled home. In right field, Maris charged the ball and made a perfect throw to Berra at the plate. With ample time, Berra slid over on his knees to block the plate. He then did a curious thing by removing the ball from his glove to make a barehanded tag. Davenport's right foot appeared to touch home plate before Berra's tag on Davenport's *left* leg.[20]

Today, without a doubt, the play would be reviewed by video replay and, based on the official 1962 World Series film, would likely be reversed. But such a review was decades away back then. Maris' throw had clearly beaten the runner and home plate umpire Charlie Berry didn't hesitate to call Davenport out.

Sanford seemed to be getting stronger as the game progressed. He retired the Yankees in order in the eighth, striking out both Boyer and pinch-hitter Johnny Blanchard. "He had great control," Boyer said after the game. "I thought he was going to be one of those overpowering fastball pitchers after what I heard about him, but he wasn't too fast. But he sure got the ball where he wanted it."[21]

In the Yankee ninth, Richardson and Tresh both grounded out to put the Giants one out away from a win. Mantle then hit the hardest ball off Sanford all day, a line drive that rattled the fence in right-center field for a double. That brought the tying run to the plate in the form of Maris, New York's leading home run hitter. But Dark's commitment to Sanford was resolute. At no time during the game did a San Francisco pitcher warm up in the bullpen. Dark's faith in his pitcher was immediately rewarded when Maris hit the first pitch to Hiller, who made a fine scoop moving to his right and fired to McCovey for the final out. The Series was tied at one game apiece.

Both managers agreed that the 2–0 San Francisco win was a testament to the brilliance of the Giant pitcher. "We didn't know Jack Sanford

Jack Sanford pitched in the minors for eight years before getting an opportunity in the big leagues. In 1962, he finished second in the National League with twenty-four victories and was runner-up in the Cy Young Award voting to Don Drysdale of the Dodgers (© 1963 S.F. Giants).

very well, but we figured he had to be good with his record," said Houk. "I thought he moved the ball around very well. We heard he was a strong pitcher and our book was right."[22] Berra joined his manager in praising the opposing pitcher when some of the writers congratulated the Yankee catcher on adding to his World Series legacy.

"I didn't do anything out there," he said. "No, wait a minute. I got a walk against Sanford and the way he was pitching today, I guess that was pretty good."[23]

Dark was asked what had made the veteran so much better this season. "He used to be a high-ball pitcher and now most of his stuff is low," he said. "He was afraid to use the slider much, and now he comes in with it even when he's behind." The Giants manager also believed rest was a big factor. "He didn't throw as many pitches in seven innings today as he did in four innings against the Dodgers the other day," said Dark, referencing Sanford's outing in the second playoff game.[24]

For his part, Sanford was quite satisfied, although his irascible nature did peek through in his post-game comments. He thought umpire Berry was squeezing him on some pitches. "I wasn't getting the low strike. I heard they don't give it to you in the American League and if I don't get the low strike, I'm in trouble. I had to adjust myself and come up with the ball, and that's dangerous in this park with the wind when you're facing left-handed batters."[25]

But he also admitted, in a candid moment, that his nerves had almost betrayed him as he warmed up. "I was so scared before the game that my hands were shaking."[26]

In the New York clubhouse, a writer mentioned to Terry that he'd now suffered four straight losses in the World Series. He'd been the losing pitcher twice in 1960. He lost the only game the Yankees dropped in 1961 to Cincinnati. Now he was beaten again.

"I pitched as good as I know how," he told the assembled reporters. "I don't feel so bad about it. The only Series job I really feel bad about is that relief business in Pittsburgh two years ago when I got clobbered."[27]

It seemed that the solid victory validated the Giants in the eyes of some of the media and, perhaps, in the opinion of baseball fans nationwide. Giants fans, while still gloating in beating the hated Dodgers, couldn't help but think that the sports world would have preferred a Yankee-Dodger Series. Despite the New York players generally being generous with their comments on the Giants and the city, media throughout the state seemed to resent them as elite easterners. The headline of a standard Associated Press recap article in the next day's *San Bernardino Sun* was "Giants Shatter Yanks' Smugness." A sub-headline above the box score read, "Yankees Go Home!"

As they completed their post-game responsibilities to the press, the Giants were looking ahead to an early evening flight to the East Coast followed by their first day without a high-pressure game since the rainout at home with Houston a week ago. Yes, they'd have a workout in Yankee Stadium on Saturday, but after that they could put their feet up and let their minds and bodies rest a little bit. For now, they approached their situation in a noticeably unemotional manner, perhaps recognizing they were in for the long haul. "We played all right in both games," commented Dark. "We're every bit the pros the Yankees are supposed to be."[28]

Baseball's first coast-to-coast World Series paused before resuming in the east. Game Three would be played in a very familiar October venue.

Six

Game Three: Boos to Cheers for Maris

It was nicknamed "The House That Ruth Built." Legendary announcer Red Barber often called it "the big ballpark in the Bronx." It had hosted heavyweight championship prize fights, National Football League title contests and scores of memorable baseball games. Yankee Stadium in October of 1962 was arguably the most famous sports facility in America. True, the most successful franchise in team sports played its home games there. But it was also a fact that in an age when television sports viewing options were quite limited, it mattered that watching the World Series often meant watching games from Yankee Stadium.

Opened in April of 1923 and built on a ten-acre tract of land that had been a lumberyard, Yankee Stadium was hosting its twenty-fifth Fall Classic in its fortieth year of existence. Of the 227 World Series games played during the years 1923 through 1961, sixty-six had been played at the Stadium. The next closest tally was Sportsman's Park in St. Louis with twenty-nine.

As the Giants and Yankees held workouts on Saturday, October 6, they saw a ballpark that looked much as it had since its last major renovation in 1946 (when lights were added) and would remain largely the same until its next major overhaul in 1974–75. Red, white and blue bunting was draped along the railing of the upper deck and along the fence surrounding the lower-level box seats. A distinctive copper-frieze façade ringed the upper deck. Baseball card collectors from the 1950s and 1960s would instantly recognize Yankee Stadium by the facade in the background of so many American League player cards. The photos used for the cards were generally shot by local photographers hired by the Topps Chewing Gum company headquartered in Brooklyn.

Among the Giants, only a handful had ever been in the unique ballpark, which featured such drastically diametric dimensions. It was only 296 feet down the right field line and 301 to left. But the power alley in

Six. Game Three: Boos to Cheers for Maris

left field was 457 feet away and in dead center field, beyond the three monuments erected for Babe Ruth, Lou Gehrig and Miller Huggins, the wall was 461 feet from home plate.[1] It was no coincidence that the greatest Yankee home run hitter—Ruth—was left-handed.

Known as "Death Valley," the vast left-center field expanse of the Stadium turned countless deep fly balls—home runs in most ballparks—into long outs. Of Joe DiMaggio's 361 lifetime homers, 148 were hit at Yankee Stadium and 213 (59 percent) on the road. On the '62 Yankees, Elston Howard and Moose Skowron were good examples of the Stadium's effect on right-handers. Howard hit 21 home runs that year, but just three came at home. Skowron had blasted 51 homers over the past two seasons. Only sixteen came at Yankee Stadium.

The Stadium was a breathtaking bit of architecture when it opened in 1923. Ruth's two-word comment when he first saw the finished product was "Some ballyard!"[2] Writing an Associated Press advance story for the third game of the Series, Jack Hand stated, "A team that has been through a bitter pennant fight, and an agonizing three-game playoff for the National League championship, does not figure to be over-awed by such little things as 68,000 fans, a triple-decked stadium and the tricky shadows and wind currents of the concrete ballpark in the Bronx."[3]

Don Larsen was the only former Yankee on the San Francisco roster, but there were a few ex–American Leaguers, including Kuenn, Pierce, O'Dell and Nieman. Willie Mays, of course had played center field for the Giants in the 1951 Series. Not many observers thought the Giants would be intimidated by Yankee Stadium.

It would be Pierce for the Giants and young right-hander Bill Stafford for New York. Stafford was a fourteen-game winner who displayed sharp control and used a decent fastball, change-up and slider to pitch to spots. In his last start of the season against the White Sox, Stafford had been knocked out in the third inning, giving up seven hits and six earned runs. He'd pitched well in relief against Pittsburgh in the 1960 Series, leading some to question why he wasn't chosen to pitch the ninth inning of the fateful Game Seven instead of Terry. Stafford started a Series contest against the Reds in '61, leaving in the seventh inning trailing 2–1 in a game the Yankees ultimately won, 3–2.

Dark was asked during his team's Saturday workout if he thought the next game was the key to the Series, a rather inane question. "We've been up and down so much this year I don't believe in keys," he said.[4] He did volunteer that he would have liked to have pitched Pierce in Candlestick Park, where he was undefeated, but he felt fine using him at Yankee Stadium. The park's vast left field would serve to neutralize the right-handed power of Mantle and Tresh, both switch hitters, as well as Skowron and Howard. The latter two were both expected to play in Game Three after missing the second game with nagging injuries.

With the next three games at home, the Yankees were quoted by oddsmakers as 7-to-5 favorites to win the third game and 9-to-5 to win the Series.[5] Another off-the-field note of interest was that two competing pitchers, the Yanks' Terry and the Giants' Larsen, had become new fathers of baby boys. Terry's wife, Tanya, gave birth on Saturday's off day to the couple's second child, Frank Gabriel. Larsen's wife, Corinne, delivered a baby boy on Friday evening. Larsen told reporters he'd been so busy with the Giants' pennant run that he had not given any real thought to selecting a name.[6] Soon enough, the Larsens settled on Scott.

Sunny, warm weather greeted the 71,434 who entered the Stadium on Sunday, many of whom still had loyalty to the Giants five years after their departure from Manhattan. Unusually high wind gusts would make outfield play a bit problematic. Mays, who dealt with far worse wind in Candlestick, twice would break in on fly balls only to back up quickly to make the catch. The blue skies and wind gusts triggered a defensive move by Dark. He placed Felipe Alou in left field and moved McCovey to right, the opposite of where both men normally played. Dark wanted Alou to deal with Yankee Stadium's notorious late afternoon autumnal sun that made left field treacherous. Baseball insiders recalled Yankee outfielder Norm Siebern's two misplayed fly balls in the sun-drenched Stadium in the fourth game of the 1958 Series that had cost the Yankees in a loss to the Braves. In Candlestick, right field was the sun field. Alou would have more experience dealing with it.

Understandably anxious as he started a World Series game in New York for the first time, Stafford uncharacteristically had trouble with his command. After Felipe Alou lined out to Mantle, Stafford walked Hiller. He got Mays to pop out to Kubek, but then walked McCovey. Cepeda, now back in the lineup after sitting out Game Two, again failed to deliver with runners on. His bouncing grounder to Richardson ended the threat.

Pierce continued the effective groove he was in since the regular season had ended. In his last seventeen innings he'd only allowed three earned runs. Building on his momentum, Pierce shut out the Yankees through the first six innings on just two hits. Kubek doubled with two out in the third but didn't score. In the bottom of the fifth, Howard led off with a two-base hit down the line in left. Skowron then hit a bullet that was speared by a leaping Davenport who fired to Hiller to double up Howard.

At thirty-five years of age, Pierce was an experienced, intelligent veteran with the confidence needed to challenge the world champions. With the Tigers and White Sox, he was often saved in the rotation to pitch against the Yankees. In fact, he'd faced no other team more than his eighty-eight appearances against New York. His lifetime record against them was only 25–37, but his opponents respected the five-foot-ten, 160-pound lefty. In head-to-head decisions vs. Whitey Ford, Pierce held an eight-to-six advantage.

Adding a slider to his repertoire made Pierce one of the premier pitchers in the American League in the 1950s. Now, having lost a little off his fastball, he was still getting hitters out using a warehouse of information he'd stored on opposing batters. Unfortunately for Pierce, the Giants weren't doing much with Stafford, either.

Taking advantage of the dimensions in left and center field, Stafford was content to let the Giants hit harmless fly balls. After retiring the Giants in order in the seventh inning, Stafford had ten fly ball outs and five strikeouts scattered among the twenty-one Giants he had retired. Only one San Francisco baserunner had advanced as far as third base.

The San Francisco scouts who followed the Yankees down the stretch of the regular season told Giant hitters to wait Stafford out, that he was likely to falter in the late innings. The analytics bore this out. During the season, Stafford's earned run average through six innings was 3.52. His ERA for innings seven-through-nine increased to 5.50 and he tended to walk more batters late as well. That might bode well for the Giants in their last two innings against Stafford. But before that, the Yankees were set to hit in the bottom of the seventh.

Facing the heart of the New York batting order, Pierce ran into immediate trouble. Tresh poked a single to center to lead off. An increasingly frustrated Mantle, just one-for-ten at the plate thus far, finally made solid contact and hit a line shot to left in front of Alou. The ball took an odd, high hop causing Alou to bobble it as he jumped for it. "It almost hit me in the face," Alou recalled afterwards.[7] The error enabled Tresh, an aggressive baserunner, to continue to third and allowed Mantle to easily go to second on Alou's throw to Davenport. The Yanks had two on with nobody out. Walking to the mound, Dark decided to play the infield back at normal depth to avoid a big inning. He instructed Pierce to keep the ball away from Maris.

"We decided to give Maris four bad pitches and if he got to first base that way, we were okay with it," said catcher Bailey.[8] With the bases loaded, the Giants could come to the plate to start a double play on a ground ball, so a walk would not be the worst thing to happen with Maris at the plate.

When he came to bat the first time that afternoon, Maris had received scattered boos from the large crowd. This was not unusual. Never having warmed up to the man as a *true Yankee*, and jaded by his sixty-one homers the year before, a portion of the Yankee fans had regularly booed Maris throughout 1962. Of course, the volume of booing was much louder on the road. Maris did his best to compartmentalize things. He disliked dealing with the media, wasn't fond of having his privacy invaded and certainly didn't enjoy being booed by his own home fans. He cared about winning and he cared for his teammates and that's what drove him. But he never stopped hearing the boos.

"Roger was very sensitive and had reason to be upset," said New York sportswriter Til Ferdenzi. "None of the other Yankee players were being booed. Not Mantle, not Kubek, not Richardson, not Yogi. That's what bothered him."[9] Columnist Larry Merchant once said, "Thirty-three thousand people could be cheering for Roger, but he only heard the boos."[10]

Longtime *New York Times* sportswriter John Drebinger had a telling comment after Maris broke Ruth's home run record. "Both great hitters," he said. "But if Ruth were alive now, he would have said, 'Why isn't that guy having more fun doing this?'"[11]

Stepping in against Pierce, Maris smacked a base hit into right-center field. Rushing to make a throw to the plate as Tresh scored and Mantle rounded third, McCovey let the ball bounce off his glove. Maris raced to second and Mantle stepped on the plate to give the Yankees a 2–0 lead. It was the Giants' second outfield error of the inning—both committed by players not used to playing in their respective outfield positions. "I made a bad pitch," Pierce said. "That is, too good a one. It was a fastball right down the middle."[12]

Dark came to the mound again and that meant the end for Pierce. The signal went out for Larsen to come in and face the three Yankee right-handed hitters coming up with none out. Howard hit a fly ball to center field. Most runners avoided testing Mays' arm, but Maris alertly—and surprisingly—tagged up and just beat the throw to Davenport. "It was hit long enough that I expected him to run," said Mays, perhaps the only man in the ballpark thinking that way.[13] Maris had taken a big risk, but made it pay off. With the Giants now bringing the infield in to cut off another run, Skowron was hit on the left side of the abdomen by a Larsen fastball and took first base. The Giant infielders retreated to normal depth to look for the double play.

Sure enough, Boyer hit a ground ball to Pagan, who made a good throw to Hiller at second to force Skowron. But Hiller took too much time making his pivot and Boyer narrowly beat the throw to first. Maris scored to make it 3–0 in favor of New York. The play turned out be another critical defensive mistake by the Giants. "I honestly don't know what happened," Hiller said later. "I just didn't get a good hold on it."[14]

When he took his position in right field for the top of the eighth, having driven in two and scored one, Maris heard cheers coming from the right field stands. For the time being, nobody was booing.

Stafford now had some breathing room. To open the eighth, Pagan singled to left and pinch-hitter Matty Alou, trying to slap one past Boyer at third, hit into a force play. That brought up Felipe Alou, who whacked a Stafford fastball back up the middle with tremendous force. The ball struck the Yankee pitcher flush on his left shin and bounced back toward home plate. Stafford reacted immediately, chased it down and fired to Skowron for the out. Then dazed, almost in shock, he sat on the ground in pain as his teammates gathered around and Yankee trainer Joe Soares, accompanied by Houk, came out to assess the damage. As was the custom of the day, Soares applied the anesthetic chemical spray ethyl chloride to freeze the wound and numb the pain.

Stafford later recalled feeling woozy as he tried to stand up. "He turned white but said he would be all right in a few minutes," Kubek told reporters.[15] After tossing a few warm-up pitches to test his landing leg, Stafford said he was okay. He managed to retire Hiller on a ground ball to second to end the inning.

"I was dizzy, and I was having trouble seeing Ellie [Howard] when Hiller ended the inning," Stafford said. "They gave me a whiff of smelling salts between innings and that helped me to finish the game."[16]

With the lump on his shin ballooning, perhaps still in a bit of a fog from the shock and pain, Stafford walked to the mound to pitch the ninth. Not one of the thirty major league managers in today's game would have sent him out there—in every case, the team's closer would have been jogging in from the bullpen. In fact, it's doubtful any of them would have let Stafford continue pitching in the eighth inning after being hit. But pitchers were expected to finish what they started in that era, so it was Stafford's responsibility to get the final three outs.

Mays opened the inning with a line drive double down the left field line, easily beating Tresh's throw to second while losing his cap racing from first base to second. McCovey made the first out, grounding to Richardson as Mays moved to third. Cepeda again failed to deliver for the Giants. His fly ball to short right wasn't deep enough for Mays to test Maris' arm, especially since one run meant little to the Giants. They needed baserunners, and now there were two out.

That brought up Bailey, a left-handed hitter with good power. Stafford did not want to walk him and bring up the tying run. He tried a fastball on the inner half of the plate and Bailey swung, launching a hard liner in the direction of the Yankee bullpen in right field. Maris tracked it for a few steps then seemed to back off in case the ball remained in play. Instead, it barely carried into the second row of the stands, clearing the low three-foot wall by a couple of feet. No longer trying to wait him out, all four Giants had swung at Stafford's first pitch.

"If I dove for it, I probably could have caught it," said Maris when asked about his chances to make a catch. "But what's the sense of diving for it? I'm not going to hit a brick wall, for anyone."[17] Maris had gotten the key hit in the game, but his assessment of Bailey's homer no doubt infuriated legions of fans and media who viewed him as nothing more than a selfish ballplayer. More significantly, Yankee management would begin believing that in the coming years.

The Giants now trailed 3–2 and Davenport would be the tying run at the plate. His pitcher was dealing with a badly wounded shin, had just given up a two-run homer and was facing a hitter with decent power (Davenport had totaled twenty-six homers in the past two seasons). But Houk made no move to relieve Stafford.

"I didn't see any blood on the mound," he later joked.[18]

As he had throughout the game, Stafford let the ballpark help him against the right-handed Davenport, getting the Giant third baseman to hit a fly ball to left-center field. Tresh gloved it with both hands for the final out. The Yanks led the Series, two games to one.

Clearly, deficiencies in the field had hurt the Giants in this one. A bit aggrieved by it all, Bailey talked about the sightlines at Yankee Stadium. "You can't see in this ballpark," he said. "The second pitch in the seventh [that Bailey popped up to third] almost hit me in the teeth. And I've never seen Felipe have trouble in the outfield."[19] For his part, Dark felt the bobble by Alou was the most important play in the Yankee victory.

Reporters checking on Stafford's condition had to wait for the right-hander to emerge from the trainer's room. "I couldn't put all my weight down on my foot, but I thought my stuff was as good as before," said Stafford. "I just made a bad pitch to Bailey. I didn't want to come out of the game. You don't want to come out of any game when you're going well."[20]

Houk seemed resigned to the fact that Stafford's adrenaline and determination might not be enough the next time he was scheduled to pitch. "I can't predict what we're going to do from now on. All I can do is hope," he said.[21] Neither he nor his pitcher would have any way to know that Stafford's gutty complete-game performance would be the young hurler's final career World Series appearance.

Six. Game Three: Boos to Cheers for Maris

Roger Maris (left) and Bill Stafford were the Yankee heroes of Game Three. Maris drove in the game's first two runs and scored a third. Stafford shrugged off an injured shin to pitch a complete game in New York's 3–2 victory (National Baseball Hall of Fame and Museum, Cooperstown, N.Y.).

An outstanding high school athlete, the native of upstate New York had turned down basketball scholarship offers from Duke and Syracuse among others.[22] Stafford joined the Yankees in 1960 after three-plus seasons in the minor leagues. When Houk took over the managerial reins, he put Stafford in the starting rotation and was rewarded for his faith in the right-hander. The youngster went 14–9 and finished with a 2.68 ERA, second-best in the American League.

His '62 season featured an identical 14–9 record, but Houk estimated the bullpen had blown at least four games that should have been Stafford victories. Number 22 was considered a key part of the Yankee rotation for the future. But fate, in the form of a frigid night in Kansas City, would intervene. Stafford's first start in 1963 came in thirty-degree weather against the Athletics. Putting a little extra on a fastball, Stafford felt something like a muscle tear in his right shoulder ("probably a rotator cuff injury," he said later).[23] After some radiation treatments, he tried to continue pitching but was mostly ineffective and finished the season with a 4–8 record. He never regained the same kind of velocity.

The Yankees traded him in 1966 and two years later he was out of baseball at the age of twenty-eight. "I wish I hadn't gotten hurt," Stafford summed up in Dom Forker's book *Sweet Seasons*. "I could have won a lot of major league games. How many? With those Yankees and my experience, two hundred, I'd say."

The Giants hadn't been able to solve Stafford, had played poorly in the field and were becoming increasingly concerned about the lack of production they were getting from Cepeda. But reporters again noted the lack of panic in the San Francisco clubhouse after Game Three. After all they'd been through in the past few weeks, the Giants had come to believe they played their best baseball when backed into a corner. They weren't going to let this team beat them twice in a row.

Seven

Game Four: Haller & Hiller

His team was trailing again in the Series, but Dark liked his pitching matchup for the fourth game. True, New York was throwing Ford, who would take the mound having won his last five World Series starts. But the Giants had shown in Game One that the veteran could be scored upon, and they felt they'd had good at-bats against him. They simply didn't hit in the clutch. And Dark felt confident giving the ball to Juan Marichal pitching on his normal three-day rest after his no-decision in the third playoff game against the Dodgers.

Like his teammate McCovey, Marichal had burst upon the major league scene in spectacular fashion. In July of the Giants' first season at Candlestick Park, he made his big-league debut at home against the Phillies. He retired the first nineteen batters in order, striking out ten, before Tony Taylor reached on an error. In the eighth inning, pinch-hitter Clay Dalrymple singled to center, the only hit Marichal would yield. The result was a remarkable 2–0 victory, a one-hit shutout in his first appearance in the majors. Marichal struck out twelve and walked only one. Three days later, he beat the eventual-champion Pirates, 3–1. He completed the season with a 6–2 record and a stellar 2.66 earned run average.

Marichal was among the first generation of young men from the Dominican Republic to see a professional baseball career in the United States as a pathway to escaping the oppressive poverty and violence that plagued the country. Without the means to buy real bats, gloves and baseballs, Dominican boys would make their own using scraps of wood, cardboard, bits of leather, yarn, tape and whatever else they could scrounge.[1] They would play for hours on bumpy vacant lots and, occasionally, cared-for ballfields maintained by volunteers in the baseball-crazed country. Blessed with a strong arm, Marichal was converted from a shortstop to a pitcher by Bombo Ramos, a star on the Dominican Republic's national team.[2]

The Giants had been aggressive in combing the Dominican Republic for talent that could be obtained at a low cost. They eventually signed all three Alou brothers, with younger sibling Jesus soon joining Felipe and Matty in the big leagues. "The three of us were always competitive," Felipe said. "We had to be to get out of the Dominican Republic. We wanted to do something to change our country's image. Plus, baseball was the only way we could get the hell away from Rafael Trujillo."[3]

A cold-blooded military strongman who ruled the Dominican Republic for thirty-one years, Trujillo directed the slaughter of thousands of Haitian immigrants before his assassination in 1961.[4] "Each of us felt that if we did well, people would think about other things besides the dictatorship," said the oldest Alou brother.[5]

In 1958, the Giants reached a contractual agreement with Marichal calling for a $500 signing bonus.[6] The young right-hander had a brilliant season at Michigan City, Indiana (21–8, 1.87 ERA), before a promotion took him to Springfield of the Class A Eastern League. He won eighteen games there, but more importantly was converted from a sidearm pitcher to one throwing straight overhand. To better conceal the ball from hitters during his windup, Springfield manager Andy Gilbert convinced Marichal to use a high left leg kick before his release.

"If you placed all the pitchers in the history of the game behind a transparent curtain, where only a silhouette was visible, Juan's motion would be the easiest to identify," Giant beat writer Bob Stevens once wrote.[7]

"He was the greatest pitcher I ever saw," teammate Jim Davenport would say years later. "I don't know how in the world he ever had such great control with that high leg kick. He was a very, very smart pitcher."[8]

Marichal followed up his rookie season in San Francisco with a 13–10 mark as he began learning the hitters' tendencies during his first full trip around the National League. Three of his victories were complete-game shutouts. He was recognized for his distinctive delivery, ability to change speeds, and for his brilliant control. All of which led the media to tag him with the colorful nickname "The Dominican Dandy." Just twenty-four years of age, Marichal impressed one of baseball's most renowned evaluators of talent, Branch Rickey. "No pitcher has made such magnificent use of his God-given equipment," said the former general manager of the Cardinals, Dodgers and Pirates.[9]

Before Game Four, Marichal told the assembled media in New York that a foot injury that had bothered him in September was "still a little sore," but would not be a factor in his performance. Despite the change from the southpaw Pierce to the right-handed Marichal, Houk decided to use the exact same Yankee lineup that had worked for him in the third game. Dark continued the platooning he'd employed much of the season. Kuenn would be back in the lineup in right field leading off, despite his zero-for-five day at the plate against Ford in San Francisco. Haller, who hit lefties marginally better than Bailey, would catch. McCovey would again be on the bench as the Giants hoped Cepeda's bat would heat up. Cepeda was in a three-for-seventeen slump over the course of the three playoff games with the Dodgers and two games against the Yankees.

On the West Coast, Giant fans turned the knobs on their television sets at 9:45 a.m. to watch the NBC-TV pregame show, with the first pitch slated for shortly after 10:00 a.m. Pacific time, 1:00 p.m. in New York. The weather in the Bronx was fair, with sunny skies and temperatures reaching near seventy degrees.[10] Clouds were expected to roll in later in the day which meant the sun might not be a factor late in the game for the two left fielders, Felipe Alou and Tresh.

After Ford retired the Giants one-two-three in the top of the first, Marichal uncharacteristically began his day by walking Kubek. With two strikes on Richardson, Kubek was running. Richardson swung and missed, and Haller's throw to second forced Kubek into a rundown where he was tagged out by Marichal to complete a double play. Tresh's subsequent single to center was wasted when Mantle struck out.

Leading off the second inning, Felipe Alou turned on a Ford fastball and doubled into the left field corner. After Cepeda grounded out to shortstop and Davenport struck out, Haller drove a full-count pitch high to the right of the Yankee bullpen as Maris watched it sail over his head. The two-run homer gave the Giants the early lead. For the rookie catcher, the blast was another dividend paid to the Giants for their unwavering confidence in his abilities.

Born in Lockport, Illinois, Haller was the youngest of three children raised by Julia and Frank Haller. Frank was a steelworker who encouraged his sons to pursue their love of sports.[11] The older boy, Bill, would eventually become a major league umpire who worked in more than 3,000 games and four World Series. Younger brother Tom was a baseball and football star in high school, earning a football scholarship to play quarterback at the University of Illinois. Haller was among the top Big Ten quarterbacks as a junior in 1957.[12] The following spring, he signed a contract with the Giants for a substantial $54,000 bonus and began working his way through the minor leagues. He did not abandon his education, however, and eventually earned his undergraduate degree from Illinois by attending classes during the winter.[13]

He impressed the San Francisco management with his ability to shake off minor injuries and not let a batting slump interfere with his leadership behind the plate. Hall of Fame pitcher Carl Hubbell was the Giants' farm director at the time. "Haller brings a quarterback's mind to catching," observed Hubbell. "He's an intellectual behind the plate."[14]

In his first spring training camp as the Giants' skipper, Dark decided Haller was ready at twenty-three years of age to be the regular catcher. But a .145 batting average after thirty games forced the Giants to reevaluate the situation. Haller was sent to Triple-A Tacoma to work on his hitting, and the Giants traded three players to obtain the veteran Bailey from Cincinnati as insurance if Haller's hitting didn't improve.

At Tacoma, Haller still struggled offensively, but his receiving skills and depth of knowledge for the game convinced the Giants that he was a keeper. In '62, he split time with Bailey, despite both being left-handed batters. The strategy paid off. The two combined for a highly productive thirty-five home runs and 100 RBIs from the catching position in an almost equal number of at-bats. Now, for the second straight game, one of the two catchers had belted a two-run homer in the World Series.

In the bottom of the second, Skowron drove a long two-out triple over Mays' head to the power alley in left-center field that would have been a homer in most major league ballparks. But Marichal kept the Yanks off the board by getting Boyer to fly out to Kuenn in right. Neither team seriously threatened to score again until the San Francisco fifth. With one out, Haller singled to center and moved to third on Pagan's single. Next came a key play that would cost the Giants the services of their starting pitcher.

With the pitcher due up, Dark signaled for a safety squeeze, ensuring that Haller would not break off third base until he saw whether Marichal's bunt attempt was successful or not. Marichal twice failed to put the bat on the ball as Ford threw him belt-high fastballs. With two strikes, he squared around again and offered at the pitch. It landed flush on the index finger of his right hand, pinning it against the bat.

In immediate pain, Marichal started to walk to first base as a hit batsman, but umpire Jim Honochick called him out, citing the rulebook. Marichal had attempted to bunt the ball, thereby negating his having been hit on the hand. It was still a failed two-strike bunt attempt, therefore a strikeout. Back in the Giant dugout, Marichal showed his rapidly swelling finger to his manager, who immediately called for Bob Bolin to warm up in the bullpen. Marichal's day was finished after he had tossed four scoreless innings.

In the meantime, Ford walked Kuenn to load the bases with two out and bring up Hiller. Working carefully on the pesky left-handed hitter, Ford struck him out on a slider away to end the inning. Not only had the

Giants failed to increase their lead, but now they'd have to protect the 2–0 advantage with their inconsistent bullpen.

Like Billy O'Dell, Bolin was a native South Carolinian, having grown up a die-hard Dodger fan in Hickory Grove, a small town about an hour southwest of Charlotte, North Carolina.[15] Later in his career, the Giants would utilize him as both a starting pitcher and a reliever, but in 1962 Bolin had made only five starts and was used thirty-six times in relief. He was a hard thrower who could get a key strikeout if needed. The day before, Bolin had tossed a one-two-three inning in relief.

Because of Marichal's sudden injury, Bolin was given extra warm-up tosses on the Yankee Stadium mound before Skowron stepped in to lead off for New York in the bottom of the fifth. The extra warm-ups paid off. Bolin's first sixteen pitches would either be put in play or be strikes.[16] But his pinpoint control did not prevent him from getting into trouble. Skowron reached base on an infield single to deep short that Pagan gloved but could not make a play on, and Boyer singled to center. Suddenly, the Yankees had runners on the corners with nobody out. The batter was Ford, an average-hitting pitcher. He drove a sharp ground ball to Cepeda who never hesitated. Rather than allow a run to score and try for the double play, Cepeda threw to Haller who chased a retreating Skowron down the third base line before tagging him for the first out. Skowron's rundown allowed Boyer to go to third and Ford to second.

With the left-handed Kubek up, the Giants were willing to concede a run if the ball was hit to the right side of the infield but brought Davenport and Pagan to medium depth on the left side. Hoping to pull the ball, Kubek couldn't get around on Bolin's fastball and slapped one on the ground to Pagan's left. The Giant shortstop had it glance off his glove for an error, leaving the bases loaded. The hitter was Bobby Richardson.

In his first World Series as the Yanks' everyday starting second baseman, Richardson had hit .367 with a record twelve RBIs against the Pirates and batted .391 vs. the Reds a year later. He had a reputation as a tough out, a man who normally put the ball in play. Thus far, the Giants had limited him to one hit in fifteen trips. His difficulties continued here, as Bolin fed him a low, outside fastball that Richardson hit on the ground near second base. Hiller fielded it, stepped on second and fired a low throw in the dirt to Cepeda, who neatly scooped it up to complete the inning-ending double play. The Giants' 2–0 lead remained intact.

After Ford retired the meat of the Giants' order (Mays, Alou, Cepeda) on three ground balls, the Yankees threatened once again in the bottom of the sixth inning. Bolin's impeccable control in the fifth had deserted him. After he fanned Tresh, Bolin issued walks to Mantle and Maris. Howard's harmless fly ball to right was the second out, but the now-revived Skowron whacked a hard grounder that just eluded a diving backhand try by Pagan for his third hit of the day. Mantle scored to make it 2–1. When Boyer singled on Bolin's first pitch, his second hit of the game, New York had tied the score, the Stadium crowd was loud, and Dark had seen all he wanted from his young relief pitcher. He signaled to the bullpen for Don Larsen.

While many of the 66,607 in attendance may not have realized it, those in the Stadium press box certainly knew that six years ago on the exact date—October 8—Larsen had achieved the ultimate nirvana for a pitcher. In Game Five of the 1956 World Series, he pitched baseball's first perfect game in thirty-four years to beat the Brooklyn Dodgers, 2–0. Wrote Joe Trimble in the next day's *New York Daily News*, "The imperfect man pitched a perfect game yesterday."

Larsen had maintained a volatile relationship with Casey Stengel and Yankee management in his five full seasons in Yankee pinstripes. Obtained in a blockbuster eighteen-man trade with Baltimore, where he'd gone 3–21 in 1954, Larsen showed enough potential for the Yankees to overlook his carefree attitude and zest for the nightlife off the field. After compiling a 9–2 record in less than one hundred innings in his first season in New York, Larsen was penciled in as one of the Yankee starters in the spring of 1956. Things got off to a rocky start when he crashed his automobile into a telephone pole at five o'clock in the morning during spring training. Larsen claimed he was tired from training sessions and simply fell asleep at the wheel, but the city of St. Petersburg, Florida, fined him for speeding.[17] Stengel publicly wondered what his ballplayer was doing out at that time of night/morning, although privately he thought he had a pretty good idea.

At the suggestion of pitching coach Jim Turner, Larsen switched to a no-windup delivery instead of swinging his arms over his head, to become more consistent with his motion and a little more deceptive to the hitter.[18] The result was better command. He threw ninety-seven pitches in his masterpiece, going to three balls on only one hitter. He followed up with a pair of decent, but not outstanding seasons, before slumping in 1959 with a 6–7 record. The tall right-hander then was exiled to Kansas City in the Roger Maris trade. A year later he was dealt to the Chicago White Sox just before the trading deadline. The Giants acquired him along with Billy Pierce in a deal made in November of '61. Larsen had proved effective pitching in the National League for the first time in his career, winning five games for San Francisco and saving eleven more.

Just to heighten the irony of this latest appearance, the first batter he'd face would be Larsen's longtime battery mate with the Yankees, none other than Yogi Berra. With Skowron on second, Boyer on first and two out, Berra was sent up to pinch-hit for Ford. "We had a chance to blow the game wide open," Houk would later tell reporters. "Whitey told me he had lost his good stuff. Even if he hadn't, I probably would have taken him out."[19]

As Berra stepped in against Larsen, it was hard for Yankee fans not to visualize Berra's famous leap into Larsen's arms after the Dale Mitchell strikeout that sealed the perfect game. Larsen wasn't as sharp this time. After getting one called strike that led the normally passive Berra to argue with umpire Honochick, Larsen walked him to fill the bases for the second straight Yankee inning. Again, the Giants escaped what could have been real trouble when Kubek bounced back to the pitcher for the third out. The score was tied, 2–2, heading into the seventh inning.

Now it was Houk's turn to summon a reliever from a sometimes leaky bullpen. He called on long man Jim Coates, a veteran of considerable World Series experience, albeit some of an unpleasant variety. It was Coates on the mound in the eighth inning of Game Seven in 1960 when the Pirates took a 9–7 lead on catcher Hal Smith's three-run homer. Coates stood to be the losing pitcher until the Yanks scored twice in the ninth before Mazeroski's game-winning shot off Terry. An acerbic personality, Coates was not the most well-liked player in the Yankee clubhouse. In the quiet of the losing dressing room, he had walked up to Terry and said, "I sure hate to see it happen to you, but you sure took me off the hook." Eyes burning, Terry said nothing.[20]

Pitching in a tie game, Coates got himself into trouble right away. He walked Davenport leading off. After Haller struck out, Dark decided to play the percentages. He called back shortstop Pagan and sent up Matty Alou. With a 2–2 count, Alou flicked at a pitch and grounded it inside the third base line out of the reach of a diving Boyer. Davenport went to third and Alou stopped at second on what was a quintessential Matty Alou double. Years later, when he became one of the best hitters in the National League, Alou would smack forty-one doubles one season to lead the league. Many of them were of the same slap-hit variety.

Utilizing his bench, Dark sent Bailey up to hit for Larsen. When Bailey was announced, Houk came to the mound and decided he'd play some percentages as well. He brought in southpaw Marshall Bridges, the Yanks' best reliever through most of the season, to face the lefty-swinging Bailey. The back-and-forth strategy continued when Dark sent right-handed Bob Nieman to pinch-hit for Bailey. That was as far as it could go—Bridges would have to pitch to Nieman.

A 35-year-old veteran who'd broken in with the St. Louis Browns in 1951, Nieman had been purchased by the Giants as outfield insurance in April. He'd once hit twenty-one homers as a Baltimore Oriole. Houk wanted no part of Nieman hitting when a fly ball could mean the go-ahead run and a base hit could mean two. He preferred trying to get out of the inning with a double play, so he gave the four-finger signal to Howard to walk Nieman intentionally. After watching four wide ones go by, Nieman trotted to first base. When he turned around, he saw reserve infielder Ernie Bowman coming in to replace him as a pinch-runner. Nieman trotted back to the third base dugout. His first career World Series appearance consisted of receiving an intentional walk and then being immediately substituted for. It would also be the last time he appeared in a major league game.

At this point, the top of the seventh had already seen two relief pitchers, three pinch-hitters and a pinch-runner. And there was *still* only one out.

Bridges stepped on the rubber to face Kuenn at the top of the Giants' batting order. The "Sheriff" initially made Houk's move look good. After fouling off five pitches in a lengthy at-bat, Kuenn skied a lazy popup in fair territory near third base that Boyer easily caught for the second out. The next batter was Hiller. Bridges missed outside then threw a strike at the knees. His 1–1 pitch was a fastball on the inner part of the plate. Hiller swung at it, later saying, "all I was hoping for there was to get a piece of it."[21] The ball flew on a line high toward the seats in right field, well beyond a dejected Maris.

Chuck Hiller had hits in five of the seven games in the '62 World Series, including a grand slam homer in Game Four, the first ever hit by a National Leaguer in the Series. Three years later the Giants traded him to the New York Mets (© 1962 S.F. Giants).

Seven. Game Four: Haller & Hiller

It was a grand slam, the first one ever hit by a National League player in the World Series. The Giants, stunningly, had taken a commanding 6–2 lead.

As *The Sporting News* would report, the homer caused "the crowd of 66,607 to roar,"[22] in part because of the sudden long ball from an unlikely source. But the roar also came from a good number of fans who made their way to Yankee Stadium solely to root for the Giants. Many had been longtime fans from the team's days at the Polo Grounds. Some undoubtedly just wanted to see the Yankees get beat. Regardless, it was another example of a phenomenon that manifests itself in old black and white films from World Series games played at Yankee Stadium. That is, in the '40s, '50s and '60s, it appears that there are as many spectators waving their arms and clapping for the opponents as there are for the Yankees. This oddity would disappear entirely by the late 1970s when Yankee Stadium crowds were fiercely loyal to the Bronx Bombers.

Part of the rationale for so many visiting team supporters was just the nature of New York. The city always attracted people from other parts of the country and was such a large metropolis that it would not be unusual for transplanted fans raised in places like Milwaukee or Pittsburgh or St. Louis to obtain World Series tickets at a ballpark that seated more than 67,000. And, of course, it wasn't very difficult for Brooklyn Dodger or New York Giant fans to find ways to score tickets at the Stadium. The result was usually a ballpark where a rather significant percentage of the crowd wasn't necessarily rooting for the home team. The noisy, home-field advantage that emerged in 1976 and remains to this day had not yet come into existence in the Bronx.

Longtime Associated Press writer Will Grimsley would remark after the fifth game in New York, "The crowd seemed almost evenly divided between Yankee fans and old Giant supporters."[23]

Fan loyalty was called into question when Hiller's home run ball was returned to him after the game. A Hornell, New York, restaurant owner named Cappy Roselli was ushered into the San Francisco locker room and presented Hiller with his historic baseball in exchange for another one autographed by the Giant second baseman. Asked if he was a Giants fan, the dapper Roselli, wearing a suit and tie and sporting a pencil-thin mustache, replied, "Nah, I'm neutral. This is only the third ballgame I've seen in my life."[24]

With Larsen out of the game, Dark decided he'd bring in the more reliable O'Dell instead of Miller or someone else from his usual corps of relievers. O'Dell had been slated to pitch the fifth game, but now Dark wanted him to lock things down. O'Dell did just that, retiring the first eight Yankees he faced, until there were two out and nobody on in the ninth.

By that time, San Francisco's lead had increased to 7–2. In the top of the ninth against Bridges, Matty Alou reached on an infield hit to shortstop, moved to second on O'Dell's sacrifice and scored when Hiller tapped a slow roller toward Richardson. The normally dependable Yankee threw wide to first allowing Alou to score on the error.

Down to their last out in the bottom of the ninth, with the big crowd filing out to face the Monday afternoon traffic in New York, the top of the Yankee order suddenly showed signs of life. Kubek singled to left and Richardson drove a base hit to left center. When Tresh lined an opposite field single to right, Kubek scored and it was 7–3 with Mantle coming up and Maris on deck. Dark walked to the mound to discuss the situation as some of the fans in the aisles scrambled back to their seats anticipating a possible Yankee rally. The suspense didn't last long. Mantle hit an O'Dell slider on the ground to Bowman at short and his flip to Hiller completed the force-out on Tresh to end the game.

Four games in and nothing much was decided, other than the Series would be returning to San Francisco, which must have pleased the newspaper editors who'd had the foresight to leave a reporter on the West Coast just in case. It was a two-of-three match now, with the fifth game scheduled the next day at the Stadium, followed by one, or possibly two games at Candlestick.

The truculent Dark refused to give the writers any indication that he felt relieved by the Giants' win. Asked if he was happy the Series was going back to San Francisco, Dark said, "I would have been just as happy if we won three in a row here."[25] He was pressed on his decision to bring in O'Dell, thereby eliminating him as a starter in the fifth game.

"When you have a four-run lead and you're down two-games-to-one, you can't take a chance on blowing it," he said. "So you've got to go with your best man available. You can't worry about tomorrow."[26] Dark said he would use Sanford, operating with his normal three days of rest, to start Game Five. Houk named Terry as his starter and said he planned on using the same lineup once again.[27] Through four games, several of his big hitters were struggling mightily. Maris was hitting .231, Mantle a microscopic .133 with no RBIs. The table-setters at the top of the lineup, Kubek (.235) and Richardson (.118) weren't getting on base much either.

"No, I'm not worried about the way our boys are hitting," said Houk. "We're hitting the ball all right but not to the right places. The teams are about even in runs scored [thirteen for the Giants, twelve for the Yankees]. It's been a good Series, close games and some good pitching."[28]

Along with O'Dell, the Giants had received clutch heroics from Haller and Hiller, which one reporter wrote, "sounds like a song and dance act."[29] Hiller happily covered all aspects of his grand slam to a throng of reporters.

"All year I've been fighting for my life and suddenly I'm a hero," Hiller said. "Baseball sure is a funny game. Was I thinking of hitting a home run? Heck, no. I don't suppose you know I hit only three home runs all year. They've been so few and far between that I can remember the date, the pitcher, the inning, even the pitch."[30]

The second baseman was popular with his Giant teammates, who now reveled in his receiving considerable attention. As Hiller patiently fielded questions, Mays yelled over to the reporters with a grin on his face saying, "Hey, I'm over here."[31]

Hiller's path to the major leagues began in his hometown of Johnsburg, Illinois, a northwestern suburb of Chicago. In high school he displayed an aptitude for both academics and athletics, earning a scholarship to St. Thomas University in St. Paul, Minnesota, where he studied business administration.[32] He was signed to a contract by legendary Cleveland Indian scout Cy Slapnicka, the same man who signed Bob Feller, Lou Boudreau and an outfielder named Roger Maris.[33] In his first professional season, Hiller earned All-Star honors in the Florida State League. But in 1958, the Indians failed to protect the second baseman during the annual minor league draft, and he was selected by the Giants.

Advancing through the San Francisco system, Hiller combined strong numbers at the plate with an aggressive style in the field. Dark liked the young infielder when he first watched him in spring training. "The scrappy kid has taken this camp by storm," declared a piece in *The Sporting News*.[34] In late April, the Giants traded incumbent second baseman Don Blasingame to make room for the rookie, and Hiller was in the San Francisco lineup on opening day. After a single his second time up, he went hitless in twenty-three subsequent plate appearances. Benched for a time, he later committed three errors in a four-game stretch. The Giants sent him to Tacoma in the Pacific Coast League for two months before he returned in mid–September. He finished the year batting .238 and fielding .973 while sharing the job with veteran Joey Amalfitano.

His candidness over his first-year difficulties and determination to work hard won over his teammates the following year. Dark stated that Hiller would be his every-day starter and meant it—Hiller played more games at second base in '62 than any other National Leaguer. With the innings piling up, he now revealed to the reporters in the San Francisco clubhouse that toward the end of the season he'd begun swinging a lighter bat as the fatigue of a long season crept in. The momentous homer had been hit using a bat borrowed from Billy Pierce that weighed only thirty ounces.[35] "I don't know how anyone can hit a home run with a light thing like that," commented Giant pitcher Jim Duffalo.[36]

In an Associated Press guest column for afternoon newspapers, teammate Harvey Kuenn wrote, "Maybe I ought to try and borrow one [a bat] from somebody. Mine seems to be out of hits."[37] Kuenn was 0-for-8 in the Series.

A depressed Bridges talked about the fateful pitch to Hiller as he faced the horde of writers in the New York locker room. "I threw it high and tight, but not as tight I intended it," he said. "The ball slipped away from me and got too far out over the plate. He creamed it. I didn't know he had that much power."[38]

Although Bridges had surrendered the shot by Hiller, Coates took the loss. The winner was Larsen, who tried to deflect the New York writers' understandable interest in his reaction to beating the Yankees on his special anniversary date. What was he thinking about when he saw Yogi walk to the plate? "Sure, I thought about him," Larsen said, "but O'Dell did a great job for us out there. And what about that little Hiller hitting a grand slam?"[39]

The two home runs by rather unlikely sources caused one writer to induce laughter in the press box when he said out loud, "It was Haller, Hiller, hallelujah and the Bridges came tumbling down."[40]

Both teams noticed that playing conditions had improved in Game Four when the clouds rolled in during the fifth inning, eliminating the low autumn sun as a hazard. The Yankee Stadium lights had been turned on in the fifth as the clouds increased.[41] Nobody knew it then, but clouds would soon become an integral part of this World Series.

Eight

Game Five: Dad Couldn't Stop Crying

On the front page near a listing of the previous day's temperatures across the nation, the October 9 edition of the *Schenectady Gazette* in upstate New York included the brief headline "Sun Shines Again in East." The two-paragraph summary also mentioned, "But another bout with dampness approached from the Great Lakes region."

This was not a forecast Ford Frick wanted to read.

Baseball's commissioner, already under criticism for scheduling the World Series to begin the day after the National League playoff ended, fervently wanted the Series to play out as originally planned. As he woke in his Manhattan hotel and looked out his window to see dark, threatening skies, he was immediately concerned. Publicly he would remain optimistic while doing everything within reason to assure that Game Five would be played that afternoon. There were multiple considerations for Frick and his senior advisors to consider.

There were thousands of fans from the New York City area with Series tickets who had made one-time arrangements to take this day off from work. Air reservations were in place for all those who had come to the city not only from the West Coast, but from other parts of the country. Baseball's revenue-sharing plan called for only the first four games of the World Series to be included in the players' share of the receipts, a long-standing formula to discourage any deliberate "extending the Series" by the players to boost their share, so all revenues from the fifth game on would accrue to Frick's bosses—the major league club owners. And gate receipts were generally diminished when makeup dates were involved.

Then there was NBC, which owned both the TV and radio rights to broadcast the Fall Classic and would have to clear time on an alternate day to cover a postponed game. Another consideration was the "press," as most people in 1962 referred to what is today called the "media."

Writers hated having their schedules changed, having to write rainy-day features instead of game summaries. This sometimes translated into columns critical of baseball and its commissioner. Plus, editors hated having to pay their writers extra in travel expenses to do so.

Frick was keenly aware of the importance of the press. His rise to the position of baseball's third commissioner had been a case study of a man who sought and cultivated opportunities to network in an up-and-coming industry.

He grew up on an Indiana farm about halfway between South Bend and Ft. Wayne, the only son of five children born to Jacob and Emma Frick.[1] As a boy, Ford led a Tom Sawyer–like existence, blending days of farm chores with hunting, fishing and his most avid love, baseball. His parents prized the value of education and encouraged their son to succeed in school. Young Frick eventually attended DePauw University in Greencastle. He played first base on the varsity baseball team and covered local sports events for statewide Indiana newspapers to earn some spending cash.[2]

Upon graduation, he obtained a job as a newspaper reporter in Colorado and attracted the notice of the Hearst newspaper chain. Offered a position in New York, he and his new bride, Eleanor, moved to the big city. Frick didn't particularly stand out as a sports columnist. "Maybe I wasn't a good writer," he once said, "but I was a hell of a typist."[3] But as a columnist for the *New York Journal*, he did impress one person who mattered—Babe Ruth. Soon, Frick would become the primary ghostwriter for the Yankee star's many newspaper articles as well as a book called *Babe Ruth's Own Book of Baseball*, published in 1928.[4] During this time, he met and corresponded with commissioner Kenesaw Mountain Landis and other executives in the commissioner's Chicago office.

Eventually, Frick was asked to head up the National League's service bureau, maintaining the official league statistics and records. When NL president John Heydler announced his retirement in 1934, Frick was unanimously elected to succeed him. He served as the league's chief executive for almost seventeen years, mostly staying out of the limelight. One of the enduring controversies of Frick's tenure was his cooperation in extending baseball's unwritten code barring black players. He had the temerity to suggest to famed black sportswriter Wendell Smith in 1939 that it wasn't the club owners preventing minorities from playing major league baseball—it was the fans.

"I am sure that any major league manager would use a colored player if he thought the fans in his city would stand for it," Frick said. An outraged Smith asked if that was so, why did so many white spectators buy tickets to watch Joe Louis fight? Frick did not respond.[5]

Eight. Game Five: Dad Couldn't Stop Crying

By 1951, the owners decided they'd had enough of strong-willed commissioners telling them how to run their business. Both Landis and his successor, Albert (Happy) Chandler, had balked at the idea that the commissioner was employed to do the will of the owners. Those owners chose not to renew Chandler's contract, and when he resigned in protest, they named Frick as his replacement. The new hire understood his role. He was essentially a caretaker. The owners ran the show.

Chandler would never have any regard for his successor. "When the clubs pushed me out in 1951," he once said, "they had a vacancy and decided to keep it."[6]

By 1962, Frick had made a practice of publicly claiming to be most concerned with the players and the sport, while privately being aware that he had to keep the owners happy to hold onto his job. His loyalty to Ruth and the tradition of the sport he grew up with was fully evident in 1961 when he realized that Maris and Mantle were legitimate challengers to Ruth's sacred 1927 record of 60 home runs. The commissioner announced in mid–July that any new home run record would have to be accomplished in the same 154 games that Ruth's season featured. If not, "there would have to be some distinctive mark in the record books" to differentiate the two records.[7]

Frick took considerable heat for this. At the time, Maury Wills was stealing bases at a pace threatening Ty Cobb's 1915 record of 96 stolen bases, but the commissioner made no mention of this or any other statistical category. Clearly, he was protecting his old partner, the Babe.

While Frick never used the word "asterisk," sportswriters and broadcasters jumped on usage of that term. (For the 40th anniversary of the Maris/Mantle home run chase, comedian Billy Crystal, a devoted Yankee fan, produced a made-for-TV movie titled *61**.) When Maris finished with 61 homers in a 162-game season, both his and Ruth's records had separate lines in baseball's official record books. Eventually, MLB eliminated the distinction, essentially stating, as Maris did, that "a season is a season."[8]

The maverick owner Bill Veeck didn't think much of Frick's leadership. "Frick has a slogan of his own, a slogan that has served him throughout the years," wrote Veeck in 1962. "It goes: 'You boys settle it among yourselves.' For that he gets paid $65,000 a year, not bad as things go these days."[9]

Frick became labeled a status quo leader, a man who disliked changing course and making quick decisions in crisis situations. One of his favorite expressions was "It's a league matter," thereby sloughing off any decision-making to the presidents of the two leagues.[10] But there were at least two notable occasions where such a fallback position was not possible. The All-Star game was one. The World Series was the other. They were administered solely by the commissioner's office.

So Frick's mood turned sour when he looked out his window and saw the gray skies mixed with fog at 7:00 a.m.[11] Nevertheless, he ate breakfast and made his way to Yankee Stadium early, as did some of the writers, Stadium workers and the teams themselves. Fans looking to score tickets from scalpers—always more available when inclement weather threatened—prowled around the Bronx streets surrounding the ballpark. Yankee management had again decided to sell $4 standing room-only tickets, making a scalper's job more difficult. Some box seat locations were still available for the full price of $12 each.[12]

By 10:00 a.m., a light, but persistent drizzle was falling. Taking a taxi to the Stadium, *Toledo Blade* columnist Eddie Jones encountered a cynical New York cab driver. "They ain't never going to play this game today, you watch," the cabbie told him.[13]

When the gates opened at 11:00 a.m., thousands of fans entered, mopping up the water dripping on their chair backs and bleacher seats. Then they waited, hopeful that baseball would be played. As the morning crept on and the drizzle became a steadier rain, Frick walked through the bowels of the Stadium to enter the Yankee dugout along the first base side to inspect the field from a closer vantage point. Periodically, he received bulletins from weather spotters at Newark Airport, approximately twenty-five miles away. He shared the information he received with the press box.

"Frick announced each bulletin as it arrived and the wording never changed," wrote *New York Times* columnist Arthur Daley. "'It's clearing up in New Jersey,' the commissioner would sing out bravely."[14] But the updates did nothing to satisfy those dealing with rain in the Bronx.

The 67-year-old Frick, whom some likened to Judge Landis "because of his gaunt, angled features and shock of white hair," continued to put off making any decision as the minutes ticked by.[15] Around 12:30 the rain let up a bit and Frick saw fewer dark clouds overhead. He ordered the tarpaulin on the infield to be removed. Slowly, the Giants and Yankees stepped out on the field to loosen up their arms by playing catch in front of their dugouts. Others jogged easily through the outfield grass, the splashes of water from their spikes landing on the turf quite evident. But the respite was brief—within fifteen minutes, the rain resumed, the players retreated to their locker rooms and the Yankee Stadium grounds crew was ordered to put the wet, heavy tarp back on the infield.

At 1:15, the press box announcer told the writers and broadcasters, rapidly becoming more irritated, that the weather forecaster said the rain would stop in fifteen minutes. It did not. The Stadium organist went through his full repertoire of pop songs, standards and rain-themed numbers. The scoreboard flashed trivia questions ("How many World Series have the Yankees won?").[16] Fans visited the concession stands to munch on a hot dog and get out of the rain for a while. Still no word from the commissioner.

Shortly after 2:00 p.m., the six umpires assigned to the Series walked out of the first base dugout accompanied by Ralph Houk and headed toward the outfield to assess conditions. When one lifted the tarp near first base to look underneath, some fans applauded. But prospects became gloomy again when the group walked back to the Yankee dugout and called Alvin Dark over to join them. Finally, at 2:10, some seventy minutes after a first pitch should have been thrown, public address announcer Bob Sheppard read the following: "With regret, we announce that the condition of the field makes playing hazardous, and the game has been postponed until tomorrow afternoon at 1:00 p.m., Eastern Daylight Time."[17]

It was the first postponement of a World Series game in six years. What followed was what one writer called "an orderly riot," as the fans hustled to the exits.[18] Most cursed the powers-that-be (i.e., Frick) for not calling the game earlier in the morning, thereby forcing fans to make their way to the Stadium and then turn around and head out with nothing to show for their efforts. Jack Hand of the Associated Press observed, "If the players had the rest of the day off, the fans didn't. They had to hustle back to town, in some cases to reclaim their hotel rooms and revise their travel plans. The airline phone operators groaned under a heavy load of cancellations and re-scheduling."[19]

Both managers were philosophical and pragmatic. "It doesn't affect us at all," said Dark. "I don't want to see anybody get hurt after we've gone this far. This delay doesn't make any difference. It shouldn't bother us."[20]

"It's just as well we didn't play," Houk said. "I was sorry we had to disappoint so many fans, but it's better than risking injury to the players. Besides, I'd hate to see an important World Series game won because an outfielder slipped down on the grass or an infielder threw a soggy ball over somebody's head."[21]

Mays indicated he'd welcome the extra day of rest. About the only player who went on the record as being upset with the postponement was the San Francisco starting pitcher. "It takes all I've got physically and mentally to work myself up for a game, and now I've got to do it all over again," complained Jack Sanford. "And sometimes you can lose a little with too much rest. This is the longest rest I've had since June."[22]

Wednesday dawned cloudy and cooler, but dry. By noon, the sun came out and it was clear to the relief of all that Game Five would be played. When Terry delivered the first pitch to Hiller, the temperature was sixty-five degrees with light winds. The combination of play on an unanticipated weekday and the morning cloudiness had obviously affected attendance. The total of 63,165 paid spectators represented roughly a 12 percent decrease from the first game in New York.

Attending as a guest of Giant third baseman Jim Davenport was Shoichi Kaneda, a veteran star pitcher for the Kokutetsu Swallows of the Japanese professional league. Kaneda had become friends with Davenport on a previous tour the Giants made to Japan. "Baseball in the United States is the biggest and greatest game," Kaneda told reporters. "It is the shoulders of the big Americans that make the difference." The pitcher's remarks ran under a *Sporting News* blurb headlined "Jap Mound Ace at Game."[23]

Seeking his first victory in this, his sixth World Series appearance, Terry started off by walking Hiller. He struck out Davenport and Matty Alou, back in the lineup and playing right field, before Mays smoked a drive directly at Tresh in left field for the third out. The Yankees immediately threatened in the bottom of the first when Kubek tapped a weak single to center to lead off and Hiller booted what could have been a double play ball off the bat of Richardson. But Sanford dug himself out of deep trouble when Tresh hit a bullet back above the pitcher's head. Sanford speared it in the webbing of his glove and quickly threw to McCovey at first base to nail Richardson, who had been sure the ball was going through. In the postgame analysis, there was speculation that Sanford missed an opportunity to be a part of a World Series rarity—a triple play.

"I didn't realize I had the ball at first," said Sanford. "It happened so fast. When I saw I had a sure out at first, I made the throw there. I was happy to settle for two outs."[24]

Pagan, the shortstop, said he yelled to Sanford but didn't think the pitcher heard him. He told reporters that Kubek on second had gone far enough toward third that "it would be a triple play for sure."[25] If Pagan's assessment was correct, the Giants had missed a chance to join the 1920 Cleveland Indians in completing a World Series triple play.

Sandwiching Sanford's fine glove work with some poor fielding, the Giants committed their sixth error in eighteen innings of defensive play at Yankee Stadium when McCovey, starting in place of Cepeda, couldn't handle Mantle's grounder, sending Kubek to third. Sanford escaped the stressful inning, however, by getting Maris to fly to Felipe Alou in left. Both pitchers retired the side in order in the second inning. But in the third, the Giants broke through against Terry.

Eight. Game Five: Dad Couldn't Stop Crying

Pagan bounced a single to center and moved to second on Sanford's successful sacrifice bunt. That brought up Hiller, and the Game Four hero continued making the baseball world take notice by sending a lazy, fly ball into short left field. When the ball landed it took an erratic bounce and angled past Tresh. Pagan scored and Hiller continued to second with a double. He was left stranded when Davenport, mired in a deep slump, and Matty Alou each grounded out.

The Giants still led, 1–0, when, with two out in the top of the fourth, Felipe Alou lined a rocket down the left field line. The ball caromed out against the concrete at the base of the left field fence. Tresh had been running hard toward the foul line and when the ball kicked past him, the New York outfielder had difficulty turning quickly on an outfield still wet from the previous day's rain. Felipe, not nearly as fast as younger brother Matty, still managed to go all the way to third with a triple, only his fourth in the past two years. But once again, in a trend afflicting both teams, a two-out hit wasn't forthcoming as Haller lined out to Maris.

Tresh led off the New York fourth by punching a shallow fly ball toward left-center field. Racing backwards, Pagan got a glove on it, but the ball bounced off, landing on the wet grass as Tresh beat the relay throw to second for a rather fortunate double. Pitching carefully to the still dormant Mantle, Sanford walked him as Yankee fans hoped this might become a big inning. But Maris couldn't deliver. He grounded one to McCovey's right. The tall first baseman threw to Pagan at second to get the force play on Mantle, with Tresh moving to third. It seemed that Sanford would wriggle out of another jam when he struck out Howard, but his first delivery to Skowron was a slider that broke too much. It skimmed under Haller's mitt and rolled to the backstop. Tresh scored standing up to tie the game and Maris moved to second. Sanford then registered his fifth strikeout of the game by fanning Skowron.

His team having drawn even, Terry faced Pagan to start the fifth. What writers of the day referred to as the *gopher ball* bit Terry once more as the shortstop belted a fastball deep to left. Tresh sprinted back to the fence but could only watch the ball land six or seven rows back in the stands. Pagan's homer put the Giants back on top, 2–1.

Against considerable odds, Pagan had become a key player on a pennant-winning ballclub. At 5-9, 165 pounds, he was far from an imposing figure and didn't possess great speed or Gold Glove–quality hands. Perhaps because he lacked these attributes, he developed into a highly regarded teammate constantly feeling the need to prove himself. Few baseball people thought of him among the top National League defensive shortstops such as Dick Groat, Roy McMillan or Maury Wills. Yet it was Pagan who had just led the league's shortstops in fielding percentage and double plays and finished third in putouts. And only Wills had played in more games than Pagan's 164.

Signed by the same scout at the same time as fellow Puerto Rican Orlando Cepeda,[26] Pagan was raised in Barceloneta, a municipality in the northern region of Puerto Rico along the shores of the Atlantic Ocean. Growing up he realized that he did not want to follow the path taken by his father, a foreman on a sugar cane plantation. He played baseball whenever he could, studied hard in school and even attended one year of college before signing with the Giants' organization.[27]

Hampered by his lack of English and subject to the same prejudices experienced by most dark-skinned ballplayers in the late 1950s, Pagan still managed to show promise with the bat through his first few seasons in the San Francisco chain. At Springfield of the Eastern League in 1958, Pagan hit .298, clubbed twenty-seven doubles and stole thirteen bases. A year later he got called up briefly by the Giants, who then sent him to Tacoma of the Pacific Coast League the following year. By 1961, the Giants felt Pagan had polished some of the rough edges in his game and was ready.

Like many of the Latin-American players of his day, Pagan was a free swinger ready to hit any pitch within his reach. In his first full season with the Giants, he walked only thirty-one times in 474 plate appearances. In '62, he had a career high forty-seven walks (in 644 plate appearances). Basically a .250 hitter, he showed occasional power and the ability to take outside pitches to the opposite field. Dark usually placed him in either the seventh or eighth slot in the batting order. In the field, he had decent range and made all the routine plays. He was nothing if not consistent—he committed twenty-one, twenty-one, twenty and twenty-two errors in his four seasons as the Giants' regular shortstop.

But on a team of superstars named Mays, McCovey, Cepeda and Marichal, it wasn't easy for Pagan to get the attention he felt he was due. He never received an invitation to the All-Star game. After two more seasons as the starting shortstop, the Giants would trade Pagan to Pittsburgh in May of 1965. But as the Yankees came to bat in the fifth inning of Game Five, it was the 27-year-old Pagan who was the leading hitter in the World Series, causing one notable observer to comment on his success.

"That little guy is a tiger," said Casey Stengel to writers after the game. "He eats those frontline Yankee pitchers alive."[28]

Pitching with a narrow lead, Sanford continued to control the New York hitters. He retired the Yankees in order in the fifth, striking out both Terry and Kubek. In the sixth, Richardson led off with a single on

Eight. Game Five: Dad Couldn't Stop Crying

an infield roller that Davenport couldn't handle. In another example of strategy *then* vs. strategy *now*, Houk asked his third-place hitter to bunt with nobody out in the sixth inning of a one-run game. Tresh executed the sacrifice as McCovey threw him out at first base. Failing once again with a runner in scoring position, Mantle hit an easy ground ball to Hiller and, disgusted by his inability to deliver a big hit when it counted, just jogged down the first base line. Hiller had to wait on McCovey, who had been playing very deep for the Yankee slugger. By the time McCovey got to the bag, a hard-running Mantle might have made it a very close play.[29]

In any event, there were two out as Richardson stood on third with Maris the batter. With the count 2–1, Maris swung and missed at an outside fastball. The ball deflected off Haller's glove and rolled several feet away as Richardson tore for the plate. Sanford raced in, blocked the plate as best he could while reaching for Haller's throw and slapped the tag on Richardson—too late, in the opinion of home plate umpire Al Barlick, a National League veteran. On his knees, Sanford could be seen arguing with Barlick, who pointed toward the corner of the plate where Richardson had slid in safely. The score was knotted at 2–2.

"The only way he could have slid under me was to beat the throw and the fellows on the bench said he didn't beat the ball," Sanford said later.[30]

As the workhorse of the Yankee staff, Terry was not looking to the bullpen as he ran into trouble in the San Francisco half of the seventh. With two out and Felipe Alou on first, Terry allowed a base hit to Sanford to move Alou to third. (Sanford had also singled in Game Two off Terry. In fact, he proved to be one of the toughest Giants for Terry to deal with over the course of the Series. Sanford wound up with hits in each of the three games he faced Terry, compiling a sterling .429 batting average.)

Facing a hot hitter in Hiller, Terry reached back and threw his best fastball. Hiller topped it, sending a grounder back up the middle. Terry gloved it, fired to Skowron and the inning was over. The Yankees went quickly in the seventh, with Skowron and Boyer striking out to give Sanford nine strikeouts. The Giants went down in order in the eighth, and so the Yanks came to bat in the bottom of the inning with the game tied, 2–2.

Houk's tactics raised some eyebrows when he sent Terry up to lead off rather than a pinch-hitter. After the game, the Yankee manager said he wanted Terry to continue because he really hadn't been in trouble in many innings. Left unsaid was Houk's lack of confidence in his bullpen after watching Coates and Bridges fail to stop the Giants two days before. He did have lefty Bud Daley available with McCovey set to lead off in the ninth. And Daley had thrown a scoreless inning in the second game in San Francisco. But Houk undoubtedly figured the Giants would pinch hit with Cepeda if he brought in Daley and he didn't care for that matchup. He would roll the dice with Terry vs. McCovey rather than see Daley against Cepeda.

Terry struck out to begin the inning. But Kubek lined a base hit to right, probably the hardest hit ball the Yankees had managed off Sanford all afternoon. The first pitch to Richardson was a high fastball. Despite having a small five-foot-nine, 170-pound frame and not being a power hitter by any means, Richardson liked the ball up in the zone.

When he came to the Yankees in 1955, Richardson was a poster boy for the slap-hitting infielder looking to make contact and use his speed to reach base. He subscribed to the Casey Stengel *butcher boy* method of chopping down on the ball. He had middling success in his first years in New York, seldom showing any power. In the spring of 1959, Yankee coach and Hall of Famer Bill Dickey suggested Richardson ditch his approach and use a heavier bat with a bigger swing.

"Bill felt that I wasn't big enough to hit the ball through the infield holes with a normal swing," Richardson told a writer in 1962. "He told me to wind up and cut for all I was worth. It's worked wonderfully for me."[31]

The results were not immediate but eventually became evident. In the 1960 World Series, Richardson collected five extra-base hits, including a grand slam, and drove in a record twelve runs. He remains the only MVP of a World Series from a losing team. A year later, he topped the Yankees with nine hits in the Series against Cincinnati. In '62, Richardson led the American League with 209 hits including thirty-eight doubles, five triples and a career high eight homers. His slugging percentage, which had typically been in the high .200/low .300 range, increased to .406. He finished runner-up to Mantle in the voting for Most Valuable Player in the American League. "Bobby should have won it," Mantle always maintained.[32]

Seeing Sanford's fastball come in high, Richardson slammed it into left field for a single. Two on, one out and Tresh coming to the plate. Dark asked for time and walked to the mound to see Sanford. As they met, press box reporters thought they saw Dark looking out to the bullpen and almost raise his hand once. Did Sanford talk him into letting him stay in to pitch to Tresh?

"Jack had pitched too well against the Yankees for me to take him out there," Dark later insisted. "At that point, they hadn't driven in a run against him in two games," he said, referencing the runs scored earlier in the day on a wild pitch and passed ball.³³ For his part, Sanford told reporters that very little conversation had taken place. What had his manager said? "Not a thing," was Sanford's response. "He just came out to give me a breather. I thought I still had it. Alvin finally just told me to keep the ball lower."³⁴

As Dark departed the mound and Sanford prepared to pitch to Tresh, at least one fan in Yankee Stadium simply couldn't bear to sit still and watch. Mike Tresh, father of the young man stepping to the plate, was too nervous to remain seated next to his wife and daughter-in-law in their choice box seats behind home plate.

"It was 2–2 when the Yankees came to bat and I decided that I might break the jinx if I moved," said the elder Tresh. "So I walked back to the standing-room section."³⁵ He also said a little prayer as his son approached the batter's box.³⁶

Mike Tresh knew exactly what his son was experiencing, coming to bat in a crucial spot in a major league baseball game. Although he never played in a World Series, Mike spent twelve years as a catcher for the White Sox and Indians. He was Chicago's number one catcher during the war years in the '40s. A lifetime .249 hitter, he finished his career with only two home runs in more than 3,000 at-bats. Earlier in the year, he'd congratulated his son for equaling his own career total in one day when Tom swatted a pair of homers in an August game vs. Minnesota.

Born on September 20, 1938, in Detroit, Thomas Michael Tresh had grown up around baseball and knew at a relatively young age that he wanted to follow his father and become a major leaguer. "I just can't remember a time when I didn't have a baseball in my hands," Tresh once said. "My folks have movies of me at two years old throwing a ball in our apartment in Chicago."³⁷

Tresh earned varsity letters in baseball, football and basketball at Allen Park High School in suburban Detroit before playing shortstop for one year at Central Michigan University.³⁸ Approached by multiple scouts to sign a professional contract, the youngster had to promise his parents he would earn his degree by attending classes in the off-season, a promise he eventually kept. "It took me four terms to graduate," Tresh once joked, "Eisenhower, Kennedy, Johnson and Nixon."³⁹ The Yankees signed him by offering Tresh a reported $30,000 bonus and he began his minor league career in 1958.⁴⁰

Three years later, Tresh was named Rookie of the Year in the International League when he batted .315 with twenty-three doubles, eight home runs and thirteen stolen bases at Richmond. He was called up to New York for a cup of coffee with the Yanks at the tail end of the '61 season and watched from the dugout when Maris hit his record-breaking homer on the final day of the season.

When the Yankees learned that Kubek would be called up to the Army reserves for most of the 1962 season, management decided to fill the vacancy from within, giving both Tresh and Phil Linz a viable shot at winning the job. Though both players performed well during spring training, Houk liked Tresh's power potential. He was rewarded for his decision. In earning American League Rookie of the Year honors, Tresh finished with twenty-six doubles and twenty home runs. His ninety-three runs batted in were second on the club to Maris's 100. Receiving an invitation to the All-Star game at Wrigley Field, Tresh batted twice and doubled in a run.

Defensively, he did a fine job at shortstop, committing sixteen errors in 111 games. When Kubek returned in August, Houk elected to return him to shortstop and move the switch-hitting Tresh to left field where he could continue to play every day. He played in forty-three games as an outfielder and impressed teammates, opponents and writers alike. "I don't think anybody has to worry about Tom," said Mantle, Tresh's boyhood idol. "I've played alongside a lot of left fielders and Tresh rates as the best one."[41]

A 1963 *Sport* magazine poll of managers, based on the previous season, ranked Tresh first among all American League left fielders. "Biggest surprise in the balloting," the magazine stated. "Managers say his versatility and switch-hitting power make him No. 1 over such established stars as Rocky Colavito and Harmon Killebrew. Good fielder. Exceptional baserunner. Accurate arm. Very determined."[42]

Beyond the Rookie of the Year award, another validation of his value in '62 came when Tresh placed No. 12 in voting for the Most Valuable Player award, even receiving one first-place vote. Thus far, with seven hits in nineteen at-bats (.368), he had been the Yankees' most successful hitter against the Giants.

Stepping in from the left side with his slightly closed stance, Tresh took the first pitch for a ball. On the next delivery, he made unmistakable contact. The ball flew high and far toward the right field stands, landing about ten rows deep, roughly 360 feet away. The rookie had hit a three-run homer—the only one the Bronx Bombers would hit in the three games at Yankee Stadium—to give his team a 5–2 lead. Tresh excitedly circled the bases, shaking Mantle's hand as he crossed home plate before entering a joyous dugout.

The location of his last few pitches, resulting in hits by Kubek, Richardson and Tresh, had proved disastrous for Sanford. Haller said he signaled for an outside fastball to Tresh, but as Sanford said, "It went right down the middle."[43]

Eight. Game Five: Dad Couldn't Stop Crying

Matty Alou balances on the low Yankee Stadium right field wall watching Tom Tresh's three-run homer in the eighth inning of Game Five. The home run, the only one the Yankees hit at the Stadium in the Series, broke a 2–2 tie and led to a 5–3 New York victory (National Baseball Hall of Fame and Museum, Cooperstown, N.Y.).

"I choked up on the bat and was trying to get a hit—any kind of a hit," said Tresh later in a boisterous Yankee locker room. "I hadn't seen any good pitches to hit all day from Sanford and I wasn't expecting any. But when the fastball came over the middle of the plate, I took a fuller swing than I intended. That was it."[44]

Sanford departed in favor of Stu Miller who finished the inning without any further damage. Terry walked to the mound with a three-run lead hoping to put the Yankees back in the Series driver's seat. Not wanting to walk anybody, he threw a fat pitch to McCovey who laced it into center field. Mantle had been playing so deep that the ball almost rolled to a stop in the wet grass by the time he picked it up and fired it in. If the score had been closer, McCovey might have had a chance to reach second, but taking the extra base trailing by three runs would be taking a terrible risk.

Pitching from the stretch position, Terry blew a two-strike fastball by a swinging Felipe Alou to record his seventh strikeout of the game. San Francisco hopes were raised when Haller blasted a liner up the alley in left center that neither Mantle nor Tresh could track down. Tresh finally picked it up about halfway between the center field monuments and the 461-foot sign. The lumbering McCovey scored easily. A faster runner than Haller might have had a triple, but the Giants weren't going to gamble, so Haller stopped at second. Down 5–3, there was still only one out and the red-hot Pagan represented the tying run. He hit an easy ground ball to Kubek for out number two, Haller remaining at second.

Down to his last out, Dark sent Bailey up to pinch-hit for Miller. Both teams were certainly aware it had been Bailey who hit the two-run homer in the ninth inning of Game Three to spoil Stafford's shutout and make the Yankees sweat a little bit. The Tennessee native could tie things up if history repeated itself.

Terry's 120th pitch of the game was a curveball that came in a little higher than he wanted. Bailey, with the short 296-foot right field fence in his sights, took a mighty cut and the ball flew high in the air toward right field. At second base, Richardson followed the ball's flight and threw up his right arm pointing to where he thought it was headed. The spectators roared in anticipation for a moment or two thinking that Bailey had done it again. But he had just gotten under the pitch a trifle. After sprinting to his right, Maris come in a step and made the catch at the edge of the warning track to the right of the Yankee bullpen. New York had won it, 5–3.

"They sure don't come easy," said a relieved Houk. "Sanford pitched a great game right up to the eighth inning when we got our three hits. But Terry also pitched a helluva game."[45]

In the San Francisco locker room, Dark was blunt about his team's performance.

"That's the worst game we've played in a long time right there," he declared. "We just played badly today. We really played bad."[46] The two errors, by Hiller and McCovey in the first inning, hadn't caused any damage. The same could be said for Pagan's failure to corral Tresh's bloop double in the fourth. But the wild pitch and passed ball had given the Yankees two runs. And his pitcher's inability to bring his pitches down in the strike zone proved fatal in the eighth.

"I still think we're going to win it in seven games," Dark said a bit defiantly, pointing to Billy Pierce's unbeaten record in Candlestick Park.[47] Houk still had not definitively named his starting pitcher. Speculation was that he might use Stafford if the young hurler's shin had sufficiently healed by then. Pierce spoke for his Giant teammates when he said, "We aren't in bad shape even trailing three games to two. We're going back to our own park."[48]

Photographers waited for Terry to finish taking a phone call before snapping a picture of him and Tresh hugging each other with broad toothy smiles on their faces. "That was my wife," Terry said about the phone call. "She just got back from the hospital after having our baby and she was feeding him in the ninth inning."[49]

Multiple sources later confirmed that the first question asked of Terry following his phone call came from Stan Isaacs, a reporter from Long Island's *Newsday*, who was one of a new breed of sportswriter looking for more intimate, revealing information when interviewing athletes. Isaacs and several of his colleagues came to be called the *Chipmunks* by legendary New York newspaper columnist Jimmy Cannon, who once said, "You sound like a lot of goddamn chipmunks."[50] Older writers like Cannon didn't care about personal details and player quotes.

When Terry said his wife was feeding the baby, Isaacs asked, "Breast or bottle?"[51] Terry smiled, the other reporters cracked up with laughter and the interview continued.

Even such impertinence couldn't stop Terry from enjoying his first World Series victory. "I was a little worried in the ninth pitching to Bailey," said Terry. "I didn't think it was going for a home run, but I thought it might be in the gap between right and center field. Roger played it perfectly. Boy, I was glad to see that final out."[52]

Patiently answering questions about *his* heroics, Tom Tresh was happy to share the spotlight not only with Terry but with his dad. Mike Tresh proudly recounted what he'd been doing when his son homered to win the ballgame.

"I knew it was gone the minute Tommy hit it," said the elder Tresh.

"I was a catcher long enough to know when a ball is out of there. I just couldn't stop the tears. I couldn't speak and I couldn't stop crying. The people around me must have thought I was crazy. I just stood there in the rear of the stands with tears coming down my face, not saying a word, unable to move."[53]

The former big-league catcher said he worked as a security guard at a Ford Motor Company plant in Livonia, Michigan. He talked about how he helped his son with his baseball training, but never pushed him. In a *Street & Smith*'s magazine article published in 1963, Tom Tresh wrote of his father, "He never tried his powers of persuasion on me. My career was something for me to choose. In fact, he was brutally frank and extremely realistic in massing the pitfalls of baseball. It's great if you make it, he'd say, but it's hell if you fail. He never tried to paint the life in false colors."

It was his dad who taught Tom to switch-hit when he was seven or eight years old. "Being a catcher, I know what an advantage it was to hit left-handed," said Mike Tresh. A reporter asked him if he'd be heading to San Francisco to see the rest of the World Series. "I wish I could," he said, "but I must go back to work."[54]

Mike Tresh would be back to work the next day. It would be an unexpectedly long time before his son could do the same. The baseball world was about to be introduced to a phenomenon of nature called Freda.

Nine

The World Series on Hiatus

Even today, some sixty years later, it is still referenced when the topic of Pacific Northwest natural disasters is discussed. It is sometimes colloquially called the "Columbus Day Storm" of 1962. Officially, it is known as Typhoon Freda. But even that name is a bit misleading according to one climatologist.

"The Columbus Day storm has frequently been labeled as a typhoon, but that is somewhat erroneous," said Kathie Dello, speaking to archivists at Oregon State University in 2012. Dello served as deputy director of the Oregon Climate Service at the time of her interview. "It was the remnant of a typhoon that became extra-tropical and hit the West Coast in three waves, but they get lumped together in people's minds as one event."[1]

When thinking about hurricanes and powerful tropical storms, most Americans think of the southeastern portion of the United States. Attention usually focuses on the states bordering the Gulf of Mexico or, occasionally, Georgia and the Carolinas. But tropical storms in the Pacific, while less common, are not unheard of. When the tropical storm eventually called Typhoon Freda gathered strength, it took nine days in early October to cross the Pacific Ocean from its origin near Wake Island. Weather forecasters first became concerned when they watched the disturbance intensify when encountering a significant cold front. The result was a monster storm headed for the West Coast.

The storm's effects first touched northern California on the afternoon and evening of Thursday, October 11, a designated travel day for the '62 World Series. Rain began falling in the late afternoon and forecasters said it was expected to continue through much of the Columbus Day weekend (at the time, Columbus Day was celebrated exclusively on October 12, not on a designated Monday as is the current practice). In addition to the rain, gale warnings were posted for winds expected to surface between thirty and forty-five miles per hour.

Some meteorologists feared a direct hit on California. Fortunately, while still approximately 300 miles offshore, Freda veered north, sparing the California coastline from untold damage. Nevertheless, torrential rain and high winds battered the coast for parts of four days. Downed trees and power lines were reported throughout coastal regions of northern California, Oregon and Washington. The San Francisco bay area recorded more than seven inches of rain in four days during a month—October—that normally averaged slightly more than one inch of precipitation.

The worst of the damage was inflicted on Oregon, Washington and even Vancouver, British Columbia. In Oregon, wind gusts exceeded 100 miles per hour in several locations. In Corvallis, the operator of a manual wind gauge recorded top speeds at 127 mph before leaving a note attached to the desk that simply said, "Abandoned station."[2]

Sue Ellen White, a Portland native, told the *Everett* (WA) *Herald* in 2018 about driving home from a friend's house when the storm hit. "Power poles were leaning and swaying back and forth. It felt like the ground was moving. I had an old Buick, a very sturdy car, but I didn't know what to do. There were trees falling all over the place. Power lines were whipping up and down between the poles." White eventually made it home safely.[3]

In Washington, weather stations at Renton (100 mph), Bellingham (98 mph) and Everett (81 mph) all documented the sheer power of Freda's wind.[4] Cliff Mass, professor of Atmospheric Sciences at the University of Washington, would later write in his weather blog that Freda was "the most powerful and destructive storm to strike the Northwest since the arrival of European settlers." He also stated that Freda was stronger than the famed *Perfect Storm* depicted in the 2000 movie of the same name starring George Clooney.[5]

The destruction was extensive and widespread. Economists later speculated that Freda had an economic impact in Oregon of $200 million, more than $1 billion in today's dollars. In all, the storm was attributed to at least forty-six deaths across the Pacific Northwest.

If the rainout in the Bronx before Game Five had been an inconvenience for the baseball world, Freda would come with a much longer checklist of repercussions, some good, some bad, depending upon perspectives.

Still stinging from the criticism he received for the late call in postponing the fifth game in New York, Commissioner Frick was largely spared any similar options to waffle on a decision. The rain had poured down all Thursday evening. Shortly after 8:30 a.m. on Friday, he and Giants head groundskeeper Matty Schwab walked the field. This time, Frick didn't hesitate, telling reporters on site the game was off because the field was unplayable.

Nine. The World Series on Hiatus

New York's Clete Boyer looks to the skies prior to Game Five being postponed due to rain and wet field conditions. Severe weather subsequently resulted in three consecutive postponements in San Francisco. The Series took thirteen days to complete (National Baseball Hall of Fame and Museum, Cooperstown, N.Y.).

Beyond just the field itself, the continuing sporadic rain and heavy wind made playing a game impossible. "If they had tried to play ball today," the Associated Press reported, "this could have been the day of the first 900-foot home run in the winds that made it difficult to open doors and shattered glass in downtown hotels."⁶ The wind, estimated at forty-five miles per hour by mid-morning, nearly lifted the infield tarpaulin off the ground despite 35-pound weights holding it down.

Newsreel footage showed water cascading down commercial and residential streets alike in the San Francisco–Oakland region. In referencing the World Series delay, the announcer suggested, "Candlestick Park should be renamed Candlestick Pond."⁷

The business managers at newspapers and broadcast outlets assigned to cover the World Series now had to contend with added expense accounts as sportswriters did their best to drum up feature articles in lieu of actual competition. NBC saw the Friday date washed out early and looked optimistically at perhaps capturing a larger audience for the afternoon game (or games) on the weekend. But that cheerful outlook soon dissipated as it became apparent that the unrelenting rain and condition of the Candlestick Park playing surface would put Saturday and Sunday in jeopardy too.

Giants owner Horace Stoneham would also learn about the habits of sportswriters with too much time on their hands. Stoneham had graciously offered a suite in the Sheraton-Palace Hotel, just off Market Street, as a hospitality room for the press. As described by *Golden Baseball Magazine*, Stoneham "now learned to his dismay that there is nothing as unquenchably thirsty as a baseball writer with no baseball to write about." Members of the Fourth Estate gravitated to the suite in large numbers and practically camped out there, running up Stoneham's huge liquor, beer and food bills.⁸

As for the players themselves, having just taken a second coast-to-coast flight in six days, the Yankees and Giants initially relished having a little extra rest. To shake off the effects of any jet lag issues, both teams were slated to conduct workouts at Candlestick on Thursday, but the rain and wind made that impossible. Instead, the Yankee players generally slept late on Friday and hung around the Town House hotel. The extra rest was also welcome news for the Giants, who had battled so hard down the pennant race stretch and through the added pressure of the playoff. Willie Mays told reporters the team was still feeling the effects of the last couple of weeks and appreciated a little extra down time.

From a competitive vantage point, both managers saw few positives as they arranged their pitching staffs to accommodate what most were still hopeful would be only a one-day postponement. At a hastily arranged press conference on Friday morning, reporters were informed that this would be only the fifth rained-out home date in the Giants' history since they moved to San Francisco. Alvin Dark said his club could now throw Billy Pierce and Jack Sanford back-to-back in Games Six and

Seven. The pair were a combined 26–1 on the year at Candlestick, an astounding success rate.

In his first season in San Francisco, Pierce had won all twelve of his decisions at home. "Both have pitched so well there," Dark said. "I don't see how a postponement of one or even two days can hurt us at this point."[9] After concluding his remarks to the press, Dark headed home to rest. He was developing a heavy cold.

His Yankee counterpart, looking to nail down the decisive Series victory, saw mostly negatives related to the rainout. Following the earlier postponement in New York, Ralph Houk had decided to use the winningest World Series hurler in history—Whitey Ford—to pitch the next game at Candlestick Park. The postponement of Friday's game would only affect his options for a possible seventh-game starter. Ralph Terry could now be in the mix to pitch that game, but Houk maintained he was focused only on Game Six.

"Win or lose in the fifth game, I had my mind made up on Ford," said Houk. "I'm going with my best right on through. Let the chips fall where they may. Ford pitches better in rotation than when he has an extra day of rest."[10]

Houk was asked about the status of Bill Stafford, who had taken the line shot off his left shin in Game Three. Houk said Stafford had been receiving treatment by team trainers and was still in some discomfort, but he believed the young right-hander could pitch if needed. However, the added day of rest now put Terry, the Yankees' top winner, on a four-day cycle if Houk chose to use him for a third time. (Years later, Stafford would confirm that he was originally scheduled to pitch in either the sixth or seventh game, "but my shin swelled up after Game Three and I lost my start.")[11]

Looking at the Giants' proposed starting pitchers, Houk felt the delay gave Pierce a welcome extra day of rest. In retrospect, this is somewhat debatable. Pierce had not pitched since Game One and would be throwing on eight days' rest instead of seven. It's a stretch to think that amount of inaction would be helpful to a control pitcher like Pierce. Perhaps Houk was trying to use some reverse psychology.

The rainout also put Sanford back in play as a possible Game Seven starter for the Giants. Looking back, it's fairly certain Billy O'Dell would have gotten the assignment if the rain hadn't upended the schedule. Juan Marichal was done for the rest of the Series after injuring his right index finger on the failed bunt attempt in the fourth game. Otherwise, he likely would have been in line for a Game Seven start. Speaking to reporters, Houk made it clear who he thought Dark would choose in a decisive game.

"Dark has shown that he likes to pitch Sanford," said Houk. "He probably would like to use him in a seventh game. And I don't blame him. He's a helluva pitcher." Houk also said he'd be sticking with his same familiar lineup, despite the dismal hitting of some of his regulars. "These are the men who did pretty well all season, and it's up to them to win or lose the Series."[12]

Weather forecasters indicated Saturday would bring scattered showers, but it was hoped any lingering wind would help dry out the field. The storm had failed to dampen the spirits of excited Giants fans hoping a return home would lift the team to a championship. Newspapers reported that scalpers were asking—and receiving—$50 for a single reserved seat and $150 for a pair of box seats. Hotels and motels in the bay area reported full capacities. Restaurants and bars were jammed, and night clubs saw large patronage increases. Those establishments would enjoy a very profitable weekend.

Intrepid Giant fans decided to brave the elements to buy tickets for what they hoped would now be a Saturday afternoon game. A group estimated to be between 500–700 ignored the terrible wind and rain and waited in line Thursday night into Friday morning for approximately 2,200 bleacher seats that the Giant ticket office made available. They brought sleeping bags, makeshift tents and huddled in the concrete recesses of the stadium to avoid the elements as much as possible. The ticket windows opened at 7:00 a.m. on Friday and all tickets were gone in less than thirty minutes. Among those in line were at least two small children and a man in a wheelchair. Authorities filled four pickup trucks afterwards with discarded, mostly damaged, umbrellas and tents.[13]

Saturday morning dawned bleak once again, with light rain and diminished, but steady wind. Frick kept to his same morning routine. He awoke before dawn in his hotel room, read the local newspapers, listened to radio weather reports and left for the stadium early in the morning. This time he didn't even bother to walk on the field. There was no chance to play on Saturday.

After holding a short meeting with the suddenly famous Schwab, Frick told the early arriving reporters, "We'll proceed on a strictly day-to-day basis. I'll be out with Matty early tomorrow and I'll make a decision then." He then took a few questions. Was he concerned that the outfield grass hadn't been cut since Wednesday, three days ago? "Yes, we have a very serious problem with that." Could the Series be moved to another location? "Positively not," he said. "It will be played right here if we have to wait until Christmas."[14] What had he heard about Sunday's weather forecast? Frick said he was informed there was a fifty percent chance of rain.

Nine. The World Series on Hiatus

By now, their troops not having thrown a ball or swung a bat in more than seventy-two hours, Houk and Dark were getting concerned about the players, particularly Houk since the Yankees were confined to a hotel. Using his professional baseball contacts, the Major tried to locate a facility with a dirt floor so the Yankees could throw, take infield and maybe swing the bat a little bit. The best he could find was an indoor baseball field house at Humboldt State College in Arcata, about 300 miles away, almost to the Oregon border. Houk rejected that option.[15] He spoke with Roy Hamey, the Yankee general manager, about his concerns that the players were getting bored and were going to lose their timing if they didn't get out and practice soon. Hamey agreed to explore solutions for Houk.

Dark, meanwhile, had called the Cow Palace, home of the San Francisco Warriors pro basketball team and many other events, to inquire about a possible team workout. But he learned that the arena's ice was down in preparation for a game that night with the San Francisco Seals of the Western Hockey League.[16]

At least the Giants were able to spend the unanticipated days off in their own homes or apartments with their families. For the Yankees, cooped up in the Town House at the intersection of Market Street and 8th Street, passing the time required more creativity. Richardson, the Yankees' boy-next-door type, interviewed his teammates to provide filler material for a daily World Series column he had agreed to write for the Columbia, South Carolina, newspaper *The State*. "Tony Kubek came up with several good ideas I could use, and I'm still grateful to him because I was really struggling," Richardson recalled in his autobiography, *Impact Player*. Afterwards, Richardson would decide that writing a newspaper column was not for him.

Tom Loomis of the *Toledo Blade*, unlike Richardson a professional columnist, wrote, "The Yankees, who act bored most of the time anyway, have become television fans. After all, you can play cards just so long and those seats in the movies get pretty hard."[17]

A few players took to site-seeing in a very walkable city, but the lousy weather discouraged some of that. College and pro football on television also provided a way to pass the time. But for one core group of veteran Yankees, the best option was a poker game. Card games took place in several of the players' rooms, and even continued after the sixth game had been played. Terry would later recount the story of his winning a $300 pot by outdrawing Berra, a man with a reputation among his teammates for always having good fortune. "I beat Yogi, I beat Yogi," Terry recalled saying to the others. "Man, it's an omen."[18]

Desperate for an angle for their daily articles or columns, some writers delved into World Series history. They learned that there was only one other time that the Series had been delayed so long. In 1911, the Philadelphia Athletics led the New York Giants two games to one when five days of heavy rain resulted in six consecutive days without baseball. (Laws prevented Sunday baseball in Philadelphia at the time, so one day was technically not a rainout.) Only the pitcher's mound at Shibe Park was covered by a tarp in those days. The Series finally resumed after the rain stopped and Athletics management used the primitive method of burning gallons of gasoline over parts of the infield to dry it out.[19]

Fred Lieb, a legendary baseball writer who worked professionally from 1909 to 1980, attended the 1911 World Series and recalled it in an article in *The Sporting News.* "Back then, the Series was a time for seeing the games, good fellowship, drinking and merrymaking," wrote Lieb. "And when the Series was stalled for six days in Philly, the drinking and merrymaking took over. A favorite quip at the time was that 'the World's Series party drank up everything in Philadelphia except the Delaware River.'"[20]

Lieb also told the story of how some of his colleagues got very creative, if not immoral, in passing the time during the rainouts. Sportswriters Bill Phelon and Hugh Fullerton (the latter a key figure in the reporting of the 1919 Black Sox scandal in Chicago) took out an advertisement in a local newspaper for female models, stating it was "a real opportunity for girls without experience."

Using a spare room secured by a friendly hotel porter, the pair spent the days taking measurements and ogling young Philadelphia women answering the ad. "'Yes, Miss, very nice,' they would say," Lieb wrote. "After the Series ended, there were girls still awaiting calls from the Fullerton-Phelon Modeling Agency."[21]

On Sunday morning in San Francisco, the sun shined brightly over the bay area and the winds had subsided, raising baseball fans' hopes, but when Frick and Schwab walked the outfield the water oozed up almost to their ankles. With Schwab's expert opinion that another day was needed, the commissioner said the game would be postponed a third consecutive day. "We cannot go today, despite the blue sky," proclaimed Frick. "The groundskeeper and his men will work all day on the field, and we'll have a game tomorrow."[22]

"A little more sun and some wind and the outfield turf would be seventy percent improved," Schwab told reporters.[23] His crew had found a dry time slot Saturday afternoon to cut the tall grass. The infield, covered throughout the rains whipped up by Freda, was still in good shape. But the outfield needed to dry considerably. Schwab later talked to Giants GM Chub Feeney about this. Eventually, someone came up with the idea of renting three helicopters to be stationed low above the outfield, blades whirling, to assist with the drying process. Photographers later snapped the unique photo. Where Mays and the Alou brothers normally were stationed, there were three hovering helicopters.

Confident that the sixth game would be played on Monday, both teams were now more concerned with knocking off some of the rust. On Saturday, Yankee co-owner Del Webb had called his manager with a thought. There was a regulation field in Modesto, some ninety miles away. It was named Del Webb Field in honor of the co-owner, who had once been a player for the minor league Modesto Reds of the California League. Modesto, a city of approximately 40,000, had received only a little more than one inch of rain during Typhoon Freda. Would Houk be interested in busing there to work out if Sunday's game was postponed? The Yankee manager was enthusiastic and told his players they'd be practicing outdoors on Sunday if there was no game and instructed them where and when to catch the bus. The Yankees then informed the commissioner of their plans. Frick immediately decided the Giants should have the same opportunity to practice if they desired. Dark quickly agreed and set up the Giants' own trip to Modesto.

Word reached the media after the commissioner's office became involved. The Sunday morning edition of the *Modesto Bee* ran the headline "Giant, Yankee Teams May Work Out Today in Modesto."[24] The powerful-signal San Francisco radio stations picked up the story, particularly once the postponement announcement became official Sunday morning. "Word spread like wildfire," wrote Ken White in his Modesto-centric book *Getaway Day*. "The Yankees and Giants were coming to the Central Valley."[25]

By the time the Yankee bus rolled up to the little stadium at 12 noon, an estimated 5,000 fans were scrambling for the 3,500 available seats. Those who couldn't sit staked out viewing areas above the wooden outfield fence or in standing-room only sections of the 13-year-old ballpark. "I never thought I'd look forward to a two-hour bus ride," said Ford, who like his teammates was happy to work up a sweat and get out of the hotel for a while. "We've had too many off days for hitters who haven't been hitting anyhow," said Houk. "It's bad when they can't face some pitching for two or three days."[26]

After a ninety-minute workout that featured light throwing, infield and batting practice, the Yankees headed back to the Town House and the Giants took the field. Dark ordered little-used pitchers Jim Duffalo, Mike McCormick and Bob Garibaldi to throw batting practice. One of the crowd's loudest applause recipients was Chuck Hiller, the second baseman who won the fourth game with his grand slam and was among the top hitters in the Series. By the time the Giants concluded their improvised workout, there were estimates that as many as 15,000 fans had been in the vicinity of the little ballpark. A website called *historicmodesto.com* refers to the team workouts as "Modesto's World Series."[27]

As the teams rested that evening knowing the *real* World Series would finally resume the next day, a host of star players and their managers had to wonder if they would finally break loose and start hitting. Through five games, the offensive production for both teams had been abysmal.

The Yankees were leading the Series, but other than Tresh and a few key hits by Kubek, Skowron and Boyer, they had fizzled offensively against San Francisco pitching. New York had scored only seventeen runs in five games and was hitting .214 as a team and .235 with runners in scoring position. Mantle was 2-for-18 (.111), Maris 3-for-16 (.188) and the previously dynamic October hitter Richardson was only 4-for-21 (.190). The club had hit a record 240 home runs the year before and followed that with 199 during the current season. But thus far, the celebrated Bronx Bombers had only two homers—Boyer's solo shot in the first game and Tresh's winning blow in Game Five.

The Giants were not doing much better at the plate. In their last two losses to the Yankees, they were a combined 2-for-14 with runners in scoring position. The big guns so far had been the unlikely trio of Pagan (.500), Haller (.364) and Hiller (.278), all of whom had homered. But Mays was at an uncharacteristic .238 with no homers and only one RBI. The normally steady Davenport was hitting .133 (2-for-15) and both Cepeda and Kuenn had yet to get a hit in twenty combined at-bats.

Cepeda's struggles at the plate were especially glaring. The Baby Bull had pounded thirty-five home runs and driven in 114 runs during the season, and his lack of success severely depleted what had been the National League's most potent attack. In fact, Cepeda had been designated the "goat" of the Series opener after he went 0-for-4, left three men on base and failed to hit the ball out of the infield in the 6–2 Giant defeat. He was fitted for goat's horns in cartoons drawn by famed sports cartoonist Bill Gallo that ran in both the *New York Daily News* and *The Sporting News*.[28]

Sports fans in the 21st century recognize the term "G.O.A.T" as a much-coveted title, an acronym standing for "Greatest of All Time." It's a popular term on social media that has been ascribed to such luminaries as Tom Brady, LeBron James and Tiger Woods. At the time of the Yankees-Giants World Series, to be a goat was something to assiduously avoid. Basically, the goat was the player or coach who kicked away the team's chance to win. For seven decades, Gallo famously created cartoons picturing World Series heroes and goats, drawing wreaths and halos over the heads of the heroes and horns emanating from the heads of the goats.

The pitching matchup for the sixth game would be two veteran left-handers, one unbeaten in his home ballpark all year, the other the most successful hurler in the history of the Fall Classic. Pierce's earned run average at Candlestick was 2.79 compared to 4.52 on the road. Ford had won ten of fourteen World Series decisions. Previewing a resumption of the rain-delayed Series, renowned columnist Red Smith wrote, "Nobody beats Ford in World Series competition and nobody has ever beaten Pierce in Candlestick Park. On form, neither starting pitcher can lose the sixth game, and neither team can win it."[29]

Then, in an eerie foreshadowing of events to come twenty-seven years later in the same city in another World Series known for a long delay, Smith concluded, "Chances are it will go 16 innings and still be tied when the earthquake hits."[30]

Ten

Game Six: Return of the Baby Bull

"Fair skies and warmer temperatures."

That simple forecast for Monday's weather in San Francisco made the managers, players and press corps a bit giddy. After four straight days with no game, in a sport that prides itself on its everyday pace, the baseball season was about to continue toward its conclusion. That urge to resume didn't mean all parties were unanimous in their assessment of the playing conditions, however.

One of Ford Frick's top assistants in the commissioner's office, Frank Slocum, arrived at Candlestick Park just after dawn on Monday and was so concerned while walking on the wet outfield turf that he called Frick and said, "You better get here early and see for yourself."[1] So Frick took another tour of the Candlestick outfield. By now, having soaked multiple pairs of dress shoes over the past four days, Frick was about as much an authority on wet playing fields as Matty Schwab. He'd had enough of the delays. Yes, the field was still wet, but he'd be damned if he'd wait any longer to continue the Series.

In his hotel room, Frick had a pair of suitcases filled with warm weather clothing for a trip he had expected to make days before. He was to fly to Hawaii for a few days of R&R before accompanying the Detroit Tigers on an exhibition game tour of Japan.[2] Typhoon Freda had botched that itinerary and he was more than ready to get this drawn-out Series moving again.

Standing in one of the dugouts, Frick told reporters that Game Six would proceed with its scheduled 12 noon start even with circumstances "which I admit are miserable. It isn't exactly fair to either team, but they will both be playing under the same conditions."[3]

Frick decided neither team would take batting practice as a nod to preserving the conditions of the infield and the home plate area. To improve the infield surface, Schwab's grounds crew applied a chemical

Ten. Game Six: Return of the Baby Bull

substance designed to loosen the rock-hard adobe soil that had been lying under a drenched tarpaulin for almost six days.

When the Yankees entered the stadium around 10:00 a.m. and went out to inspect the field, they were generally upbeat and anxious to play. With their best pitcher on the mound, and with a little luck, they'd finish the thing that day and head on home. The soggy turf didn't bother them. "Opening day in Washington was a lot worse," said reserve first baseman Dale Long, who began the season playing for the Senators. He told the story of how he'd borrowed football cleats from the Washington Redskins' equipment manager that day rather than use his baseball spikes. Manager Houk was appreciative of the job Schwab and his crew had done. "There are some soft spots in the outfield, but the infield looks good. We've played under worse conditions several times this year."[4]

As if they, too, had been thrown off their routines by the storm and subsequent delays, the fans were slow arriving to the ballpark. Large patches of seats were still vacant through the first two innings, but soon filled in, and ultimately it was announced as another sellout crowd. The final gate count was 43,948, thirty-eight more fans than attended Game Two. Among the more notable spectators settling into their seats was Joe DiMaggio, a native of San Francisco but obviously rooting for the Yankees to end it.[5] After the national anthem was performed by singer John Raitt, appearing in a San Francisco production of *The Pajama Game*,[6] those fans on hand for the first pitch let out a large anticipatory roar when Pierce fired strike one to Kubek leading off for New York.

Much had been made in the newspapers of Pierce's 12–0 success at home during the regular season, and he seemed determined to show why early on. Working as he always did from the extreme first base side of the pitching rubber, he retired the Yankees in order through each of the first four innings. Only one New York hitter—Ford—struck out, but Pierce retired five batters on ground balls, four on pop flies to the infield and two on fly balls to the outfield. Only two balls had been hit with authority. Mantle, in the second inning, and Skowron, in the third, hit long shots that Mays ran down without any trouble. His fastball was not quite up to his usual standard, but Pierce's control on his breaking pitches—the curve and the slider—kept the New York hitters off balance.

Ford escaped trouble in the first inning after Hiller beat out an infield single with one out and moved to second when Boyer mishandled Felipe Alou's grounder for a rare error. That brought up Mays, Ford's longtime National League nemesis. This time, however, Mays slapped a hard ground ball to short and the New York infield—Kubek to Richardson to Skowron—turned the double play to get out of the jam.

Cepeda elicited a loud roar from the crowd in the bottom of the second by grounding a single into left field, his first World Series hit in thirteen at-bats. After Ford struck out Davenport, Cepeda broke for second on a full-count pitch to Bailey. When Bailey swung and missed, Howard gunned down Cepeda with an accurate throw to Kubek for the *strike 'em out, throw 'em out* double play to end the inning. But after an easy third inning, the roof caved in on Ford in the fourth.

It started innocently enough when Hiller flied out to Tresh. Alou than smashed a one-hopper down the third base line that the acrobatic Boyer could only deflect with his glove as he leaped to his left, putting Alou at first with an infield single. Pitching away from his power, Ford walked Mays. With Cepeda at the plate and two men on, the Yankees decided to put on a pickoff play to go after Alou at second. Ford turned as Richardson broke for the bag, but his throw was about ten feet wide of second base and skipped into right-center field. Playing Cepeda deep, by the time Maris picked up the errant throw, Alou came around to score and Mays went all the way to third. The Giants had broken the ice and led, 1–0.

"I tried to hold up the throw when I saw I had no play," Ford said later, "but when I wheeled and then tried to check the throw, the ball flew out of my hand into the outfield."[7] Dark would later call Ford's error the biggest play of the game.

Cepeda quickly made it 2–0 by driving an outside fastball deep into the gap in right center. Mays scored as Cepeda coasted into second with a double. That brought up Davenport, mired in a 2-for-16 funk. The Giants' third baseman made solid contact, lining a bullet past the glove of Ford into center field. Cepeda scored without a play being made on him. The Candlestick crowd was deliriously happy. The Giants had a 3–0 lead and two of their most reliable players, Cepeda and Davenport, were finally showing signs of life at the plate.

Playing in his fifth season in the big leagues, Davenport had become one of the foundations of the ballclub. He broke in with the Giants that first year at Seals Stadium and earned the regular job at third base with his stellar defense and steady offensive production. He hit twelve home runs and batted .256 as a rookie, and his numbers had not varied much in his first three seasons. But he drove in what would be a career-high sixty-five runs in 1961 and a year later produced his best batting average, hitting .297 in 144 games.

Not blessed with great speed or power, Davenport seldom struck out and rarely walked. Usually hitting in the lower part of the batting order, he put the ball in play and moved runners along. An outstanding bunter, he led the National League with seventeen sacrifice hits as a

Ten. Game Six: Return of the Baby Bull

rookie and would wind up his career ranking in the top ten in that category seven times. But Davenport's real value to the Giants was at third base—and in the clubhouse. He led the NL in fielding percentage three times and earned a Gold Glove in 1962. Later in his career, he would establish a major league record (since broken) by playing ninety-seven consecutive errorless games at third.

"Jim was the best third baseman in the league when we were teammates," recalled Felipe Alou many years later.[8]

His teammates respected him and loved playing with him. This was notable on a team whose diversity in the clubhouse was just starting to show some stress points in '62 and would break wide open within a couple years. Despite Davenport's having grown up in the segregation of metro Birmingham, Alabama, he showed no favoritism or animosity toward any group. "He was really one of the best teammates, for whites, Latinos, and blacks," Alou stated upon Davenport's death in 2016. "There was not a trace of racism in him. He was an incredible friend and teammate."[9]

Fellow Alabamian Willie McCovey would say of Davenport, "There was not a prejudiced bone in his body, and that's what I admired about him so much. He was just a regular guy."[10]

After Davenport's base hit put them in a 3–0 hole, the Yankees came up in the top of the fifth. Mantle hit an easy fly ball to Mays, becoming the thirteenth consecutive Yankee set down by Pierce. But Maris belted a slow curveball deep over the fence in right field for a long home run. It was a no-doubt shot by the Yankee slugger. Second baseman Hiller didn't even turn around to watch the ball's flight, instead looking down to smooth the dirt in front of him with his spikes. It was only the third home run of the Series by the Yankees and the first for Maris, who led New York during the season with thirty-three.

Pierce then faced a bit of adversity when Howard reached second on an error charged to Davenport, who fielded a hot grounder before his throw to first eluded Cepeda and rolled down the right field line. After Skowron flied out to center, Dark decided to force Houk into making a tricky decision. He ordered Pierce to walk Boyer intentionally, putting runners on first and second with two out and the pitcher Ford due up.

Down two runs in the fifth inning, what would Houk do? His power pinch-hitters were all left-handed—Berra, Blanchard and Long—and would be at a disadvantage against the southpaw Pierce. Hector Lopez was probably the only other option Houk considered. Adding to the intrigue, Jim Coates was warming up in the Yankee bullpen when Boyer was intentionally passed. But Houk later claimed this was just a ruse. "I warmed up Coates to try and make the Giants think I might pinch-hit for Whitey," he insisted.[11]

Houk must have also factored in how poorly his pinch-hitters had come off the bench in 1962. As a team, the Yankees batted a miserable .213, eight points lower than the American League average. Berra was the best of the lot (6-for-23, .261), but Lopez (5-for-24, .208), Blanchard (3-for-25, .120) and Long (3-for-28, .107) were largely unsuccessful. The only other reserve hitters available to Houk were backup outfielder Jack Reed and rookie infielder Phil Linz. Houk wasn't going to throw either of them into a clutch spot like this.

So, no one emerged from the visiting dugout down the third base line. Instead, No. 16 walked to the plate from the on-deck circle. Pierce overpowered him, inducing Ford to weakly pop up to Hiller at second base and the threat was over. After the game, Houk was roundly second-guessed for the decision to let Ford hit, especially after what was about to transpire in the Giants' half of the fifth. Bill Gallo's cartoon the next day pictured the Yankee manager wearing the goat's horns.[12]

"I never thought about it," Houk insisted when asked afterwards if he gave thought to replacing Ford. "I had four more at-bats and Ford is my best pitcher. I'm not going to take out a pitcher like Ford with that many innings left."[13]

Wrote Red Smith in his syndicated column the next day, "Pierce appeared to be laboring in this inning, but Houk and Ford helped him out—the manager by letting Ford bat with two out and Whitey by popping up."[14]

Consecutive one-out singles in the fifth by Kuenn (his first hit in the Series) and Hiller put runners on the corners. With Ford pitching from the stretch, Alou belted one through the hole between short and third scoring Kuenn, increasing the Giants' lead to 4–1. Mays popped up to Skowron in foul territory for the second out, but the suddenly rejuvenated Cepeda smacked a hard single to center to bring in Hiller. As the crowd exulted and the Giants cheered from the dugout, Houk slowly walked to the mound to pull his ace. Ford received applause from the San Francisco fans as he made the slow walk toward the Yankee clubhouse located in the right field corner. Coates came in to relieve Ford.

Having weathered the fifth inning, Pierce now seemed to put the hammer down on the Yankee chances. Three ground ball outs retired the top of the New York order in the sixth and after Maris reached base on a one-out walk in the seventh, Davenport started an around-the-horn double play on a grounder off the bat of Howard. That left the Yankee catcher with a dismal .176 World Series batting average.

Like Davenport, Elston Howard was among the most respected Yankees in the estimation of his teammates. Unlike Davenport, he'd had to surmount numerous racial obstacles on his journey to becoming the starting catcher on a defending world champion team.

Howard was born in St. Louis, just like the man he replaced as Yankee catcher (Berra). After excelling in a semipro league, he was persuaded to attend an open tryout run by the hometown Cardinals in 1948. When the Cardinals showed no interest in signing him—the team wouldn't integrate its major league roster until 1954—Howard signed a contract to play for the Kansas City Monarchs of the Negro League.[15] He was paid $500 per month, much of which he mailed home to his mother. In the summer of 1950, Howard and a Monarch teammate were sold to the Yankee organization for $25,000. After an assignment with Special Services during the Korean War, Howard continued to make his way up the Yankee farm chain. By 1953, *Jet* magazine was headlining a profile of him that read "Howard May Be First Negro with Yankees."[16] A year later, with pressure mounting on the Yankees to integrate, coupled with Howard's MVP season (.330, twenty-two HRs, 109 RBIs) in the International League, the Yankees announced they'd be inviting him to their 1955 camp in St. Petersburg, Florida.

"I had a rough time in spring training," Howard told author Peter Golenbock in *Dynasty: The New York Yankees 1949–1964*. "The camp would break at the end of the day and you had to go back across the tracks to the black section to dress while the white boys would go back to the hotel. They would all get on the bus, but I had to jump in a cab in my uniform to go back there and dress. I couldn't live with the other players at the hotel. I stayed with a private family in the black section of St. Pete. But I remember everybody tried to make everything pleasant for this black guy who was going to be the first one to join us. I remember Bill Skowron and his wife came to pick me up at the train station, which I'll never forget, and Phil Rizzuto, goddamn, he was great. I'll never forget him. I would call him the Great White Father."

That spring, the quiet, personable Howard won over his teammates and even some skeptical writers with his solid, determined play. "He seems certain to be the first Negro to make the Yankees," wrote Arthur Daley in the *New York Times*. "They've waited for one to come along who is the Yankee type."[17]

As Bill Dickey had done for him in his days as a young catcher, Berra worked with the 26-year-old Howard to improve his defensive skills behind the plate. At the same time, manager Casey Stengel had Howard work out in the outfield and at first base to increase his versatility and get him in the lineup more often, rather than let him rot on the bench behind Berra as other Yankee catchers—including Ralph Houk—had done.

If his teammates' acceptance was a positive, one of the negatives Howard had to deal with was the internal thinking of his manager. Stengel grew up in Missouri, a state that still harbored a legacy of slave-owning families. He was raised in a time when disparaging, even racist, terms were commonly spoken out loud in public among whites. As he aged, Stengel became a bit more circumspect in his comments, but those generational feelings were never far from the surface. Commenting on Howard's lack of running speed, Stengel famously said, "When I finally get a nigger, I get the only one who can't run." It was also written that Stengel sometimes referred to Howard as "Eightball."[18]

His teammates generally treated Howard as just another player. He quickly earned their respect for both his skills on the field and his modest personality. "He never brought up those issues in the locker room or on our train rides and flights," recalled Richardson of racism directed at Howard. "Dignity is a word that comes to mind when I think about how Ellie handled the pressure. Ellie was a true gentleman."[19]

For his part, Howard displayed a quiet grace on and off the field and got revenge on his detractors by becoming a valuable member of four pennant-winning Yankee teams of the late 1950s. His diving catch in short left field resulted in a spectacular double play in the fifth game of the 1958 World Series. It is often cited as the turning point in a struggle the Yankees won in seven after trailing Milwaukee three games to one. By 1960, he was catching more often than Berra. In the World Series that year, Howard batted a hefty .462 before being hit on the finger in Game Six. He was not in the lineup when the Yanks lost the decisive seventh game to the Pirates.

In 1961, Howard enjoyed an outstanding season that was completely overshadowed by the Maris/Mantle home run assault on Babe Ruth's record. Howard batted .348 with twenty-one homers and seventy-seven runs batted in. He placed tenth in the voting for the American League's Most Valuable Player (fifth on the Yankees behind Maris, Mantle, Ford and Arroyo). And the Yankee pitching staff trusted him. "He got more strikes for his pitcher than any catcher I ever saw," said former Yankee left-hander Bobby Shantz. "When the ball hit his glove, it didn't move. His glove stayed right there. Most catchers give a little. Not him, though. He was a pitcher's best friend."[20]

Firmly entrenched as the starting catcher at thirty-three, Howard's average dipped sixty-nine points in '62, but he still hit twenty-one home runs and drove in ninety-one runs. He'd become an integral part of the

Ten. Game Six: Return of the Baby Bull — 121

New York lineup and his lack of production vs. the Giants was becoming a real factor in the Yankees' offensive woes.

Down 5–1, the Yankees made one final stab at getting to Pierce. Skowron flied out to left to open the top of the eighth before Boyer hit a shot down the left field line good for a double. This time Houk did reach for a pinch-hitter, sending up Lopez for Coates, who had retired all seven San Francisco batters he faced. Lopez flied out to Alou in right. Kubek then poked an opposite field single to left center to bring in Boyer and make it 5–2. With no one warming up in the bullpen, Pierce calmly fired a slider on the inside part of the plate that Richardson lofted to medium left field. When Kuenn caught it, the inning was over and, soon enough, Yankee hopes of ending the Series on this day. In the ninth, Pierce retired Tresh and Mantle on routine fly balls and struck out Maris swinging to put the finishing touch on a 5–2 victory.

"I threw him [Maris] a hard fastball to strike him out," Pierce said in the locker room. "You can't relax a minute with the Yankees."[21] The veteran southpaw had tossed a three-hit gem that took exactly two hours

Willie Mays heads back to retrieve his lost cap after stealing second base in Game Six. It was the Giants' only stolen base of the Series. The Yankee infielder is Bobby Richardson and the umpire is Jim Honochick (© 1962 S.F. Giants).

to complete. As one newsman noted, the game ended so early that the famed Candlestick winds hadn't yet started up.

In a happy and confident Giants locker room, the twin targets of media attention basked in their success. Pierce was asked how his performance compared to the shutout he tossed in the first game of the NL playoff. "I followed the same pattern against the Yankees as I used against the Dodgers," he said. "I realized early that I wasn't as fast as I had been against the Dodgers, so I concentrated on my breaking stuff. I used sliders mostly to right-handers and mixed curves with my fastball against the lefties."[22]

Pierce said a big part of his pregame strategy had been to keep the bases clear whenever Mantle came to bat. "Mickey hasn't done much hitting in the Series," he said, "but you figure a great hitter like that is going to get his hits sooner or later. And you can look for him to hit that long ball almost any time. So if you have Mantle coming up with nobody on, you can breathe a little easier."[23] Pierce succeeded with flying colors. Mantle led off an inning his first three times up and never batted with a man on base.

Knowing his season was likely complete—there was very little chance Dark would use him in relief the next day—Pierce reflected on his effort with justifiable satisfaction. "The whole season has been a great one for me because a lot of people thought I was washed up when the White Sox traded me to the Giants. I hope I've proved they were wrong."[24]

Boyer told reporters that Pierce "had real good control, and when a pitcher as good as him has his good control, he's hard to hit."[25] But most of Boyer's teammates and his manager saw nothing special out of the veteran southpaw, and instead lamented their own offensive troubles. "He pitched a good ball game. We didn't get any hits. That's about all there was to it," summarized a tight-lipped Houk.[26] Asked one of those roll-your-eyes-at-the-reporter questions, namely did he expect to win the deciding game, Houk said, "They ought to fire me if I didn't expect to win it."[27]

The other San Francisco hero—Cepeda—cited the three rainouts as a major factor in his big day (3-for-4, a double and two RBIs). "I didn't swing any different than I have been," said the Baby Bull, "but with the rest, I felt good. I felt strong. I used a 35-ounce bat instead of the 33 I'd been using. I didn't feel tired anymore."[28]

Dark talked about Cepeda's run-scoring double in the fourth and RBI single in the fifth and said they were the hardest balls Cepeda had hit in more than a month. He also said his first baseman's batting exploits had convinced him to start Cepeda at first base in the seventh game and use McCovey in the outfield. Additionally, Haller would catch instead of Bailey, who was now 1-for-13 at the plate.

In the visiting team locker room, the Yankees were a noticeably annoyed, frustrated group, led by the so-called "M&M Boys." Maris never interrupted grabbing his clothes and getting dressed while answering a few questions mostly with a grunt or shrug of the shoulders. Approached by one writer, Mantle shut off all conversation saying, "I don't want to say a damn thing about anything," as he ripped off his jersey and fired it into a pile of dirty laundry in the middle of the floor.[29]

Mantle's 0-for-4 against Pierce left him with a paltry .091 batting average (2-for-22) through six games. His World Series history had pretty much been a heaven or hell experience so far. He'd enjoyed some personal high points such as the .345 average and game-winning home run in Game Seven in 1952; the great running catch of Gil Hodges' screaming liner to preserve Larsen's perfect game in 1956; and the monster 10-for-25 (.400), eleven-RBI effort in the losing cause against Pittsburgh two years earlier.

But the World Series had also meant physical pain for Mantle. In his first Series in 1951, he tore up his right knee after catching his spikes on a rubber drain embedded in the Yankee Stadium outfield. He had been chasing a fly ball hit by Mays when he was called off by DiMaggio moving over from center field. "Well, shit, you don't want to run into Joe DiMaggio in center field in Yankee Stadium," Mantle told Jane Leavy in *The Last Boy*. "I was running so fast my knee just went right out the front of my leg."

In 1957, he suffered a right shoulder injury when Milwaukee second baseman Red Schoendienst fell heavily on him on an attempted pickoff play. The injury cost him two starts in a Series the Yankees would lose in seven games. For years afterward Mantle would maintain that he had more pain and less power hitting left-handed because of the mishap.

And a year before facing the Giants, Mantle had gamely tried to play against the Reds despite the oozing wound to his hip caused by a needle from a disreputable celebrity doctor who earned the nickname "Dr. Feelgood."[30] This was the same ailment that took him out of the final stages of the so-called home run derby with Maris. Mantle played in two games in Cincinnati, going 1-for-6. When he singled in the fourth inning of the fourth game, blood was weeping through his uniform trousers and Houk sent Lopez in to run for him. That was the extent of Mantle's contribution in the Series.

Now, feeling healthy after recovering from the leg injuries he'd suffered trying to beat out that ground ball against Minnesota in May, Mantle was beyond angry with himself for utterly failing to help his ballclub at the plate. Thus far he'd scored only two runs and had yet to drive one in while batting in the cleanup position in every game. "That Giants pitching tied me all up," he would later write.[31] Asked at one postgame press conference in San Francisco if he thought the balls were livelier that year, he sarcastically replied, "No, but the players are."[32]

His most famous line concerning the 1962 World Series would be a typically self-deprecating one. As Mantle told the story to author Joe Durso in the 1977 book *Whitey and Mickey*: "The more it rained, the more me and Whitey and the guys horsed around in San Francisco. Anyway, all the papers were writing about how the Series had these two great center fielders, Mays and Mantle, and the way it turned out, neither one of us was doing too goddamn good. So one day I'm out in center field and I hear this big booming voice yelling at me, 'Hey Mantle, everybody came out here to see who was better, you or Mays. Now we wonder which one of you guys is worse.' The next inning, I grounded out and now I'm hitting like .100 for the Series and I go back out to center and now this same guy yells over, 'Hey Mantle, you win! You're the worst!'"

Perhaps banking too much on Ford's terrific World Series success, many of the Yankees had made airline flight connections for that evening rather than fly back to New York on the team charter. But Ford had been the losing pitcher, tying the World Series record of five career losses held by such Hall of Famers as Christy Mathewson, Eddie Plank and Rube Marquard. (He would eventually own the record by himself, winding up with eight Series defeats.) All air reservations for Monday evening had to be altered. Change fees were rare in 1962, but the inconvenience of dealing with telephone reservation agents for limited seating was still an unpleasant experience.

"This was a good, sound pasting for the Yankees," wrote Red Smith.[33] The team was also cranky thinking about spending a sixth consecutive night in the Town House hotel. Not to mention the very real possibility that they might drop both games in San Francisco, thereby blowing a World Series in which they'd had three different one-game leads. That also had a real financial impact to it—the difference in the winner's share vs. the loser's share was estimated to be approximately $2,500 (roughly $21,500 in 2020 dollars based upon a typical inflation calculator). This was significant money for rookies like Tresh, Linz and Bouton who were making in the neighborhood of $7,000 a year.[34]

"To fellows like Mickey, Yogi and myself who are in the higher income brackets, the few thousand dollars isn't important," Ford told a group of writers before warming up for his sixth game assignment. "But pride is. That's why we like to win."[35]

Despite all the dismal hitting he'd seen, Houk would not consider

Ten. Game Six: Return of the Baby Bull

using a different lineup for the next day's final game. He'd go with the same eight position players and once again pick Terry as his starting pitcher. None of which was a surprise. Terry had already exceeded 300 innings and would be making his 42nd start of the 1962 season. To put that in some perspective, Terry would be making more starts than "Iron Man" Joe McGinnity did in seven of his ten years in the major leagues. A Hall of Famer, McGinnity earned his nickname by starting both ends of a doubleheader on multiple occasions in the first decade of the 20th century.

The lack of variety in the lineup was also a typical Yankee strategy. Game Two injuries to Skowron and Howard had forced Houk to use Long and Berra as starters. But other than that, in a time when the designated hitter didn't exist, New York sent up only four pinch-hitters in the seven games vs. the Giants. Berra walked in his one appearance, Lopez was 0-for-2 and Blanchard struck out against Sanford in Game Two.

It would be Sanford on the mound again in a rubber match between him and Terry. The last time two starting pitchers faced each other three times in the World Series had been in 1945 when Hank Borowy of the Chicago Cubs squared off three times vs. Hal Newhouser of the Detroit Tigers. Cornered by reporters in the San Francisco locker room, Sanford said he was still nursing a cold that had plagued him since the end of the Dodger playoff. "But I feel pretty good," he said. "I'm about as nervous as I was before my first start. I'm sure thinking about it. This is something that happens once in a lifetime."[36]

He'd be putting a 23–2 mark at Candlestick Park over the past two seasons on the line. "Guess it's just home," Sanford said, trying to explain his success. Before heading out the door, he told the writers that the key for him was to keep the first three Yankee hitters in check—Kubek, Richardson and Tresh. "You have to be careful with all those guys. But I know where I'm not supposed to throw the ball. Down the middle."[37]

"After thirteen days, 6,000 miles of jet travel and six ball games, the San Francisco Giants and New York Yankees are all even again," wrote Jack Hand in his Associated Press preview for the seventh game. The whole season had been reduced to a winner-take-all contest. For the first time since the Series began, the early betting line was a pick 'em bet. The Yanks had been favored by the bookies to win the Series and to win each of the first six games. Now the bookies expected money to come in evenly on both sides.[38]

One game for all the marbles. Two pitchers who'd already beaten and lost to each other. Nine innings to a World Series championship.

Eleven

Game Seven: High Drama at Candlestick

Finishing up with a seventh game was becoming a distinct trend for the World Series.

For the sixth time in eight years, the Fall Classic would be going the distance. No other stretch before then—or since—had seen so many Game Sevens in such a concentrated period. Since 1955, every Series had gone seven games except for two—1959 when the Dodgers beat the White Sox in six, and 1961 when the Yankees dusted off the Reds in five. With '62 added to the list, the Bronx Bombers would now be participants in all six of those Game Sevens.

Consequently, the Yankees had a roster full of players who'd experienced the pressure of a climactic Series contest. And, although the San Francisco franchise had not been in a Series in eight years, the Giants had been similarly tested more recently, having struggled through the crucible of the final regular-season series with Houston and the NL playoff with Los Angeles. In both cases, San Francisco had won two out of three games to survive and advance. So the experience factor was not much of an advantage for either club.

The Yankees were 10–3 in thirteen World Series since dropping the 1942 Series to St. Louis in five games (the only losing World Series Joe DiMaggio ever played in). All three of those defeats came in seven games, leading Alvin Dark to tell reporters, "The only way to beat the Yankees is in seven games, and I've got the ballclub to do it."[1]

The weather in the bay area would again cooperate on this mid–October Tuesday, with temperatures in the low seventies under a bright sun. But the wind, a non-entity the day before, was going to be a significant factor this time. It was noticeably stronger during pregame activities, blowing from left field to right as it routinely did in the afternoon.

Unlike the previous day, both teams took batting practice. "How do you put up with this wind?" Elston Howard told reporters he had asked Willie Mays before the game. Mays' reply was, "If you think this is bad, wait until it starts to shift directions."² During the game, when the gusts particularly picked up strength, NBC radio announcer Joe Garagiola quoted Milwaukee pitcher Lew Burdette's favorite line about the wind at Candlestick—"It's the only park where you can sit in the dugout and read the morning paper as it flies by."³

Matty Schwab, who all observers agreed had done yeoman's work in preparing the field after all the heavy rain, ordered his groundskeepers to cut the stadium's grass early that morning in the hope that balls would roll a bit truer on the still-wet outfield turf. Commissioner Frick surveyed activities around the stadium and felt profound relief that the season would finally finish up this day and he could be on his way to Hawaii.

When the Giants took their BP, one of the volunteer pitchers was outfielder Bob Nieman. "I don't expect to be wearing this uniform next year, so I wanted to give them something to remember me by," said Nieman, who was playing for his seventh major league team in a career that stretched back to 1951, the last time Mays and Dark played in a World Series against the Yankees.⁴

A rather large total of eleven players—seven for the Yankees—had not yet appeared in the Series. Among the names were Jim Bouton, Luis Arroyo and Phil Linz for New York, and Mike McCormick and Jim Duffalo for San Francisco. All had made contributions during the season, but none would play in Game Seven either. In just one year's time, Arroyo had gone from being the American League's premier relief pitcher to an afterthought in the Yankee bullpen.

At 12 noon, Kubek stepped into the batter's box as Sanford toed the rubber. "This is it," said George Kell, broadcasting the game nationally on radio. "Forget the rest of the season, the playoffs, what you did in this ballpark or that ballpark. It's all wrapped up in today."⁵ Kubek bluffed a bunt and took strike one as the 43,948 in attendance—the exact same figure as Game Six—settled in to watch baseball history unfold. After Kubek flied out to Mays in center field, Richardson drew a walk. Tresh then popped out to Davenport, bringing up Mantle. His futility at the plate with men on base continued as he skied out to McCovey in left field.

Terry gave everyone an early indication of what was to come. He had his fastball working, pumping it in for strikes, and had good control of his slider and curveball. He needed only eight pitches to dispose of Felipe Alou, Hiller and Mays in the bottom of the first. Both pitchers sailed through the second inning with no base runners, but in the top of the third the Yankees put together the first scoring threat of the game.

After Boyer lined out to Alou in right and Terry struck out on three pitches, Kubek singled sharply in the hole between short and third. For the second straight time, Richardson walked on a 3–1 count. The Yanks had two on for their leading hitter in the Series, Tresh.

On radio, Kell and Garagiola both noted that Sanford was leaving the ball up in the strike zone more than normal, that the key to his effectiveness in 1962 had been his ability to throw strikes in the lower part of the zone. Pitching "up" in Candlestick Park was flirting with danger for any pitcher facing a left-handed hitter. Get a ball up in the jet stream blowing toward right and it usually meant trouble. And the New York lineup had three straight lefty power hitters set up in a row for Sanford. As Tresh walked to the plate, Kell observed that the wind had shifted (as Mays told Howard it could) and was now blowing in toward home plate. Newspaper accounts later estimated the wind's velocity at between 25 and 35 miles per hour.[6]

Taking longer than normal between pitches, Sanford again missed high and ran the count to 3–1. Tresh took a strike to run the count full, then swung as the runners took off with the pitch. He got on top of the ball, grounding a two-hopper to Hiller who threw him out to end the threat.

Terry, meanwhile, continued to mow down the San Francisco hitters. In the bottom of the third, Davenport led off with an epic at-bat, fouling off six consecutive 2–2 pitches before popping up to Richardson. Although pitch counts were not paid nearly the attention or importance as they are in today's game, Houk and his pitching coach, Johnny Sain, had to be hoping Terry would be efficient. The right-hander was a strong young man, but he'd already exceeded 300 innings on the season. How much more could Terry have left in the tank?

His athleticism, durability and uncanny control had interested the Yankees in the Oklahoma native during his schoolboy years at Chelsea High School before they signed him to a professional contract at the age of eighteen. Unfortunately for them, the St. Louis Cardinals also saw promise in Terry and signed him to another contract. The matter became a legal entanglement and was ultimately settled by Commissioner Frick's office in favor of the Yankees.[7] Terry won thirty-eight games over three minor league seasons before joining the Yanks late in 1956.

Appearing in a handful of games the next year, he was dealt to Kansas City at the trading deadline in a four-for-four deal that brought New York only one player of immediate value, reliever Ryne Duren, and one significant player to be named later (Clete Boyer). This was the trade that sent Billy Martin away from the Yankees, and Martin would swear for the rest of his life that the deal was vengeance for his being blamed for the famous 1957 incident/fight involving several high-profile Yankees and a patron of the Copacabana nightclub in Manhattan.

"So Casey called me in and said, 'We just made a little trade. You're going to Kansas City,'" Terry recalled. Shocked at first, and reluctant to leave the organization he'd come up through, Terry realized there was a silver lining when Stengel added, "You go over there and you'll have a chance to pitch."[8]

Terry went 11–13 as a starter for the Athletics in 1958 on a team that finished seventh. In May of the following year, he was obtained by the Yankees along with Hector Lopez in a seemingly never-ending trading carousel with Kansas City that infuriated general managers throughout the American League in the late 1950s. Of the 25-man roster the Yanks listed for the World Series against the Giants, five had previously played for the A's—Maris, Terry, Lopez, Boyer and Daley, fully 20 percent of the New York roster. (Within four years, three more Yankees would add Kansas City to their resume as Blanchard, Stafford and Sheldon were all traded away.)

Terry had won twenty-six games in his first two full seasons with New York, finishing second in the AL in winning percentage in '61 at 16–3. But the high slider he threw to Mazeroski had become the one thing most people thought of when hearing Terry's name. He was grateful that Houk was giving him a chance at redemption.

Through five innings, Terry had thrown only thirty-eight pitches, thirty of them for strikes. On their second set of at-bats against him, Alou, Hiller and Mays all put the ball in play within two pitches. They saw no advantage on this day to waiting out the Yankee hurler. He was putting the ball almost exactly where he wanted it. When the Giants hit fly balls, however, Terry and the Yankee dugout had to hold their breath. In the fourth, Tresh caught Alou's drive to left on the dead run as the wind pushed it toward left center. In the same inning, Mays hit a high fly that Mantle initially thought he had easily lined up. As the wind gusted in, Mantle was forced to pursue it while sprinting toward the infield. With Maris also converging, Mantle stabbed the ball with his glove hand fully extended for what one newspaper caption called "a sensational catch."[9]

Terry's fifth inning was much more routine. He needed just nine pitches to retire McCovey, Cepeda and Haller. The Baby Bull again looked lost at the plate, having struck out in the first and popped up to second in the fifth. Just as in the first game, Cepeda would be unable to hit the ball out of the infield on this day.

In the New York fifth, Sanford again seemed to struggle with his control. On a 2–2 delivery to Skowron, the New York first baseman smacked a ground single into left field, becoming the first leadoff hitter in the game to reach base. Boyer, who had been relatively quiet at the plate since his heroics in Game One, hit a rope into the alley in left center field. On dry turf the ball may have rolled all the way to the fence. But the Candlestick outfield slowed it down, and by the time Mays threw it back to the infield, Skowron was on third with Boyer at first. That brought up Terry.

With an offensive attack built on the long ball, Houk had no thought of having Terry bunt or try a squeeze play. He wanted his pitcher to try and put the ball in play. In three games hitting against Sanford, Terry had struck out in five of his six at-bats. As the crowd's concerned buzz grew louder on each delivery, Sanford threw four straight out of the strike zone to walk the opposing pitcher. The bases were loaded with none out.

An intrepid reporter would later ask Sanford in the gloom of the San Francisco locker room if he had been missing with his fastball when he walked Terry. "Certainly I was," Sanford snapped. "Why do you think I walked him?"[10]

Dark headed to the mound to calm his pitcher and break up the tempo. He had already ordered right-hander Miller and left-hander O'Dell to warm up in the San Francisco bullpen. Pagan, Hiller and Davenport joined Haller in the conference on the mound as Dark spoke to Sanford. The Giants had a decision to make with Kubek coming up. How should they play the infield? Should they position Pagan and Hiller at double-play depth and concede a run on a ground ball? Should they bring the infield in to try and cut off the run at the plate, but risk a grounder finding a hole and delivering two runs, maybe setting up a big inning? Finally, the conference at the mound broke up.

"The infield is halfway except for Davenport at third," Kell told his radio listeners. "Jimmy is ready to make a play at the plate. Depends how hard it's hit."[11] At first base, Cepeda was playing on the edge of the grass and, like Davenport, was ready to come home on a sharply hit ball. Only Pagan and Hiller were playing back on the dirt part of the infield.

Inevitably, Dark would later be criticized in some quarters for playing his middle infielders back for the double play, a very easy second guess in hindsight. The crux of the criticism was summed up by prominent Chicago baseball writer Jerome Holtzman who believed Dark should have anticipated a low-scoring game in which no run could be conceded. "Dark's critics maintain that by keeping his infield back, it was a colossal blunder because he failed to adjust to the playing conditions," wrote Holtzman. "If the wind had suddenly come up, there may have been a greater excuse. But the wind had been strong even before the game started. The hitters had to adjust and, therefore, so did the managers. At any rate, Dark didn't adjust."[12]

Pagan later said he'd pretty much made up his mind what he would do if the ball were hit to him. It was too early in the game to throw to the plate, he decided. "If I forced Skowron," reasoned Pagan, "they still would have had the bases loaded and only one out."[13]

For his part, Dark was incredulous afterwards that the Giants would be second-guessed for not setting up their defense to cut off a run on a ground ball. He never considered it. "You don't play it that way in the fifth inning with Tony Kubek up," said Dark. "You just don't."[14] Reporters were left to wonder what Dark meant by "with Tony Kubek up." Was it a compliment or a knock on the Yankee shortstop?

Not so long ago, it looked like Kubek might be one of the heroes of a Yankee World Series. In 1957, he found himself a rookie in the starting lineup as the Yanks faced the Braves, then in their fifth season representing his hometown of Milwaukee. The night the team arrived in Milwaukee, Kubek invited some of his teammates to his parents' house for dinner.

"We rode around the neighborhood, which was a Polish ghetto," Kubek recalled in *Sixty-One: The Team, the Record, the Men*. "I mean very Polish, very Catholic, and a lot of bars. A corner wasn't a corner unless it had three taverns and a bunch of guys sitting there, sipping beer and shots and listening to ballgames on the radio."

Jose Pagan was the leading hitter (.368) among Giants regulars against the Yankees. Pagan told reporters he did not consider throwing home on Tony Kubek's double play grounder that produced the only run of the deciding seventh game (© 1962 S.F. Giants).

Tied at a game apiece, New York had crushed the Braves 12–3 in Game Three, with the 20-year-old Kubek homering twice and driving in four runs in front of family and friends. Seeing action in both left and center field as well as third base, Kubek was hitting .417 through three games. When the Yankees took a 5–4 lead in the tenth inning of Game Four, it appeared they would put a lock on the Series. But a two-run homer by Eddie Mathews in the bottom of the tenth evened the Series and the Braves went on to win in seven. Kubek's eight hits tied him for the most by a Yankee.

Casey Stengel took advantage of the youngster's versatility to make him into the second coming of Gil McDougald, a player who could fill any number of positions in the lineup. But Stengel was known as a tough critic with young players such as Kubek, Richardson, Boyer and others. "Casey was a good manager and he got a lot out of his players," said Richardson. "But he didn't have much patience, especially with young players. He also tended to be very sarcastic when you'd make a mistake."[15]

Wrote Kubek, "Ralph [Houk] came to the conclusion that pulling players out of games and zapping them in the press was not going to work with this team. The idea of being treated with respect and as a man appealed to the guys."[16]

Eventually the Yankees determined that Kubek's best position was shortstop and he became the starter at that position in 1960, developing into a consistent .270 hitter with occasional power and a remarkably low on-base percentage. In nine years in the majors, Kubek never drew more than a meager thirty-one walks in a season.

The Yankees missed him when he was called up by the Army to serve on a National Guard unit in the fall of 1961. When he was discharged the following August, the Yankees gradually improved. The team was definitely stronger with Kubek and Tresh in the lineup than with Tresh at shortstop and either Berra, Blanchard or Lopez in left field. His truncated year had statistically been Kubek's best. He batted .314 in forty-five games and his work with Richardson gave New York one of the best double play combinations in all of baseball. Against the Giants, Kubek had been one of the few Yankees having success at the plate.

With the bases loaded, Sanford's first two pitches to Kubek in the fifth inning were called balls by home plate umpire Stan Landes. The San Francisco right-hander had now missed with six straight pitches and Giant fans became increasingly agitated. Taking all the way, Kubek watched strike one, then swung at the next pitch. Trying to take it the other way, he bounced one right at Pagan on three hops. The shortstop never hesitated, flipping to Hiller to start a tailor-made double play.

Eleven. Game Seven: High Drama at Candlestick

Skowron crossed the plate to give the Yankees a 1–0 lead. With Boyer on third, Richardson could not pad the Yankee lead, popping out to Cepeda in foul territory.

In the sixth, Terry again survived a long at-bat by Davenport, who'd seen twelve pitches in his first trip to the plate. This time, Davenport fouled off three straight before pushing the count full at 3–2. It would be the only batter Terry went to a three-ball count on all afternoon. Finally, Davenport stroked a well-hit fly to left that Tresh gloved just in front of the warning track. When Pagan followed by fouling out to Boyer near third base, Terry had set down seventeen consecutive hitters. With two out, Sanford was the batter.

Later in the dressing room, Terry admitted to reporters that he'd had a fleeting thought about the perfect game thrown by Larsen, now watching in a Giants warm-up jacket in the San Francisco bullpen down the third base foul line. "I was aware I had a perfect game going," said Terry. "But I tried not to think too much about it. When I came out to pitch the sixth, I said to myself, 'Keep your mind on the game. The game's the thing.' I didn't want to get hit-conscious. When you get that way, you tend to become too careful and you wind up walking the hitter. I could hardly afford that with the barest of leads."[17]

His first pitch to Sanford erased any lingering hit-conscious thoughts. Sanford swung and lined a clean single to center to become the Giants' first baserunner. Terry briefly pounded his glove as the ball was relayed back to him. "Ellie signaled for a breaking pitch and I shook him off and threw a fastball," Terry remembered. "That was the only time I shook him off the whole ball game. Isn't that funny?"[18]

Pitching from the stretch for the first time all day, Terry watched Boyer make a nice play on a slow roller by Alou for the third out.

Sanford continued to gut it out on a day when he clearly did not have his best stuff. Whether it was the residual effects of a cold that had been bothering him or simply the sheer volume of a long season's work—this was his 42nd start and he was approaching 290 total innings—Sanford was going deep in the count more and more. In the sixth, he walked Mantle with one out, then promptly picked him off first base, adding yet another humbling episode to the Yankee star's miserable Series.

After the public address system played "The Sidewalks of New York" at the start of the seventh inning, Sanford went to a full count on Howard before fanning the New York catcher on a slow curve. Skowron then hit a deep fly ball that Mays lined up, only to yield to McCovey moving swiftly to his left. Boyer made good contact, driving one up the middle for his second single of the day, thereby improving his Candlestick Park batting average to .455 (5-for-11). That brought up Terry, and the knowledgeable San Francisco fans gave the rival pitcher a nice round of applause. Terry then belted a line single just out of Davenport's reach to put runners on first and second with Kubek due up.

The Giants had both Larsen and O'Dell throwing in the bullpen, but Dark stayed with Sanford and was again rewarded for his decision. As he had done in the fifth inning, Kubek hit the ball the opposite way, this time flying out to McCovey to end the inning.

With the realization that the Giants were down to their final nine outs of the season unless they could score a run, Hiller led off the bottom of the seventh trying to bunt for a base hit. Instead, he popped the ball in the air behind the mound where Terry snared it for the first out. That brought up Mays. He wasted no time, again going after Terry's first pitch, a breaking ball up in the zone, and rifled it deep into the left field corner. Tresh had been playing deep, and slightly shaded toward the line in left, even against a hitter like Mays who routinely hit to all fields. Sprinting full throttle, Tresh galloped nine full strides and caught the ball in his glove's webbing, the proverbial "ice cream cone catch." Tresh made the play about ten feet from the foul line, and his momentum carried him three or four steps into the wall.

"I was running so fast I grabbed it [the ball] with my right hand to hold it in the glove because I knew I was going to hit the wall real hard and I didn't want to drop it," Tresh later told reporters.[19] The rookie, who spent most of the year playing shortstop, had just made the defensive play of the entire World Series.

The value of Tresh's catch was underlined when McCovey belted a 1–1 slider over Mantle's head in deep left center field. Overrunning the ball when it hit the fence near the 410-foot mark, Mantle picked it up on the edge of the warning track and fired in to Kubek to hold McCovey to a very long triple. Had Mays reached base and McCovey hit the same shot, the game would have been tied. Writers would later speculate whether the ball would have been a home run with a less ferocious wind blowing in.

With two consecutive long shots off Terry, Houk summoned action in the New York bullpen. Bud Daley and Bill Stafford, still hobbling a bit on his injured left leg, both got loose in a hurry. The next batter was Cepeda. Giants fans had always relished seeing the Baby Bull hit in a clutch situation. In his last three seasons, he'd averaged 111 runs batted in per year. But in this World Series, except for one game, watching No. 30 advance to the plate had been an empty feeling for the Giants and their followers. Terry missed low on his first offering, then blazed three fastballs past Cepeda, who took an immense cut on the third one. The strikeout was only the second of the day for Terry, but by far his most important out to that point.

Eleven. Game Seven: High Drama at Candlestick

In the top of the eighth, Richardson hit a high hopper fielded by Pagan, but the throw pulled Cepeda off the bag and Richardson was safe on the error. Looking for an insurance run, Houk asked Tresh to bunt, but his attempt went foul. After Sanford went to 3–2 on him, Tresh smashed a hard shot that ricocheted off Pagan's glove into short left field for a base hit. Richardson had been running on the pitch but had to stop at second when the Giants quickly retrieved the loose ball.

Once again running the count full, Sanford served up a fastball that Mantle whacked on a line past Hiller at second. With a short lead off second base, Richardson hesitated, making sure Hiller didn't spear the liner. He was forced to stop at third and the Yankees again had the bases loaded with nobody out. The hitter would be Maris. Dark had seen enough of his struggling right-hander. He walked to the mound signaling with his left arm for O'Dell. Sanford slowly walked to the Giant dugout along the first base line as the fans gave No. 33 a standing ovation.

O'Dell had not pitched in seven days, a long gap of inactivity for any major league pitcher, let alone one conditioned to pitching every fourth day in rotation as O'Dell had been. He'd been roughed up by the Yanks in Game One, giving up nine hits and five runs in seven-and-one-third innings. But he'd been effective protecting the Giants' victory in the fourth game in New York. His return to the mound could not have come under more dire circumstances. Bases loaded, nobody out and New York's top home run hitter at the plate.

This time, the Giants played the infield in, not daring to concede any more runs. O'Dell blazed a fastball that jammed Maris, who hit a ground ball to second. Hiller gloved it as Mantle raced by him and smoothly fired home to Haller to get the force-out on Richardson. One out. Howard then hit a hot shot down third that Davenport fielded behind the bag. When he stepped on third and fired to first to complete the double play, New York's inning was over. O'Dell had escaped a terrific jam. The Giants still trailed by a run, but whatever momentum existed in the air now seemed to be on their side.

With Daley and Stafford still tossing lightly in the Yankee pen, Terry again made quick work of the Giants in the eighth, retiring Haller on a fly ball, Davenport on a foul pop behind third and pinch-hitter Bailey on a foul popup to Skowron. It was the fifth time Terry retired the Giants by throwing less than ten pitches in an inning. Houk and Sain had gotten their wish. Terry was pitching a masterful, efficient ballgame.

New York went quietly in the ninth against O'Dell. Before striking out to end the frame, Terry again received a generous round of applause from the crowd.

Trailing by a run in the bottom of the ninth, Dark needed somebody to hit for O'Dell. Giant pinch-hitters had done extremely well all season. Bailey, who'd already been used, batted .333 off the bench. Carl Boles hit .364 in his limited opportunities. But their best pinch-hitter, at .375, was the less-heralded member of the Alou brothers, Matty.

Like older brother Felipe and fellow teammate Juan Marichal, Mateo Rojas Alou displayed superior baseball skills growing up in the Dominican Republic. Signed by the Giants at eighteen, the younger Alou was not subject to the racial prejudices of the South as he began his minor league career, but he still faced similar issues when he was sent to Michigan City, Indiana. "The ballplayers always treated us good," Alou recalled. "The trouble we had was in the streets, the restaurants, the hotels, all those things. We used to cry, but we didn't fight."[20]

Unlike Felipe, Matty was slight of stature, standing five-foot-nine and weighing around 160 pounds. Despite his size, and reflective of the way baseball was played in the late '50s and early '60s, Alou still took an uppercut swing trying to hit the long ball. In his final minor league season at Triple-A Tacoma, Alou hit fourteen home runs while batting .306. Promoted to San Francisco in 1961, he batted .310 as a fourth outfielder. He again failed to break into the starting outfield in '62 on a team that featured Mays, McCovey, brother Felipe and Harvey Kuenn. But he was a smart ballplayer who could hit, steal a base and play the outfield. And he had a knack for getting on base.

Pinch-hitting for O'Dell, the left-handed Alou executed a perfect drag bunt, pulling the ball past Terry and leaving Richardson with no play as he fielded the ball on the infield grass. Giant fans roared in anticipation. The heart of the batting order was coming up. Alou's single put the tying run on base and left Dark signaling Matty's brother to move him over. On Terry's first pitch to him, Felipe bunted foul. On the next pitch, Alou swung and fouled one straight back. Playing well in on the grass at third expecting another bunt, Boyer could be seen bowing his head down as if thanking God for sparing him.[21] He retreated to his normal position on the dirt part of the infield for the 0–2 pitch and watched as Alou swung and missed for the first out.

"The book says you bunt at home to tie the score, but you don't bunt when you haven't got a guy up there to bunt. Felipe is a real bad bunter," Dark later stated to reporters,[22] providing another example of the kind of blunt public criticism that often nettled his players.

Hiller was next. Terry poured across strike one. On the next pitch, Hiller pushed a bunt down the third base line where Boyer was playing at normal depth. The ball slowly rolled up the basepath before sliding about a foot outside the foul line. Seeing Boyer back, Hiller had been trying for a base hit. Faced with an 0–2 count, he made Terry work hard, fouling off three consecutive pitches before taking ball one. On his seventh delivery to Hiller, Terry blew a fastball past him for strike three. Howard excitedly raised the ball up in his bare hand then trotted to the mound to have a word with his pitcher as Mays stepped in representing the last hope for the Giants.

With the crowd yelling "Go, go, go," Terry fell behind, 2–0, trying to bust Mays inside. Ahead in the count, Mays looked for something outside that he could handle and connected solidly, slashing a line drive toward the right field corner. As Maris raced for it, Matty Alou rounded second and sprinted toward third. Slowed by the wet condition of the outfield, the ball never reached the fence in the corner where it might have rattled around giving Alou the chance to score. Instead, Maris expertly fielded it, took a hop and skip to set his feet and fired a dart to Richardson who had gone out about thirty feet to take the relay. The throw was low, but Richardson scooped it with two hands, whirled and threw a one-hop relay that bounced high in front of Howard. The Yankee catcher gloved it over his head at the edge of the right-handed hitter's batter's box. Third base coach Whitey Lockman, watching the relay unfold, threw up his arms and stopped Alou at third base.

It is the question that still torments San Francisco Giants fans six decades later. Should Alou have tried to score? By virtually all contemporary accounts, he would have been a relatively easy out at the plate.

"Roger played the ball real good and Alou didn't have a chance," Houk would say later. "He was a dead duck if he tried to score."[23]

"He would have been out," Dark flatly stated.[24]

Writing about the play in his autobiography, Richardson observed that Maris cutting off the ball was a "great hustle play. I've always believed that Alou would have been out by about five feet, but the fact that my throw took such a high hop would have at least made a play at the plate more interesting."[25]

Lockman had to do some rapid calculations as Mays' hit bounced toward the right field corner. Would the wet grass affect the ball? *(Yes, preventing it from reaching the fence.)* What kind of arm did Maris have? *(One of the best in the majors.)* What kind of second baseman was Richardson taking the relay? *(Excellent, a five-time Gold Glove winner.)* Did the Giants have a good hitter on deck? *(Absolutely—Willie McCovey.)* Lockman told the writers he had a quick thought of sending Alou. "If he had bobbled the ball, even for a second, I would have sent Matty home," he said. "But Maris handled the ball cleanly."[26]

Even Alou agreed with the assessment, saying, "I think I would have been out."[27]

The supremely confident Mays expressed a somewhat different

view. "If it had been me, I would have tried to score," he later wrote. "Some people don't like to take chances, to be criticized for being thrown out in the last inning. It wouldn't have bothered me at all. I'm trying to score if I can, especially here, where we haven't been able to do anything all game against a tough pitcher."[28]

Howard, who would have been at the center of a play at the plate, had no doubt what would have happened. "I was hoping he'd come in," the Yankee catcher told reporters. "I wanted to get the game over with. I was actually disappointed when he didn't try to score. If he had, the game would have been over two minutes earlier."[29]

But it wasn't over. The potential winning runs were in scoring position for the Giants with two out. The sellout crowd was going wild. And Ralph Houk was walking slowly toward the mound to talk with his pitcher.

Twelve

Game Seven: The Aftermath

After considering his options—pitch to McCovey with first base open or walk him to face Cepeda with the bases loaded, Terry decided to go after McCovey. Years later, he recalled his thinking at the time. "I'd rather pitch to him in good spots. If I walk him intentionally, I'd be losing my advantage because I'd have to be much more careful pitching with the bases loaded. I kept thinking I could get McCovey out. I felt like I had a pretty good line on him. I hadn't faced Cepeda but this one game and I just felt like pitching to McCovey."[1]

When Terry ended the conference with Houk and Howard, Richardson heard a voice behind him calling, "Hey, Rich." Looking back, he saw second base umpire Al Barlick. "Can I have your cap for my little cousin?" asked Barlick. Momentarily stunned by the unusual request coming from an umpire at the most critical point in the game, Richardson was dumbfounded. "Sure," he finally told Barlick.[2]

Pitching from the set position Terry took something off his curveball, hoping to come inside and throw McCovey's timing off. "He swings and sends a long drive to right field!" yelled George Kell, his voice rising. "Maris is chasing it … it curves foul going in the seats!"[3] Kell told his radio listeners that the ball did not have the distance to be a home run, but of course any fair hit could deliver the two runs San Francisco needed to win the game.

On the mound, Terry tried to collect himself. "He hit it kind of on the end of his bat and Maris was moving over for the ball and, oh boy, this looked like the last out," Terry would recall. "Then all of a sudden that damn wind at Candlestick took the ball and lifted it foul all the way up over the bullpen."[4]

On the official World Series film, members of the Yankee bullpen rise up off their bench to watch the ball, one of them giving the outstretched arms "safe" signal that the ball was foul. Stafford and Daley were still warming up, but it was doubtful circumstances would necessitate Houk bringing in a reliever at this point. It was Terry's game to win or lose.

After the close call, Terry figured he'd be better off throwing to the right spot rather than worry about messing up McCovey's timing. He'd stick to the hard stuff. Seeing McCovey out in front on the long foul, Richardson took two steps to his left, deciding he'd play a little more in the hole between first and second. "One time in the Series, I'd fielded his ball so far toward first that I had to wait on the first baseman to get to the bag before I could make my throw," Richardson wrote. "So I moved a little bit into the hole between first and second expecting McCovey to pull the ball."[5]

As Terry looked to Howard for the sign and Richardson took his stance, another bizarre exchange between a Yankee infielder and an umpire took place. Skowron heard first base umpire Jim Honochick talking in his direction. Honochick was an American League umpire he knew pretty well. The chat provided a momentary break in the tension, but also proved a distraction. "While I was talking to him, Terry threw to McCovey," recalled Skowron. "If he had hit it to me, it would have taken my head off."[6]

Terry took his time between pitches to McCovey. He tried to concentrate only on where to put this next pitch, his 98th of the game. "I figured I'd better not give him another one [breaking ball]. So I gave him a fastball inside and it had my very best stuff on it. And he hit a bullet."[7]

"Everything is riding on every pitch here in the bottom of the ninth," said Kell. "Ralph Terry gets set. Here's the pitch to Willie. THERE'S A LINER STRAIGHT TO RICHARDSON! THE BALLGAME IS OVER AND THE WORLD SERIES IS OVER!"[8]

McCovey had uncoiled and scorched a line drive with topspin on it. Richardson, playing him perfectly, took a quick crossover step to his left and gloved the ball with two hands. The force of the liner caused Richardson to drop his hands almost all the way to the ground as his momentum carried him to his left. But the ball remained secure. The Yankees had won their 20th World Series, 1–0, behind Terry's four-hitter and a run driven in on a double play grounder.

Reacting with a combination of joy and sheer relief, Terry tossed his glove twenty-five feet in the air and threw his arms high over his head. Skowron, running in to offer congratulations, picked up the glove as Terry was engulfed by Howard, Kubek, Boyer and a bareheaded Richardson, who somehow remembered his agreement with Barlick and gave him his game-worn cap. As Terry was mobbed by the victorious Yankees, the group moved toward their locker room entrance in the right

Twelve. Game Seven: The Aftermath

field corner. Boyer and Stafford lifted Terry up on their shoulders and carried him down the right field line.

As he followed his teammates into their locker room with newsreel cameras filming, Richardson paused to open his glove slightly to reveal the ball still tucked neatly in the pocket. He hadn't even tried to take it out of the glove with his bare hand yet. He later gave it to Terry as a souvenir for a lifetime.[9]

The Yankees reacted with the enthusiasm expected of a team that had just won a championship. But their celebration seemed tempered by the pressurized game and the long, oft-delayed conclusion of a World Series that had stretched on for thirteen days and parts of three different weeks. And there could be no denying that many of the Yankees, so accustomed to such success, wound up right where they expected to be all along. The headline of the next day's *Santa Cruz Sentinel* read "Terry Thrilled but Title Is Old Hat for Yankees."

Ralph Terry is carried off the field by teammates after his four-hitter gave the Yankees a 1–0 victory in Game Seven at Candlestick Park. On Terry's right is third baseman Clete Boyer. The triumph earned New York its twentieth World Series championship (National Baseball Hall of Fame and Museum, Cooperstown, N.Y.).

Writing for the Associated Press, Jim Becker stated, "Even Roger Maris, the angry man of the team, smiled, although he was into the shower within thirty seconds after the team entered the dressing room."[10] Becker's report also said a half-hearted attempt by several Yankees to throw Houk into the showers in his uniform quickly failed. Instead, the manager pulled a tobacco chaw out of his cheek and unwrapped a long cigar. "Anybody got a match?" he said with a grin.

Terry told the massive circle of reporters and TV cameramen surrounding his locker that he couldn't help but think how much better this was than his last Game Seven appearance.

"I welcomed this because very rarely does a man get a second chance in life," he said. "I never thought I'd get the opportunity to live that Pittsburgh thing down. I thought I'd always just be the guy who fed that pitch to Maz. I made the pitch the way I wanted to on McCovey. I was very lucky."[11]

The man who caught it agreed. "It was a screamer," Richardson would write. "Willie smoked that ball. And I caught it. Over the past fifty years I have heard or read all kinds of adjectives for that catch—*miraculous, incredible, amazing, sensational, tremendous,* and on and on and on. I wish it had been that spectacular, but in all honesty, it wasn't. I simply took one step to my left, reached about shoulder high and snared the ball. McCovey had hit the ball so hard, that was *all* I could do. Even if I needed to step and leap, there would have been no time to do it."[12]

As the players celebrated in the clubhouse, Terry grabbed a glass, poured some champagne and sipped reflectively, banging his head softly against his locker as if to make sure he wasn't dreaming. "What an ending," he kept repeating. He elaborated what the victory meant to him personally. "I had to prove something to myself that nobody else could prove," he said. "I wanted to prove I was just as good a pitcher in October as I was from April to September."[13]

In Chelsea, Oklahoma, 70-year-old Rose Terry had watched her grandson on television. "I don't know anything about the game," she said, "but it seemed like it was awful close." The 1,500 citizens of Chelsea, where Ralph Terry played baseball in high school, burst into the streets shouting and cheering when the game was over.[14]

Terry was the recipient of another significant expression of congratulations. *Sport* magazine announced that he was the winner of a new Corvette, having been named the Most Valuable Player of the Series. A presentation was scheduled in two days at a luncheon in New York.[15] Terry chuckled and told the writers he guessed he would not be returning to his Oklahoma home to see his newborn son until after the luncheon.

Twelve. Game Seven: The Aftermath

The runner-up in the voting for the Corvette had been a major contributor to the championship. Tom Tresh batted a team-leading .321 and played a key role in winning both the pivotal fifth game (three-run homer in the eighth) and the deciding seventh game (backhand catch off Mays in the seventh). "He saved them a run, of course," said Dark referring to Tresh's defensive play, "but you don't know how it might have also influenced the outcome. I've never seen such an even pair of clubs in the World Series."[16]

In a grimly quiet San Francisco locker room, Mays wondered out loud how Tresh robbed him of extra bases. "That kid was way out of position for me," he said. "He was playing toward the foul line and Terry was pitching me outside all day. Any other player would have played more to center field."[17]

And, of course, McCovey was forced to answer multiple questions about making the final out in such an unfortunate manner. He'd hit the ball so hard that it was in Richardson's glove before he could take more than one or two strides out of the batter's box. A wire service photo the next day showed McCovey sitting at his locker in full uniform, still wearing his embroidered SF cap, eyes cast downward to the floor, chin resting on the palm of his big left hand.

"I hit that ball as hard as I could," McCovey would say. "I wasn't thinking about anything when I connected, but when you hit it good, you assume it's going to be a hit. I didn't even have time to get excited."[18] As if to further torment him, McCovey was asked if his triple over Mantle's head would have been a home run without the fierce wind blowing in from left field. Measuring his words carefully, McCovey wearily replied that he knew of no way to predict the effects of the Candlestick Park wind.[19]

Asked about the final out, Houk replied with his own version of "Stengelese." "He couldn't have hit it much better, but I don't care how hard they hit them if they hit them at somebody."[20] Dark simply said, "No one ever hit a ball harder than that one Stretch hit."[21]

Two months later at baseball's winter meetings in December, Dark ran into St. Louis Cardinal manager Johnny Keane and Hank Bauer, then a coach for the Baltimore Orioles. The conversation eventually turned to the seventh game. "I don't think I could have let that guy [Terry] pitch to McCovey," Keane told Dark. "Neither would I," agreed Bauer. Dark nodded and said, "I know I wouldn't have." Then all three smiled somewhat ruefully. Houk and Terry had gotten away with it.[22]

With reporters finishing up, both ballclubs showered praise on their opponents. "The Giants didn't do anything to disgrace themselves," said Houk. "They fought us right down to the last out of the seventh game."²³ Skowron, who'd just completed his seventh—and last—World Series as a Yankee, said, "I'll tell you, those Giants are the best bunch of guys I ever played against."²⁴

"We have nothing to be ashamed of," said Dark. "I have no regrets. You have to give them [the Yankees] credit. They played real good ball."²⁵

Two voices from deep within the Yankee dynasty were on hand to watch the drama unfold in the two hours and twenty-nine minutes it took to play the game. Joe DiMaggio stood in the midst of yet another Yankee championship celebration, a sight he was well familiar with. "This was the best-pitched World Series game I have ever seen," said the *Yankee Clipper*. "Both Terry and Sanford were terrific."²⁶

Pete Sheehy, the Yankees' equipment manager and clubhouse attendant since the days of Ruth and Gehrig, weighed in with a review of his own. "This was the greatest baseball game I've ever seen a Yankee team play," said the 52-year-old Sheehy, who began his duties in the Yankee clubhouse in 1925 and would continue until his death in 1985. "For dramatics and great performance when it meant the most, this was the best of them all."²⁷

A small number of Yankees—Richardson, Kubek, Blanchard and Bouton—had made air reservations to fly back to New York on their own late that afternoon. The group had to wait on Richardson's multiple interviews discussing the McCovey catch before they could leave. They had arranged a police escort to San Francisco International Airport, but got caught in late afternoon traffic, despite the police (one of whom was Frank Jordan, the future mayor) using sirens to clear their path.²⁸ Richardson recalled thinking, "Man, we've paid all this money for these special arrangements and we're going to miss our flight and not get home any earlier!" The group barely made their flight. After reuniting with his wife and children, Richardson drove overnight to the family's home in Sumter, South Carolina, arriving on Wednesday morning.²⁹

The remainder of the team personnel returned to the Town House for a victory dinner before roughly half of the traveling party would take a 10:00 p.m. charter flight to New York's Idlewild Airport (to be renamed JFK Airport one year later).³⁰ The airport was mostly deserted when the team entered baggage claim shortly after 6:00 a.m. Jim Coates, one of the first players to enter the terminal, tried for some levity, exclaiming, "What a mob! Get them off me! Get them off me!"³¹

An amusing side note attached to the final out is the identity of the person to whom umpire Barlick wanted to give Richardson's Yankee cap. In his autobiography, Richardson says Barlick was asking on behalf of his cousin. In Peter Golenbock's *Dynasty*, Barlick asks Richardson, "Can I have your cap if this guy makes an out? I have a little nephew who

Twelve. Game Seven: The Aftermath

would like to have it." And in Dom Forker's *Sweet Seasons*, Richardson is quoted as saying Barlick asked, "Hey Rich, after the game can I have your hat for my ten-year-old son?"

While research may not conclusively prove who wound up with the cap, it does indicate that Barlick, who was inducted into the Hall of Fame in 1989 after thirty-two years as a National League umpire, had two daughters and no sons.[32] Who knows if he actually had a "little nephew" or a memorabilia-loving cousin? It's unlikely such a request would be made today by an umpire, but if it was, social media no doubt would light up with memes and tweets expecting to see Richardson's cap wind up on eBay.

The most famous anecdotal footnote attached to the '62 Series came from the pen of cartoonist Charles M. Schulz, creator of the *Peanuts* comic strip. Schulz, expressing the sentiments of underdogs everywhere, drew America's most famous underdog—Charlie Brown—reflecting on what had occurred in the ninth inning of the seventh game. In a strip that ran on December 22, 1962, Charlie Brown and his pal, Linus, sit silently for three identical panels with their heads resting on their hands. In the fourth panel, Charlie Brown looks up to the sky and screams, "WHY COULDN'T McCOVEY HAVE HIT THE BALL JUST THREE FEET HIGHER?"[33]

As if that was not enough to express his frustration, some five weeks later the pair again sat silently for three panels before Charlie Brown rises up and yells, "OR WHY COULDN'T McCOVEY HAVE HIT THE BALL EVEN TWO FEET HIGHER?"[34]

If the Giants had won, the city of San Francisco would have been up for grabs. Plans had to be cancelled for a huge parade that would have taken place in the downtown business district. The Yankees' winning did not change any plans in New York. This was just one more championship, the twentieth in forty seasons, a neat and precise one-World Series-crown-every-other-year average since 1923. They had done what was expected of them, although in more dramatic fashion than predicted. But it was nothing to throw a parade over.

Less than one week later, Americans would find it hard to think about the Yankees, the Giants, the World Series or almost any other ordinary facet of life.

Thirteen

An Underrated Classic

While Billy Pierce was beating the Yankees in Game Six, President John F. Kennedy and his closest advisors were studying surveillance photos taken by a United States U-2 aircraft over the island of Cuba. The images clearly showed construction sites for medium and intermediate-range ballistic nuclear missiles.[1] The administration fully knew that the Soviet Union was working with the Castro regime in Cuba. It was the start of what came to be known as the Cuban Missile Crisis, and it remains the closest Americans have come to engaging in a catastrophic nuclear war.

Less than a week after the World Series ended, on the evening of October 22, President Kennedy addressed the nation from the Oval Office in what the Associated Press described as "a grim emergency nationwide radio/television address."[2] Kennedy spelled out the threat. "The 1930s taught us a clear lesson; aggressive conduct, if allowed to go unchecked, ultimately leads to war ... our objective, therefore, must be to prevent the use of these missiles against this or any other country."[3]

The president told the nation that a *quarantine* (rather than a *blockade*, which would suggest a state of war) had been established to prevent Soviet ships from reaching Cuba with materials for the missile sites. A reporter subsequently asked a Department of Defense spokesman, "Are you prepared to sink Soviet ships?" The spokesman immediately replied, "Yes."[4]

Two days later, Soviet leader Nikita Khrushchev labeled the quarantine "an act of aggression."[5] Some Soviet ships were turned away, others were stopped, searched and allowed to pass when no offensive weapons were found. United States armed forces were placed on DEFCON 2, essentially indicating that war was imminent. For the next week, Americans hung on word from the developments in Washington and Moscow and prayed for peace. Finally, Khrushchev agreed to dismantle the missile sites in Cuba if the United States would remove some of its Jupiter missiles from Turkey and agree not to attack Cuba.[6] The compromise was approved. The crisis had been averted.

The recent World Series was understandably not uppermost on people's minds as that tumultuous October concluded. But the question remains—why hasn't the 1962 Fall Classic received the kind of historical notoriety that other Series have received? When citing tense, competitive and memorable World Series, most observers tend to reel off a relative few. This list usually includes 1975 (Reds–Red Sox), 1986 (Mets–Red Sox), 2001 (Diamondbacks-Yankees) and 1967 (Cardinals–Red Sox). Going much deeper in history, there have been books written about 1912 (Red Sox–Giants), 1945 (Tigers-Cubs) and many of the Yankee-Dodger matchups of the '50s. But by comparison, there's been a paucity of analysis and review of the 1962 Series.

One factor, already noted, was the attention paid to truly significant non-sports happenings in the United States that certainly distracted casual sports fans. There was the bloodshed and rioting that surrounded the integration of the University of Mississippi by James Meredith. The successful six-orbit flight by NASA astronaut Wally Schirra and what it meant to America's race to outer space. And finally, and most assuredly, the Cuban Missile Crisis. But there were other factors within the games themselves that account for some of the luster of those seven contests between the Yankees and Giants being worn off by time.

There is little question that the weather postponements, especially the three consecutive rainouts in San Francisco, killed the Series' momentum and diminished the attention of the general public. The broadcast network, NBC, lost a pair of Saturday telecast windows due to the late start of the Series (caused by the NL playoff) and the second postponement in San Francisco. The third successive postponement also removed a valuable Sunday viewing date in an era when the World Series was strictly an afternoon affair. All four games played at Candlestick Park began at 12 noon Pacific time, 3:00 p.m. for the major markets in the East. The three contests at Yankee Stadium began at 1:00 p.m. locally, which meant a brunch-like 10:00 a.m. start for West Coast viewers. World Series games would not be switched to the more viewer-friendly prime time hours until the fourth game between the Orioles and Pirates in 1971 successfully experimented with an evening start.

Another contributing factor was the pitching-dominant nature of the games. Baseball fans generally prefer high-scoring games with lots of hits rather than watching a pitcher's duel. With proven home run hitters like Mays, Mantle, Maris, McCovey and Cepeda, there was a great expectation that lots of runs would be scored. Instead, the pitchers dominated and virtually all the above-mentioned stars failed miserably.

"The Series was a circus without a trapeze act, a martini without the gin, a cowboy movie without the high-noon showdown," wrote Sandy Grady in *Baseball Digest*. "I suspect the missing ingredient was a home run by either of baseball's archangels, Willie Mays and Mickey Mantle. The pressure and the careful pitching trussed up both the Gullivers."[7]

The Yankees established a record that has stood for sixty years by hitting .199 as a team. No other winning team has won a seven-game Series with such a poor overall batting average. In addition to hitting below the Mendoza Line, the Yanks hit only three home runs after banging out 199 during the season. New York finished with a weak .276 slugging percentage. The Bronx Bombers collected only ten extra base hits and averaged less than three runs per game.

The Giants hit only marginally better, batting .226 with five homers. They outscored the Yanks by a single run, twenty-one to twenty. They hit slightly better with runners in scoring position (.289 to New York's .222), resulting in the Yankees leaving more men on base. Remarkably,

Yankee pitching pretty much shut down the hard-hitting San Francisco trio of (left to right) Willie Mays, Felipe Alou and Willie McCovey. The three batted a combined .246 with one homer and only three runs driven in (© 1963 S.F. Giants).

New York stranded a total of eighteen baserunners in Games One and Seven and still managed to win both.

Individually, the big boppers on both clubs failed to ignite either offense. Mantle was utterly helpless against San Francisco pitching, hitting .120 and failing to drive in a single run. Howard hit .143, Richardson .148, and Maris .174. Said Casey Stengel afterwards, "Somebody in the Giant organization turned in a good book on those big guys."[8] The most productive Yankee hitters were Tresh (.321, four RBIs), Boyer (.318, four RBIs) and Kubek (.276).

"Gee, I wish I knew how to hit a home run in the World Series. Is it hard?" Mantle said sarcastically after watching the press engulf Tresh after the rookie's game-winning homer in the fifth game.[9] His team's victory would never totally extinguish Mantle's disgust for his own poor performance. "We took the Series, but no thanks to anything I did," he'd recall years later. "It was one of the worst World Series I ever had."[10]

The Giants received only one solid game out of Cepeda, who finished at .158 with two RBIs. McCovey hit .200 and drove in one run. Mays had a couple of moments, including his clutch double in the final inning, but his .250 effort with one run batted in was most definitely sub-par for him. At the bottom of the ledger stood Davenport (.136), Kuenn (.083) and Bailey (.071). The most reliable San Francisco hitters were Pagan (.368) and pitcher Sanford, who batted .429.

Who could have predicted that the leading hitters in the Series would include light-hitting infielders like Boyer, Kubek, Pagan and Hiller?

The winning pitcher in almost every game was a starter who shut down the opposition with apparent ease. In selecting each game's "Hero," *The Sporting News* named five starting pitchers in the seven games, with Hiller and Tresh being the only position players recognized.[11] Terry would later credit Yankee scout Mayo Smith (who managed Detroit to a World Series championship in 1968) with giving the New York pitchers a reliable scouting report on how to pitch to the Giants. "He gave me a little extra insight and that helped me a lot," said Terry.[12] But games dominated by pitchers seldom appealed to casual fans back then as they seldom do now. Low-scoring games made for a relatively bland, vanilla viewing experience.

One aspect of the Series that did not disappoint was the attendance. Giants fans filled Candlestick Park four times despite the rain interruptions. The three games in Yankee Stadium, perhaps fueled by so many loyal *New York Giant* fans, averaged 67,068. The total gate for the Series—376,864—ranked second at the time among the most attended World Series in history. Only the Dodgers and White Sox in 1959, taking advantage of three 90,000-plus crowds at the Los Angeles Coliseum, drew more spectators. A full winner's share for each Yankee came to $9,883 compared to the losing share of $7,291 earned by each of the Giants.[13]

What attention the '62 Series still receives all these years later is unquestionably helped by the decisive last play. According to a 2016 article by SABR researcher Wade Kapszukiewicz, Terry threw exactly one dozen *golden pitches* in the ninth inning.[14] A golden pitch is defined as one thrown in the seventh game on which either team could win the World Series, depending on the pitch's outcome. With one on and one out in the bottom of the ninth, Terry used seven pitches to strike out Hiller. He threw three to Mays, who doubled and kept the Giants alive. And he threw two to McCovey, the last finding its way into Richardson's glove. The research shows that this was the first occurrence of a golden pitch since Grover Alexander threw one in 1926 when the Cardinals beat the Yankees.[15]

Another possible reason for the '62 World Series being overlooked is this—the wrong teams were playing. It's entirely possible that "Yankee fatigue" kept some fans relatively uninterested and, combined with the issue of coast-to-coast travel, led print outlets to forsake staffing the games themselves instead of relying on wire service copy. With football becoming undeniably more popular, baseball seemed to be stuck in a rut. The last thing many fans wanted was another appearance by the Yankees.

It's also fair to speculate that more fans and media without a distinct rooting interest would have preferred to see the Yanks play their old Brooklyn rivals, the Dodgers. The teams had created quite a rivalry in the 1940s and '50s and many would have been eager to see another round of that battle unfold. As events turned out, that matchup would come twelve months later and result in an even less celebrated World Series, one resulting in a four-game sweep.

In a *San Bernardino Sun* piece titled "Baseball Fans May Be Cheated," columnist Bruce Brown expressed his opinion prior to the start of the Giants-Dodgers playoff. "What a shame it will be for the nation's baseball fans if the Dodgers do not win the playoff series with the Giants," wrote Brown. "We think the Dodgers will break out of their slump and win. But if they don't, the nation's vast armchair baseball audience will be the big losers."[16]

By any measure, the '62 Giants were most definitely an outstanding team, one that had proven its mettle. It had, arguably, the greatest current player in major league baseball playing center field. It had a lineup of big hitters and excellent starting pitching. But the Dodgers had always had a much larger national fan base stemming in large part to their signing of Jackie Robinson and their underdog "Dem Bums" persona in Brooklyn, especially when pitted against the lordly Yankees.

Brown went on to lament the possibility that fans would be robbed of seeing Wills, the new base-stealing champion, and Tommy Davis, the new NL batting champion, and fleet outfielder Willie Davis, not to mention stud pitchers like Drysdale and Koufax. While the column perhaps reflected a southern California perspective, it seems reasonable to assume that this viewpoint was shared by many other sports media.

Bill James, writing in his 1997 book *Guide to Baseball Managers*, elaborated on the media's tendency to elevate the 1962 Dodgers while not properly crediting the Giants.

> This [the Giants] is an amazing team. The fourth and fifth outfielders were Willie McCovey and Matty Alou. The fifth and sixth starting pitchers were Mike McCormick and Gaylord Perry. Between them they won 448 major league games and three Cy Young Awards. This team scored fifty more runs than the 1961 Yankees. They scored more runs than any other major league team between 1950 and 1982.
>
> The Dodgers got ahead, and then they lost. In the mind of the typical sportswriter, when you get ahead, you're supposed to win. This is particularly true if you represent a media center, New York or Los Angeles, because to a large segment of the media, the story of any season is either going to be the story of how the Dodgers won or the story of how the Dodgers lost.
>
> The story in 1962 was about how the Dodgers lost. The 1962 Dodgers were a great team, but the 1962 Dodgers didn't have five Hall of Famers [like San Francisco] ... nobody should have to apologize for finishing one game behind the 1962 Giants.

There's one other element that may have colored some thoughts on the Series participants. The Dodgers were playing in a beautiful, sparkling new stadium in sunny Los Angeles. Quite a contrast with the windy, barren experience of the unappealing concrete visage of Candlestick Park. Today's Giant fans may protest, but the likelihood is that the baseball world back then would have preferred a Los Angeles–New York Series just a little more. And maybe, just maybe, the coverage at the time stamped the 1962 World Series and relegated it to a rarely visited dustbin of baseball history.

There can be no denying the ultra-competitive nature of the seven games. Neither team won two games in a row, the first time that happened since Honus Wagner met Ty Cobb in 1909. The two teams wound up separated on the scoreboard by a total of one run. The triumphant Yankees held a lead after less than a quarter of the sixty-three total innings had been played. Almost 40 percent of the innings ended with the teams tied. Game Five was the only contest in which the team that scored first (San Francisco) did not win.

In three games, the teams were tied heading into the seventh inning. In another, they were tied going into the eighth. Two games saw a team nursing a one-run lead going into the seventh inning. Game Seven, of course, saw a one-run lead entering the ninth. Although Games One (New York, 6–2) and Four (San Francisco, 7–3) ended with wider victory margins, the biggest "blowout" would probably be Game Six, which ended as a 5–2 Giant victory in which the losing Yankees never sent the tying run to the plate after the fifth inning. And you'd be stretching the definition to call a 5–2 game a "blowout." Further, the Yankee win in Game Seven was the first 1–0 decision in a seventh game in Series history. That would not occur again until Jack Morris and the Minnesota Twins edged the Atlanta Braves in ten innings in 1991.

Regardless of the reasons, the 1962 World Series has never received the kind of attention it deserves. If it occurred today, one can only imagine the second-guessing that would blow up Twitter, Facebook, Instagram and other social media. Why didn't Houk pinch-hit for Ford in Game Four? Why did Dark leave Sanford in to pitch to Tresh in the eighth inning of Game Five? Should Pagan have come home on Kubek's grounder with the bases loaded in the fifth inning of the last game? Should the Giants have tried to score Alou on Mays' double in the ninth? And did Terry and the Yankees win despite making a crazy decision to pitch to McCovey instead of Cepeda in the ninth?

It is the kind of irresistible speculation that baseball fans love to indulge in, even six decades removed from the event. If it happened today, ESPN would quickly call the 1962 World Series an instant classic. Instead, it is practically just a footnote when reviewing the long Yankee dynasty.

A dynasty that was soon enough to come to a resounding end.

Fourteen

Today's Paid Attendance—413

In its April 1963 outlook on the pennant races, *Baseball Digest* picked the Yankees to repeat. "They fail to win the pennant only often enough," wrote Allen Lewis, "to keep the other American League teams from committing *hara-kiri*."[1] The magazine's prediction proved correct, but the '63 season was one filled with injuries for the defending champions and a harbinger of troubles to come.

As had been heavily rumored, the Yankees decided to cut ties with their dependable, but aging first baseman, in order to pave the way for a potential star. Moose Skowron was traded to the Dodgers in exchange for Stan Williams, the designated villain of the playoff loss to the Giants. Skowron accepted the trade with great reluctance. "All told, I played on five different teams," Skowron would recall many years later, "but I always felt like a Yankee and I think I always will."[2] Joe Pepitone would become the regular first baseman in the New York lineup. (At the conclusion of the 2001 season, the Yanks made very nearly the same type of move, allowing Tino Martinez to walk to sign a younger free agent named Jason Giambi.)

Most of the lineup otherwise remained the same. The Yanks expected a big season out of Tom Tresh, and he didn't disappoint, hitting twenty-five homers and compiling a solid .857 OPS mark (on-base plus slugging percentages). But this was a team with key players showing signs of wear and tear. Whitey Ford struggled with elbow pain in spring training and lost his first two starts. Tony Kubek suffered through a 1-for-35 slump and finished the year hitting an ordinary .257. Roger Maris was nagged by an assortment of leg injuries and played in only ninety games. Booed one evening at the Stadium when he failed to run hard on a ground ball—as permitted by Houk who wanted his bat in the lineup—Maris gave the home fans the finger, saying, "I'll only satisfy people when I get out of baseball. Everything will be all right with them when I'm gone."[3]

Maris' mood hadn't been helped when shortly after the prior

season ended, United Press International (UPI) announced that he had been voted the wire service's "Flop of the Year."[4] Observers could not recall ever seeing such a negative sanctioned poll. An advocate for the poll, Harold Kaese of the *Boston Globe*, provided his thoughts on the unusual award. "Surely it is not holding anyone up to ridicule to note that a number of players produced much less than what was expected. If my vote were taken, Roger Maris would undoubtedly be elected flop of the year.... Plenty of teams could use a player who hit 33 homers, had 100 RBIs and a .256 batting average. But Maris hit those 61 homers and batted in 142 runs a year ago, which makes him a bum now by comparison."[5]

The most serious injury to the Yankees occurred on June 5. While chasing a home run ball hit by Brooks Robinson of the Orioles, Mickey Mantle caught his left foot in the chain-link outfield fence in Baltimore, breaking a long bone in his foot that necessitated a cast from his knee to his toes. He missed almost two full months of play. When he finally returned on August 4, pinch-hitting in the locally televised second game of a doubleheader against the Orioles, he hit a line drive home run into the left field seats at Yankee Stadium. The crowd, which had given him a two-minute standing ovation when he emerged from the dugout, roared with appreciation. "It gave you chills standing over there at first base," said Baltimore first baseman Boog Powell. "Just being in the ballpark gave you chills."[6]

An MVP season from Elston Howard and strong pitching by Ford, Jim Bouton, Ralph Terry and newcomer Al Downing enabled the Yanks to win going away, ten games ahead of the White Sox. Just as many fans had hoped for the previous year, the Yankees met the Dodgers in the World Series. It was all Los Angeles, a four-game sweep, as the Dodger pitching staff completely stifled Yankee bats. The Bronx Bombers never led for a single moment and struck out thirty-seven times in the four games, including a then-record fifteen strikeouts in the opener facing Sandy Koufax. "I can see how he won twenty-five games," said Yogi Berra. "What I don't understand is how he lost five."[7]

The Yanks barely held on in '64, edging Chicago by one game in a pennant race that went down to the next-to-last day of the season. An older team still relying on power and defense, the Yankees took on the younger, speedier Cardinals in the World Series. When Ford came up lame after a poor start in the first game, Berra, now the manager after Houk assumed the general manager position, decided to use rookie Mel Stottlemyre on two days' rest in Game Seven against St. Louis ace Bob Gibson. The weary Gibson yielded a pair of solo home runs in the ninth before sealing a 7–5 victory. Within a few days, Berra was fired, and St. Louis manager Johnny Keane resigned to take the New York job.

The Yankees had become an old ballclub with a barren farm system living primarily on reputation. Tired of seeing the Yankees use their big bankroll to sign up the best young prospects, the major league club owners had instituted an amateur draft in 1965 to better distribute available high school and collegiate talent and give the lower echelon ballclubs a chance to sign players without breaking the bank. Arizona State outfielder Rick Monday became the first pick of the draft when he was selected by the Kansas City Athletics.[8]

The Yankees finished sixth in '65 before falling to dead last a year later, the franchise's first permanent home in the American League cellar since 1912. On September 22 that year, the Yanks hosted the White Sox in a makeup afternoon game. The stunningly small paid crowd that wandered in—413—was the lowest attendance figure in Yankee Stadium history.

The crowd was so sparse that relief pitcher Dooley Womack was able to carry on a conversation with third baseman Clete Boyer *from the right field bullpen.*[9] Recognizing the historical significance of such a small crowd in a majestic ballpark, Yankee announcer Red Barber asked his TV director to point the cameras over the vast stretches of empty seats. The director refused and after Barber repeated his request to the front office—and was again denied—management decided he was no longer welcome as a part of the organization and dismissed him after the season. "More dreadful public relations, which made the club look not only pathetic but paranoid," wrote author Philip Bashe.[10]

Terry, less than two years removed from shutting out the Giants in Game Seven at Candlestick, had been part of the last late-season Yankee trade that paid dividends. He and Bud Daley were dealt to Cleveland for reliever Pedro Ramos, whose work in September helped clinch the '64 pennant. Unhappy with the trade, Terry later expressed bitterness toward Houk and maintained that he was in over his head as the GM. "When the Yankees started to decline, the owners felt that Houk was the salvation," Terry stated. "They looked to him for leadership, and he didn't quite have it. They needed him where he belonged. As field manager."[11]

Houk would return to manage the Yankees when Keane was fired in 1966 and remained through 1973. He resigned at the conclusion of that season rather than put up with interference from new owner George Steinbrenner. Before leaving the dugout for good, Houk managed in Detroit and Boston. He never won another pennant.

Kubek retired after the '65 season, fearful that neck and back injuries could leave him paralyzed if he further aggravated them. His double-play partner, Bobby Richardson, was also ready to leave baseball at the same time. The Yankees asked if he would reconsider and stay through 1966. He agreed, but not without regrets. "Probably the most frustrating time I've ever experienced," said Richardson of the '66 season. "My thinking was, 'Why did you come back? You should have retired.'"[12] Richardson ultimately went on to coach college baseball at three different universities, run unsuccessfully for Congress at the urging of President Gerald Ford and become an active speaker advocating Christian values.

Bill Stafford's career was short-circuited following an arm injury suffered in frigid temperatures early in 1963.[13] Reserves Johnny Blanchard and Roland Sheldon were packaged in a trade with the Athletics that brought journeyman catcher Doc Edwards. After the disastrous last-place finish of '66, the team decided to make further changes. Mantle would be switched from the outfield to first base to preserve the strain on his legs. That moved an unhappy Pepitone to center field. And Boyer was traded to Atlanta for highly regarded prospect Bill Robinson, who never had much success in New York. "I had tried to put out and play for them all the time," Boyer would recall with considerable resentment. "Richardson and Kubek quit, and *Christ*, I was the best infielder they had. I was really the only one. And then they trade me. I didn't deserve to be traded."[14]

The Yankees also dealt Boyer's good friend Maris, who all but demanded a trade or he would quit playing baseball. Maris was dealt to the St. Louis Cardinals for Charlie Smith, an undistinguished third baseman who would replace Boyer. Maris spent two enjoyable seasons as a Cardinal, playing in two more World Series and winning a championship in 1967.

Always suspicious of how the fans might react to him, Maris avoided returning to Yankee Stadium until opening day of the 1978 season when he received a lengthy ovation while joining Mantle in raising the Yankees' 1977 championship banner. It was the team's first title since the victory over San Francisco fifteen years earlier. "I've never been in a situation where people cheered for me like that," Maris told reporters. "It was nice."[15]

Early in 1967, Ford experienced pain in his left elbow and decided it was time to quit. "I could have hung on through the year and tried to fool them, but what was the use?" Ford remembered. "I knew I couldn't pitch anymore. My elbow was burning. It was on fire when I was pitching."[16] He departed having won a franchise record 236 games. His lifetime winning percentage of .690 remains the best among all pitchers with a minimum of 200 victories.

By the time Ford left, Bouton was barely hanging on as a Yankee. "I always had a big, overhand motion and people said that it looked like on every pitch my arm was going to fall off with my cap," Bouton wrote in his landmark book *Ball Four*. "I used to laugh, because I didn't know what they meant. In 1965 I figured it out. It was my first sore arm. It was my only sore arm."[17]

An eighteen-game winner in 1964, Bouton won only nine games in his final four years in New York. Sent to the expansion Seattle Pilots for cash, he became a knuckleballer while keeping handwritten notes throughout the season that he weaved into *Ball Four*, considered one of the iconic works of sports literature. It memorably concludes with Bouton's observation that, "You spend a good piece of your life gripping a baseball and in the end it turns out that it was the other way around all the time."[18]

In 1967, Elston Howard ruined a no-hit bid by Boston left-hander Bill Rohr with two out in the ninth inning in Rohr's major league debut. Four months later, the veteran catcher would be a member of the Red Sox, having been obtained from the Yankees to steady a young ballclub through its first pennant race. The Sox won the American League pennant in a season dubbed *The Impossible Dream* and extended the Cardinals to seven hard-fought games before losing the World Series.

Howard came back for one final season before transitioning into a new career as a coach for the Yankees. He never achieved his ambition of managing in the major leagues. He was destined to become the first prominent player from the '62 Yankees to pass away when he died in December of 1980 at the age of fifty-one from heart failure caused by myocarditis.[19]

The Yankees' top hitter during the 1962 World Series, Tom Tresh never quite fulfilled the high expectations his rookie season placed upon him. He remained one of the American League's best left fielders through the dismal 1966 season. In the second exhibition game the following spring, Tresh tore cartilage in his right knee and was advised to continue playing rather than lose a season with surgery. "Supposedly your prime physical condition is between twenty-eight and thirty-two," Tresh recalled. "I was twenty-nine years old. I was ready to roll."[20]

The injury depleted his power and Tresh's offensive skills deteriorated precipitously. His batting averages in his final three years were .219, .195 and .211, and his home run total never exceeded fourteen. Prior to hurting his knee, he'd belted twenty-six and twenty-seven homers in back-to-back years. He called it quits after wrapping up the 1969 season with the Detroit Tigers.

Mickey Mantle's final years in New York were marked by the adulation of Yankee fans combined with the deterioration of his playing skills. Mantle still holds World Series career records for runs, home runs, total bases and runs batted in (National Baseball Hall of Fame and Museum, Cooperstown, N.Y.).

Nobody exemplified the sad decline of the Yankees in the mid- to late 1960s as much as the team's biggest name—Mickey Mantle.

"By 1967, Mantle was the only reason to go to the Stadium," wrote Jane Leavy. "The weight of the listing franchise rested uneasily on his fragile pins."[21] Mantle spent his final two seasons learning to play first base while still representing the best home run threat in a weak Yankee lineup. He hit his 500th career home run against ex–San Francisco reliever Stu Miller in May of '67. A year later, on Memorial Day, he enjoyed his last huge day at the plate, going 5-for-5 with a pair of home runs and five runs batted in against the Washington Senators. The Yankees hoped he'd sign on for one more year in 1969, but on March 1 he announced his retirement at a press conference. "I don't hit the ball when I need to," he admitted. "I can't score from second when I need to. I can't steal when I need to."[22]

To his everlasting regret, Mantle's final season left him with a sub-.300 career batting average. "The most disappointing thing ever," he would say. "I could hardly stand to think about it ... to think you're a .300 hitter and end up at .237 in your last season, then find yourself looking at a lifetime .298 average—it made me want to cry."[23]

In retirement, he became a beloved figure, a symbol for millions of older baseball fans who remembered another era when Mantle was the brightest star on the sport's most glamorous team. His public admission of a decades-long battle with alcoholism, combined with his near-deathbed advocacy for organ donations, brought him the admiration of a new generation. When he died from cancer in August of 1995, his Yankee teammate Richardson served as the minister of his funeral service. Sportscaster Bob Costas delivered the eulogy, saying "He was a fragile hero to whom we had an emotional attachment so strong and so lasting it defied logic."[24]

Watching Mantle and the Yankees methodically grind out victory in the 1962 World Series, who could have predicted that the franchise would not win another championship for fifteen years? As far-fetched as that might have seemed then, it may not have been as outlandish as if the following statement was made—that the San Francisco Giants would not win one until well into a new century.

Fifteen

Good, But Not Good Enough

The loss to New York had stung, but, to a man, the Giants thought they'd have multiple opportunities to avenge the disappointment and bring a championship to San Francisco. "The thrill team of '62 comes into the new season confident it will break the league's no-repeater jinx," wrote the *Chicago Tribune*'s Ed Prell in a 1963 season preview. "The Giants have every reason to feel that way because this is a team with good balance, more run-scoring potential, perhaps, than any of its rivals, and top pitching."[1]

The National League had not seen a team win consecutive pennants since the Milwaukee Braves in 1957 and '58. The Giants would not do so either. The 1963 season would be the first of eight straight without a title. Included was a mega-frustrating stretch of five consecutive second-place finishes. No other major league team had ever finished runner-up in the standings for so many straight years. (The Red Sox would finish second to the Yankees eight years in a row starting in 1998.)

Playing with virtually the same roster from a year earlier, the '63 Giants were in first place at the end of May before another June swoon (14–15) left them in third place behind Los Angeles and St. Louis. They never made up the ground and finished eleven games behind the world champion Dodgers.

Juan Marichal threw 321 innings and won twenty-five games. Willie Mays (38 HRs, 103 RBIs) and Willie McCovey (44 HRs, 102 RBIs) were outstanding. But 36-year-old Billy Pierce showed the wear and tear of sixteen big league seasons and more than 3,000 innings of work, finishing in the bullpen with a 3–11 record and an inflated 4.27 earned run average. Chuck Hiller (.223) and Jose Pagan (.234) had poor seasons at the plate and in the field. Only the ninth-place Colt 45s turned fewer double plays than the Giants.

A year later, Chub Feeney began inserting new talent into the roster. "[The Giants] still possess a fine bunch of old pros, basically the same group that captured the '62 championship," stated one 1964 preseason magazine. "Trouble is, they're getting older."[2]

Felipe Alou was the first key member of the '62 squad to go, traded to Milwaukee in December of '63 as part of a six-player deal. Alou helped lead the Braves to a National League West title in the first year of divisional play in 1969. After a distinguished career that included more than 2,000 hits, he became one of the game's most respected figures during a managerial career that saw him guide both the Montreal Expos and the Giants. His 1994 Expos had the best record in baseball before the MLB strike wiped out the last month of the season and the entire post-season. Alou's longevity and trail-blazing presence as one of baseball's first Latin stars has led to discussions of his worthiness to enter the Hall of Fame. "For nearly fifty years, the Dominican-born Alou has been involved in baseball as a player, coach and manager, forging a successful and exemplary career both on and off the field," stated one writer advocating for his Cooperstown consideration.[3]

In the foreword to Alou's autobiography, fellow Dominican Republic native Pedro Martinez wrote, "Felipe was the first. He paved the way. For those of us who followed him from our small island to the big leagues, Felipe was the light at the end of the tunnel."[4]

In September of '63, the Giants called up the youngest of the three Alou brothers, Jesus, an outfielder who would spend fifteen seasons in the majors as a lifetime .280 hitter. In the eighth inning of a game at the Polo Grounds on September 10, Alvin Dark sent up Jesus and Matty as pinch-hitters before Felipe batted in his leadoff slot in the order. Mets pitcher Carlton Willey retired all three Alous. Five days later, the three brothers played two innings together in the Giants' outfield. But the Alous never started together in the same game as is commonly thought.[5] Matty Alou completed a fifteen-year career as a .307 hitter for six different clubs.

The Giants made two key position changes to their infield in 1964, giving the bulk of playing time to hard-hitting third baseman Jim Ray Hart and smooth-fielding second baseman Hal Lanier. Jim Davenport stayed on for seven years as a valuable backup, collecting approximately 300 at-bats each year while being used at third, shortstop and second base, often as a late-inning replacement for the defense-challenged Hart. Like Alou, Davenport would have a spin as manager of the Giants, with far less success.

In August of '64, while embroiled in a heated pennant chase with three other ballclubs, Dark spoke to Jackie Robinson for a passage in Robinson's book *Baseball Has Done It*. His comments included the following:

The majority of the people in the South, especially the Christian people that I have associated with, have really and truly liked the colored people. As for socializing with them on different levels, there is a line drawn in the South, and I think it's going to be a number of years before this is corrected, or it may never be corrected.

There has never been any trouble between colored boys and other players on this club during my connection with it. Colored boys have never given me any trouble as manager. I wouldn't care if I had nine colored players on the field at one time as long as they can win.

San Francisco Chronicle columnist Charles McCabe, in an opinion piece on Dark's statements, wrote, "Had Mr. Dark's views been made public in New York when the Giants were living there, and had the press there reacted as they predictably would, Mr. Dark would now be seeking employment in a field outside baseball. This kind of chit-chat is garbage, and dangerous garbage, whether it comes from a politician or a baseball manager."[6]

Dark defended himself at an August press conference at Shea Stadium and claimed his comments were taken out of context. But Giants owner Horace Stoneham decided his manager could not continue and Dark was fired at the conclusion of a season which saw the fourth-place Giants finish three games behind pennant-winning St. Louis.

He was replaced by Giants coach Herman Franks, a former big-league catcher who would hold the job through 1968. "If I didn't think they could win it, I wouldn't have taken the job," announced Franks when asked about his team's chances.[7]

The futures of Hiller and Pagan in San Francisco were sealed by Franks' early-season assessment of their defensive play. "The '65 Giants were the best team I ever managed, except I didn't have a shortstop or second baseman," Franks once said, taking a shot at both Hiller and Pagan as well as their replacements, Lanier, Tito Fuentes and Dick Schofield. "We couldn't make a double play. If I had had that, I would have won the pennant all four years."[8]

Hiller was dealt to the Mets where his primary role was as a pinch-hitter. He was never a regular in the lineup again before retiring three years later. His former middle-infield partner Pagan was sent packing shortly after Hiller, joining the Pittsburgh Pirates where he would spend parts of eight seasons. In the 1971 World Series, Pagan doubled home the second run in the Pirates' 2–1 victory in the seventh and deciding game against the Orioles.

In Franks' first season at the helm, the Giants battled the Dodgers in a tense race that recalled the teams' epic battle three years earlier. On August 22, while batting against Sandy Koufax in a critical

Fifteen. Good, But Not Good Enough 163

meeting with the Dodgers at Candlestick Park, Marichal thought Los Angeles catcher John Roseboro had thrown a return toss to Koufax too close to Marichal's ear. Words were exchanged and within a few seconds Marichal began clubbing Roseboro over the head with his bat, drawing blood and precipitating a full-scale brawl between the two rivals. Roseboro required fourteen stitches to close the wound and Marichal was suspended for ten games and fined an unprecedented $1,750, a huge amount of money in 1965.[9] But the Dodgers had their revenge when Koufax beat the Braves on the next-to-last day of the season to clinch the pennant—the deciding run scoring on a bases loaded walk to Roseboro.

It was the same result a year later. Los Angeles won the NL pennant over the second-place Giants, this time by a game-and-a-half. The difference was the Dodgers' superior pitching (a staff ERA of 2.62) and defense. When the Dodgers finally fell from the top in 1967 and '68 following Koufax's retirement and the departure of Wills, it was the Cardinals who assumed the mantle of National League champions. The Giants finished a distant second in both years, giving manager Franks four consecutive second place finishes despite averaging 92 victories per season.

By 1969, Franks had been replaced by Clyde King, who guided the Giants to yet another second-place finish in the newly created West Division of the National League. The roster bore only a slight resemblance to the one that battled the Yankees seven years earlier. McCovey, Mays, and Davenport were still mainstays in the lineup, and Marichal, Gaylord Perry, Mike McCormick and Bobby Bolin were the heart of the pitching staff. But other key members of the '62 team were scattered around the majors or out of baseball entirely.

Pierce decided he'd had enough after a modestly successful '64 season that saw him finish 3–0 with four saves and a 2.20 ERA out of the bullpen. "I would like to have been a factor in the 1964 pennant race, but I didn't pitch much, not even fifty innings," said Pierce.[10]

His teammate Billy O'Dell followed Pierce into retirement within a few years. Like Pierce, O'Dell finished his career working out of the bullpen where he racked up fourteen wins and twenty-eight saves over a two-year span with the Braves and Pirates. He could proudly look back at a career that lasted thirteen years and saw him come within one assignment of receiving two hundred lifetime starts.

After letting them split the catching duties one more time in 1963, the Giants broke up the Ed Bailey–Tom Haller combination, putting Bailey in the Felipe Alou trade with the Braves. A year later, the Giants brought him back to be a pinch-hitter, but after he hit .107 in twenty-four games, they shipped him to the Cubs. He retired after a brief stint with the Angels in '65. Bailey eventually served a dozen years as a Republican city councilman in Knoxville, Tennessee. "When he occasionally got booed by the audience at council for taking an unpopular stand," former Knoxville mayor Victor Ashe recalled, "he simply said he'd been booed by far worst [sic] and louder by more people when he played baseball."[11]

Haller left the Giants in February of 1968 as part of the first trade between the Giants and Dodgers since the teams moved west.[12] He spent four seasons in L.A. before one in Detroit where he finally got the chance to play in a game umpired by older brother Bill. After retirement, he entered the insurance business before leaving to become a coach for the Giants. He steadily progressed up the ladder in the front office, eventually becoming vice-president of baseball operations. He later had an unsuccessful term as general manager of the Chicago White Sox. He died at 67 in 2004 after contracting the West Nile virus.[13]

A medical condition also prematurely claimed Haller's former teammate Harvey Kuenn. The Giants traded Kuenn to the Cubs during Herman Franks' first season as manager. After collecting 2,092 hits over fifteen seasons, Kuenn became the Milwaukee Brewers' hitting coach from 1971 through 1982. During this period, his health began to deteriorate as he dealt with circulation problems that led to open-heart surgery and a quadruple bypass.[14] The poor circulation caused him constant foot problems. When subsequent operations failed to cure the issue, doctors were forced to amputate Kuenn's right leg below the knee in February of 1980.[15]

Fitted with a prosthesis, Kuenn soon resumed his coaching duties. In June of '82, he was named manager of the Brewers, replacing ex-Angel catcher Bob Rodgers. Kuenn led the free-swinging, powerful Brewers—dubbed "Harvey's Wallbangers"—to the American League pennant and a seven-game World Series loss to the Cardinals. He was let go at the conclusion of the following season when the Brewers finished fifth in the American League East. He remained with the organization as a scout. In February of 1988, while preparing to play a round of golf with his wife in Arizona, Kuenn suffered a fatal heart attack.[16] He was 57 years old.

The biggest name exiled by the Giants had been Orlando Cepeda, traded to the Cardinals in May of 1966 for lefthander Ray Sadecki. Looking back almost fifty years later, SABR contributor Bill Ryczek wrote: "The trade ... is generally ranked with that of Lou Brock for Ernie Broglio, Frank Robinson for Milt Pappas, and Babe Ruth for *No, No, Nanette* as one of the most lopsided deals in baseball history."[17]

Even though Dark and his philosophies on race and team unity were gone, Cepeda had never become comfortable in the Giant clubhouse. Discussing Dark decades later, Cepeda said, "I think he was a vicious man. I hurt my knee in 1962 and played two years in terrible pain

Fifteen. Good, But Not Good Enough

just to prove that a Latin could play hurt. I never said a word about being injured and that was a mistake."[18]

Cepeda's injury-shortened '65 season, combined with the Giants' desire to make McCovey the full-time first baseman, led Chub Feeney to pull the trigger on the deal. Sadecki had an overall losing record in four years with the Giants. Cepeda earned Most Valuable Player honors in leading the Cardinals to the 1967 world championship. He later was a productive offensive performer for the Braves and Red Sox.

In 1975, Cepeda was arrested at the San Juan airport after Federal authorities discovered 160 pounds of marijuana in his car trunk. He was sentenced to five years in prison. His reputation in his native Puerto Rico was in tatters.

"The isolation, the disgrace, the feelings of numbness, they were horrible," Cepeda would say. "I knew I had done something wrong, that I had to pay for my stupidity." He attempted to rebuild his life by opening a baseball school for children in San Juan.[19] After years of being haunted by thoughts that his crime would keep him out of Cooperstown, Cepeda was elected to the Hall of Fame in 1999. "The biggest victories come over yourself, when you control your mind and your destiny," Cepeda reflected upon the good news. "My life has been a drama of inner change."[20]

Cepeda became the eighth player from the 1962 World Series teams to be elected to the Hall, joining Berra, Ford and Mantle from the Yankees and Marichal, McCovey, Mays, and Perry from the Giants.

With the 3-M trio of Mays, McCovey and Marichal being the last real links to 1962, San Francisco won the West Division title in 1971 under manager Charlie Fox, long a member of the Giants' organization. After winning the first game of the championship series with Pittsburgh, the Giants lost the next three. It was the last hurrah for Mays, McCovey and Marichal in San Francisco. The team would not return to postseason play for sixteen years.

In deference to their onetime superstar, the Giants traded Mays to the New York Mets in May of 1972 to allow him to finish his fabulous career in the city where it began. After an initial flurry of excitement—facing his old team, Mays homered to drive in the winning run in his first game as a Met—it became painfully obvious that he was just hanging on. Mays realized this more than anyone.

The following year, on September 25 with the Mets in a tight race for the divisional title, he spoke to a huge crowd at Shea Stadium, saying, "Just to hear you cheer like this for me and not be able to do anything about it makes me a sad man. This is my farewell. You don't know what's going on inside of me tonight.... Willie, say goodbye to America."[21]

Willie Mays taking a big swing during his prime in San Francisco. Note the cap tucked into the back pocket, a common practice for hitters in the '60s who often discarded the batting helmet when they became baserunners. Mays finished his career with 3,283 hits in 2,992 games (© 1962 S.F. Giants).

Playing in the World Series vs. Oakland, Mays lost a ball in the sun and scrambled to reach balls that he'd previously been able to put away with his trademark "breadbasket" catch. He retired having hit 660 home runs, driven in 1,903 runs and scored 2,062. Eighty-nine years old as 2021 dawned, he was generally regarded as the greatest living ballplayer. It is fair to say that in an age when Mariano Rivera became the first unanimous Hall of Fame selection, Mays would have received the same honor were he to have concluded his career in 2015 instead of 1973.

Juan Marichal struggled through two more years as a Giant with a combined record of 17–31. At 36, but still hoping to pitch, he convinced the Giants to trade him in a cash deal with Boston. He went 5–1 for the Red Sox before concluding his career in the uniform of the Giants' arch-rivals—the Dodgers—in 1975. He finished with 243 wins, a 2.89 ERA and a lifetime winning percentage of .631. Yet in an era dominated by Koufax, Bob Gibson and Tom Seaver, Marichal was never acclaimed the finest pitcher in the National League. "Marichal was great," observed Bill James, "but he was just in the wrong place to be winning any Cy Young Awards."[22]

Fifteen. Good, But Not Good Enough

In the twilight of his playing career, Willie McCovey became adored by Giant fans and was recognized as having been one of baseball's legendary players. When injuries limited him to only eighty-one games in 1972, the Giants began preparing for life without "Stretch." He was traded to the Padres a year later and spent two-and-a-half seasons in San Diego before being dealt to Oakland. In 1977, the first year of major league free agency, McCovey had no offers. Instead, he signed as a non-roster player with the Giants, fully understanding there was no guarantee of a spot on the roster if he didn't produce. He responded by being named the NL's Comeback Player of the Year, hitting twenty-eight home runs to go with eighty-six RBIs and an OPS figure of .869. He retired in 1980 after twenty-two seasons in the majors.

The Giants would play in the postseason in six different years between 1987 and 2003, twice losing in the World Series. Their fans would have to wait until 2010 to enjoy the team's first world championship on the West Coast. Managed by Bruce Bochy, and featuring stars such as Buster Posey, Madison Bumgarner and Pablo Sandoval, the Giants became a mini-dynasty, winning the World Series again in 2012 and 2014, making three championships in five years.

In June of 2007, the Yankees traveled to the West Coast to play the Giants as part of major league baseball's inter-league schedule. It was the first time the two teams met in San Francisco in a meaningful contest since October 16, 1962. The Giants' management arranged a special 45th anniversary reunion of players from both teams. A ceremony was held prior to the Sunday finale of the Yankees-Giants series, featuring video clips from the '62 World Series, gifts for the attendees and a moment of silence for those players who had passed away.[23]

The Giants were well represented by more than half of the '62 roster, including Mays, McCovey, Marichal, the Alou brothers, Davenport, Pierce and manager Dark. Only a half dozen Yankees could attend—Ralph Terry, Jim Coates, Hector Lopez, Tex Clevenger, Jack Reed and Bobby Richardson, who initially had some Maris-like trepidation about attending and being booed.[24] When his name was announced, there were some scattered boos, but seemingly in a good-natured way from the sellout crowd. The Giants now played their games at AT&T Park, their sleek, fan-friendly home since 2000, located hard by the industrial waterfront area known as the China Basin.

The players enjoyed telling stories and reminiscing. Terry again explained why he chose to pitch to McCovey rather than Cepeda. Matty Alou repeated his opinion that he would have been out trying to score in the ninth inning of Game Seven. Marichal mentioned the helicopters that hovered low over the field to dry out the outfield grass. "I tell that story to a lot of people and they don't believe it," said the Dominican Dandy.[25]

McCovey and Richardson greeted each other for the first time in more than twenty years. Richardson had previously conducted a prayer service in connection with McCovey's induction into the Hall of Fame. Seeing Richardson, McCovey smiled and said, "I bet your hand's still hurting." Richardson nodded and replied, "You did hit it hard."[26]

The Giants honored McCovey at their new ballpark in several ways. An inlet of San Francisco Bay past the right field stands was dubbed "McCovey Cove." Souvenir hunters would bring kayaks to sit in the water and fish out home run balls. The Giants kept count of these "splash hits" on a tally board inside the park. In 2003, the team dedicated a statue of McCovey, in the follow-through of his swing, to be displayed outside the ballpark. In the summer of 2020, the statue was placed in storage to protect it from a massive environmental construction project designed to improve the area near McCovey Cove.

He remained a revered modern-day San Francisco icon until his death in late October of 2018. Injuries and medical procedures from his playing days left him generally confined to a wheelchair in his later years,[27] but he still reveled in the success of his old team as the Giants captured those three championships. Still, he couldn't help but think back to his own time on the big stage all those years ago. "There isn't a day that goes by that someone doesn't mention the World Series ball I hit to Richardson," he told one writer.[28] "I was sitting in front of my locker wondering what happened. I was feeling sad, but at the same time I really thought I was going to be able to redeem myself. Everyone on the team thought we'd dominate the league for ten years. I never thought we'd never get back [to the Series]. I guess I would have felt sadder if I knew that was it."[29]

At his 1986 Hall of Fame induction at Cooperstown, McCovey was asked how he'd like to be remembered, a logical question for one of the game's most feared sluggers, a big man with a gentle personality who made friends easily and was regarded as a wonderful teammate.

His answer was immediate. Said McCovey, "I'd like to be remembered as the guy who hit a line drive over Bobby Richardson's head."[30]

Sixteen

A Yankees and Giants Who's Who

New York Yankees

Manager and Coaches

No. 35 Ralph Houk—Managed Yankees, Tigers and Red Sox for twenty years, winning 3,156 games. His three first-place finishes came in his first three seasons. Had pinch-hit single as a rookie in Game Six of 1947 World Series against Brooklyn.

No. 2 Frank Crosetti—Parlayed seventeen years playing for the Yankees into a 23-year coaching career with Yankees, Seattle Pilots and Minnesota Twins. A .245 hitter, but a superior defensive shortstop over more than 1,600 games. A member of 23 World Series teams.

No. 44 Jim Hegan—Earned reputation among finest defensive catchers in baseball with Cleveland in late 1940s and 1950s. Light hitter with occasional home run power. His son, Mike, also played in the majors and was the last batter in Yankee Stadium before ballpark's 1974–75 renovations.

No. 36 Wally Moses—Solid line drive hitter through seventeen years, finished with 2,138 hits and .291 average, leading to second career as a batting instructor. Had two different stints coaching under Ralph Houk in New York. Batted .417 in 1946 Series for Red Sox.

No. 31 Johnny Sain—Four-time 20-game winner for Boston Braves. Forged successful career as pitching coach for seven different clubs. Was the first MLB pitcher to face Jackie Robinson in 1947. Above-average hitter for a pitcher, he twice recorded batting averages over .300.

Pitchers

No. 47 Luis Arroyo—League's top reliever in 1961, but strained elbow and loose bone chips suffered in early-season cold weather appearance led to limited role a year later and retirement in '63. Saved thirteen of Whitey Ford's twenty-five victories in 1961.

No. 56 Jim Bouton—After success of his trailblazing book, *Ball Four*, made comeback eight years later at the age of 39 with Braves. Lost three of four decisions, leaving his lifetime record below .500 (62–63). Later worked as a sports reporter for multiple New York City television outlets.

No. 30 Marshall Bridges—Left-hander spent seven seasons in the majors but, oddly, was never featured on a Topps baseball card. Career was imperiled after he was shot in a Ft. Lauderdale bar by a female patron during spring training in 1963.[1]

No. 21 Tex Clevenger—Born in California as Truman Eugene Clevenger, but nicknamed "Tex" despite never playing for a team in Texas. Led AL in games pitched in 1958. Game Seven of the 1962 Series was his last afternoon in a major league uniform.

No. 39 Jim Coates—Had excellent .712 winning percentage as a Yankee (37–15) as both starter and reliever. Traded to Washington in early 1963 in deal that brought lefty Steve Hamilton to New York. Finished career pitching for the California Angels in 1967.

No. 28 Bud Daley—Had successful professional career despite a deformed right arm caused by a doctor's mishap during Daley's birth.[2] Won sixteen games in consecutive seasons for lowly Kansas City before trade to New York. Real first name was "Leavitt."

No. 16 Whitey Ford—Inducted into Hall of Fame in 1974, same year as teammate Mickey Mantle. Twice led the American League in lowest earned run average. Threw more innings in World Series competition (146) than any other pitcher.

No. 45 Roland Sheldon—Yanks thought he was 20 when he signed, but he was actually 23 years old. His 1961 rookie season (11–5, 3.60) was his finest in a brief five-year career. Played baseball and basketball at the University of Connecticut.[3]

No. 22 Bill Stafford—Born in Athens, New York, small town on banks of Hudson River south of Albany. Held opponents to .233 batting average in winning fourteen games in 1962. In 21 innings of work in four World Series, pitched to a 2.06 ERA.

No. 23 Ralph Terry—Fanned last hitter he ever faced, Dick Allen, to finish career with exactly 1,000 strikeouts. Played professional golf after baseball career, posting sixteen Top 25 finishes on the Champions Tour in late 1980s and early 1990s.[4]

No. 19 Bob Turley—One of Yankees' heroes in 1958 championship season. Picked up two wins and a save as Yanks overcame 3-to-1 deficit to defeat Milwaukee. Won Cy Young Award that season. Became wealthy in his post-baseball career as recruiter for insurance sales.[5]

Catchers

No. 8 Yogi Berra—Inducted into Hall of Fame in 1972. Three-time MVP, fifteen-time All-Star and played in record fourteen World Series. Managed both New York teams to pennants. Saw service with American naval forces during D-Day invasion.[6]

No. 38 Johnny Blanchard—Hit .300 as a pinch-hitter in World Series play, including game-tying homer in eighth inning of third game vs. Reds in 1961. Batted .305 that season but never came within fifty points of that mark again. Spent eight years in majors.

No. 32 Elston Howard—Lifetime .274 hitter. Was a business partner in the manufacture of—and first player to use—the weighted donut employed by hitters to loosen up in the on-deck circle.[7] Committed two errors while catching 146 games in 1964, compiling a .998 fielding percentage.

Infielders

No. 6 Clete Boyer—One of three brothers (with Ken and Cloyd) to play major league baseball. Both Ken and Clete hit homers during '64 World Series. Most productive offensive season was his first in Atlanta, when he hit 26 home runs and drove in 96 for Braves.

No. 10 Tony Kubek—Played every position in the field except pitcher and catcher. Had four seasons ranked in the top four among American League shortstops in fielding percentage. Like Ted Williams, homered at Fenway Park in his final at-bat in the majors.

No. 34 Phil Linz—Replaced injured Tony Kubek as starting shortstop in 1964 World Series, hitting .226 with two homers. Earned an endorsement contract from the Hohner musical instrument company after infamous '64 harmonica-playing episode on team bus.[8]

No. 26 Dale Long—Became first major leaguer to homer in eight consecutive games while with Pirates in 1956, a feat later matched by Don Mattingly and Ken Griffey, Jr. Hit 17 homers as the regular first baseman for the expansion Washington Senators in 1961.

No. 1 Bobby Richardson—Tied record for most hits by a player in both a five-game and seven-game World Series. Had thirteen hits vs. Cardinals in '64 Series and batted .406. Coached college baseball at three institutions—South Carolina, Coastal Carolina and Liberty.

No. 14 Bill Skowron—Clutch performer in eight Series, hit eight homers and batted .293. Belted grand slam in Game Seven victory over Brooklyn in 1956. Famous "Moose" nickname was derivative of family member claiming poor haircut made him resemble Italian dictator Benito Mussolini.[9]

Outfielders

No. 11 Hector Lopez—Native of Panama, broke into majors primarily as an infielder with Kansas City, converted to outfield by Yankees. Forced into service by Mantle injury in '61 World Series, he led New Yorkers with seven runs batted in, including five in Series-clinching win.

No. 7 Mickey Mantle—Finished with 536 career home runs. Only Derek Jeter played in more games as a New York Yankee. Tied with Babe Ruth for most lifetime home runs hit by an opponent at Fenway Park (38). Seldom tried to steal a base but was successful on 80 percent of his career attempts.

No. 9 Roger Maris—Concluded career playing with two straight pennant winners with St. Louis Cardinals. Hit 275 homers in twelve seasons. Earned back-to-back MVP awards in 1960 and '61. Averaged a home run every 9.7 at-bats in record-breaking 1961 season.

No. 27 Jack Reed—Was starting safety for Ole Miss football team in 1951 and '52, playing in 1953 Sugar Bowl against No. 2–ranked Georgia Tech.[10] Game-winning homer in 22-inning game at Detroit in June of 1962 was the only one of his career.

No. 15 Tom Tresh—Averaged 23 homers and 76 RBIs during first five years, but exhibition game injury in '67 resulted in cartilage damage to right knee and ultimately led to early retirement at age 32. Hit three home runs on June 6, 1965, vs. White Sox.

San Francisco Giants

Manager and Coaches

No. 1 Alvin Dark—Selected in third round of 1945 NFL draft by Philadelphia Eagles as a halfback out of LSU. After termination from Giants in '64, managed Kansas City, Cleveland, Oakland and San Diego. Guided A's to World Series championship in 1974.

No. 46 Larry Jansen—Winning pitcher in relief during Giants' 1951 Game Three NL playoff win on Bobby Thomson home run. Lost both starts vs. Yankees in that year's World Series. Native of Verboort, Oregon, community noted for annual "Sausage and Sauerkraut Festival."[11]

No. 3 Whitey Lockman—Like manager and rest of Giants' 1962 coaching staff, played on famed '51 "Miracle at Coogan's Bluff" team. Solid first baseman/outfielder for fifteen big league seasons. Real first name was Carroll. Managed the Cubs for three seasons (1972–74).

No. 9 Wes Westrum—Primarily a backup catcher, hit 23 home runs as a regular in 1950 for Giants. Notable as the manager who succeeded Casey Stengel and preceded Gil Hodges with New York Mets. Later managed the Giants for two seasons.

Pitchers

No. 42 Bob Bolin—Versatile starter/reliever pitched for thirteen seasons recording 88 wins and 50 saves. Was the winning pitcher in Milwaukee Brewers' first-ever victory in 1970. Had lifetime average of 6.7 strikeouts per nine innings.

No. 45 Jim Duffalo—Retired Roberto Clemente with two on and two out in the ninth inning of a 2–1 game to earn a save in major league debut. Spent parts of five years with Giants before finishing career with Cincinnati in '65.

No. 28 Bob Garibaldi—Signed with Giants for $150,000 bonus after being named the Most Outstanding Player of the 1962 College World Series for Santa Clara University. Later became a college basketball official in the Western Athletic Conference (WAC).[12]

No. 18 Don Larsen—Two years before his perfect game was 3–21 in the Orioles' first season in Baltimore. Finished with a 4–2 mark in five World Series for Yankees and Giants. Nicknamed "Gooneybird" by Yankee teammates.[13]

No. 27 Juan Marichal—Named to Hall of Fame in 1983 as first inductee from the Dominican Republic. Led all pitchers with 191 victories during the decade of the 1960s, twenty-seven more than runner-up Bob Gibson. Threw fifty-two career shutouts.

No. 40 Mike McCormick—Won Cy Young Award in 1967 with 22–10, 2.85 ERA season for San Francisco. Added NL "Comeback Player of the Year" award as well. Won 134 games in sixteen years and smacked seven home runs as a hitter.

No. 37 Stu Miller—Enjoyed greatest success in mid–'60s with Baltimore, racking up 35 victories and 92 saves over four-year span. Yielded Mickey Mantle's 500th homer, May 14, 1967, at Yankee Stadium.

No. 31 Billy O'Dell—Won 105 games and saved 48 others over 479 major league appearances. Nicknamed "Digger" after popular character from radio/TV sitcom *The Life of Riley*.[14] Had career-low 2.18 ERA out of Milwaukee Braves bullpen in 1965.

No. 19 Billy Pierce—Signed with hometown Detroit Tigers as 18-year-old schoolboy in 1945 and was on Tigers World Series roster that Fall. Ranks fourth among pitchers with most victories in the decade of the 1950s. Finished with career record of 211–169.

No. 33 Jack Sanford—Won 137 games for four major league teams.

Led NL with 42 starts in 1963, but a shoulder injury the following year resulted in his becoming primarily a relief pitcher during his final three seasons.

Catchers

No. 6 Ed Bailey—Lifetime .256 hitter with 155 home runs over fourteen seasons. Selected to five National League All-Star teams. Hit three homers in one game as a member of the Reds in 1956. Born in Strawberry Plains, Tennessee.

No. 5 Tom Haller—Belted a career-high 27 homers in 1966. Traded by Giants to Dodgers two years later. Set a National League record for catchers in '68 by participating in 23 double plays. Also led NL in runners caught stealing that season. Selected to three All-Star teams.

No. 34 John Orsino—Left Giants in 1963 and became a platoon catcher for the Orioles, hitting 19 home runs in his first season in Baltimore. Native of Teaneck, New Jersey, was nicknamed "Horse." Coached men's golf program at Florida Atlantic University.

Infielders

No. 21 Ernie Bowman—Attended college in the city of his birth (East Tennessee State in Johnson City, Tennessee). Spent three seasons in San Francisco, filling in at shortstop, second and third base. Hit lone career home run off Al Jackson of the Mets in 1962.

No. 30 Orlando Cepeda—Inducted into Hall of Fame in 1999. First designated hitter in Boston Red Sox history in 1973. Had nine seasons of 90 or more RBIs. Finished with 379 home runs. One of five '62 Giants with number retired by ballclub (Cepeda, Marichal, Mays, McCovey, Perry).

No. 12 Jim Davenport—One of four players in '62 Series who became a major league manager (joining Harvey Kuenn, Felipe Alou and Yogi Berra). Guided Giants through 144 games in 1985 before resigning with club in last place. Lifetime .258 hitter.

No. 26 Chuck Hiller—No longer a starter late in his career, he became a quality pinch-hitter, coming off the bench to hit .283 over his last three seasons. Batted .280 in only full season with the Mets. "Iron Hands" nickname was solidified by his 29 errors at second base in '62.

No. 15 Jose Pagan—Played until he was 38 years of age, hitting exactly .250 over fifteen years with the Giants, Pirates and Phillies. Hit .324 in his two World Series. Led National League with 19 pinch hits in 1969.

Outfielders

No. 23 Felipe Alou—Batted .300 or better three times, including .327 with 31 homers and league-leading 218 hits in 1966 for Atlanta. The eldest of the Alou brothers, Felipe was the only one with real power, hitting 206 career homers compared to Jesus (32) and Matty (31).

No. 41 Matty Alou—Traded from Giants to Pirates, hit .342, .338, .332 and .331 in first four years in Pittsburgh, winning batting title in 1966. Contact hitter who rarely fanned (one strikeout every 15.3 at-bats).

No. 14 Carl Boles—Served two years in the Navy in the late '50s. Never appeared in the majors after 1962, suffering a broken leg during spring training in '63. Played six seasons in Japan and hit 117 home runs.

No. 7 Harvey Kuenn—Won AL batting title in 1959 (.353) with Detroit, then traded to Cleveland for Rocky Colavito. A lifetime .303 hitter, led the American League in hits four times and in doubles three times. Rookie of the Year in 1953 with Tigers.

No. 24 Willie Mays—Inducted into Hall of Fame in 1979. Won two Most Valuable Player awards (1954, '65) and finished runner-up twice. Named to twenty All-Star teams. Ranks third among position players in career Wins above Replacement (WAR) metric.

No. 44 Willie McCovey—Inducted into Hall of Fame in 1986. *The New Bill James Historical Baseball Abstract* listed him as ninth-best first baseman in MLB history. Finished with 521 home runs, same total as Ted Williams and Frank Thomas.

No. 20 Bob Nieman—Homered in his first two major league at-bats as a member of the St. Louis Browns in September of 1951. Later bunted for a base hit to cap a 3-for-5 debut. Lifetime .295 hitter over twelve seasons.

Chapter Notes

Introduction

1. Peter Golenbock, *Dynasty: The New York Yankees 1949–1964* (New York: Berkley, 1975), 489.
2. *Ibid.*
3. John Tullius, *I'd Rather Be a Yankee* (New York: Jove Books, 1986), 288.
4. *Ibid.*, 287.
5. 1962 10/16 World Series G7 SF Giants vs NY Yankees Candlestick Park, *YouTube*, 2:34:06, posted January 16, 2017, https://www.youtube.com/watch?v=tMwIgUNLdwU&index=21&list=PLAlDA2cK3weTcC26mfDxP8RCVp5nGmS6q.
6. Golenbock, *Dynasty*, 394.
7. Yogi Berra and Tom Horton, *Yogi: It Ain't Over Yet* (New York: Harper Paperbacks, 1989), 20.
8. 1962 10/16 World Series G7 SF Giants vs NY Yankees Candlestick Park, *YouTube*, 2:34:06, posted January 16, 2017, https://www.youtube.com/watch?v=tMwIgUNLdwU&index=21&list=PLAlDA2cK3weTcC26mfDxP8RCVp5nGmS6q.
9. Wade Kapszukiewicz, "Golden Pitches," *Baseball Research Journal* (Spring 2016): 7.

Chapter One

1. "New York Yankee Quotations," baseball-almanac.com, https://www.baseball-almanac.com/teams/yankquot.shtml.
2. Joseph L. Reichler, *Baseball Encyclopedia Seventh Edition* (New York: Macmillan, 1988), 2508.
3. Dave Anderson, *The New York Times Story of the Yankees* (New York: Black Dog and Leventhal, 2012), 250.
4. Jane Leavy, *The Last Boy: Mickey Mantle and the End of America's Childhood* (New York: HarperCollins, 2010), 225.
5. Tom Clavin and Danny Peary, *Roger Maris, Baseball's Reluctant Hero* (New York: A Touchstone Book, 2010), Chapter 28, loc. 292 of 486, Nook.
6. Tony Kubek and Terry Pluto, *Sixty-One: The Team, The Record, The Men* (New York: Macmillan, 1987), 35.
7. *Ibid.*, 36.
8. Murray Olderman, "Maris in 1962: How Many?" *NBC Baseball* (1962), 49.
9. *Ibid.*, 50.
10. Dan Daniel, "Army Corrects False Report of Early Releases," *The Sporting News* (May 2, 1962), 24.
11. Til Ferdenzi, "Hector Shakes Off 'Handcuffs'; Takes Hefty Cut at Horsehide," *The Sporting News* (April 11, 1962), 11.
12. Jimmy Piersall and Richard Whittingham, *The Truth Hurts* (Chicago: Contemporary Books, 1985), 47.
13. Murray Olderman and Blackie Sherrod, "American League Preview, New York Yankees," *NBC Baseball* (1962), 14.
14. Til Ferdenzi, "Yanks Dish Up Fast Razzberry for Gabe's 'Complacency' Rap," *The Sporting News* (March 21, 1962), 9.
15. *Ibid.*
16. Ralph Houk and Robert W. Creamer, *Season of Glory: The Amazing Saga of the 1961 New York Yankees* (New York: G.P. Putnam's Sons, 1988), 19.
17. *Ibid.*, 20.
18. *Ibid.*, 22.
19. Mickey Mantle, *The Quality of*

Courage: True Stories of Heroism and Bravery (New York: Bantam Books, 1964), 111.
20. Golenbock, *Dynasty*, 400.
21. Whitey Ford and Phil Pepe, *Slick: My Life in and Around Baseball* (New York: Dell, 1987), 165.
22. Mantle, *The Quality of Courage*, 114.
23. Ford and Pepe, *Slick*, 164.
24. Kubek and Pluto, *Sixty-One*, 74.
25. Associated Press, "Chisox Slug Reds, 8–4; Braves Nip Tribe, 4–3," *Toledo Blade* (April 7, 1962), 15.
26. 1962 New York Yankees Statistics, *baseball-reference.com*, https://www.baseball-reference.com/teams/NYY/1962.shtml.
27. Til Ferdenzi, "Yank Hurlers Ride Up 'n' Down Trail with Arroyo Out of Action," *The Sporting News* (May 23, 1962), 9.
28. Leavy, *The Last Boy*, 236.
29. Mickey Mantle, *The Education of a Baseball Player* (New York: Pocket Books, 1967), 135.
30. Leavy, *The Last Boy*, 236.
31. Daniel Okrent and Steve Wulf, *Baseball Anecdotes* (New York: Oxford University Press, 1989), 271.
32. Pat Jordan, "Once He Was an Angel," *Sports Illustrated* (March 28, 1994).
33. Danny Peary, *We Played the Game* (New York: Black Dog and Leventhal, 1994), 550.
34. Gregory H. Wolf, "Bo Belinsky," *sabr.org*, https://www.sabr.org/bioproj/person/bo-belinsky/.
35. Dan Daniel, "Houk Cites Top Surprises of Tight Race," *The Sporting News* (October 13, 1962), 3–4.
36. 1962 New York Yankees Statistics, *baseball-reference.com*, https://www.baseball-reference.com/teams/NYY/1962.shtml.
37. Til Ferdenzi, "Ho Hum—Bomber Clubhouse Quiet After Pennant Clincher," *The Sporting News* (October 6, 1962), 14.
38. *Ibid.*

Chapter Two

1. Josh Leventhal, *Take Me Out to the Ballpark* (New York: Black Dog and Leventhal, 2000), 114.
2. Lowell Reidenbaugh and Craig Carter, *The Sporting News Take Me Out to the Ball Park Second Edition* (St. Louis: The Sporting News Publishing Company, 1987), 167.
3. Steve Bitker, *The Original San Francisco Giants: The Giants of '58* (Champaign, Illinois: Sports Publishing, 1998), Part One, loc. 38 of 542, Nook.
4. Reidenbaugh and Carter, *TSN Take Me Out to the Ball Park*, 260.
5. "Franchise timeline," *mlb.com*, https://www.mlb.com/giants/history/timeline-1960s/.
6. *Ibid.*
7. *Ibid.*
8. Charles Einstein, *Willie's Time: A Memoir of Another America* (New York: Berkley Books, 1979), 105.
9. Reidenbaugh and Carter, *TSN Take Me Out to the Ball Park*, 263.
10. "Psychologist Hutch Sees Ill Wind Buffeting Giants," *The Sporting News* (March 28, 1962), 29.
11. Reidenbaugh and Carter, *TSN Take Me Out to the Ball Park*, 263.
12. "The Ballparks: Candlestick Park," *thisgreatgame.com*, https://www.thisgreatgame.com/ballparks-candlestick-park/.
13. "Franchise Timeline," *mlb.com*, https://www.mlb.com/giants/history/timeline-1960s/.
14. *Ibid.*
15. Bob Verdi, "Candlestick Park Makes NL Playoffs a Chilling Drama," *Chicago Tribune* (October 11, 1987).
16. Ron Fimrite, "Jack Jumps All Over Candlestick," *Sports Illustrated* (August 23, 1982), 16.
17. Rich Westcott, *Diamond Greats: Profiles and Interviews with 65 of Baseball's History Makers* (Westport, Connecticut: Meckler Books, 1988), 140.
18. Okrent and Wulf, *Baseball Anecdotes*, 225.
19. Willie Mays and Lou Sahadi, *Say Hey: The Autobiography of Willie Mays* (New York: Pocket Books, 1988), 160.
20. *Ibid.*
21. Murray Olderman and Blackie Sherrod, "National League Preview, San Francisco Giants," *NBC Baseball* (1962), 62.
22. Bob Burnes, "N.L. Primed for All-Time Boom at Gate," *The Sporting News* (April 11, 1962), 1, 4.

23. Bob Stevens, "Marichal, O'Dell Sanford Pegged Giants' Big Three," *The Sporting News* (April 11, 1962), 27.
24. *Ibid.*
25. *Ibid.*
26. Jack McDonald, "Kid Keystoner Hiller Greased Lightning in Field, Steady at Dish," *The Sporting News* (June 2, 1962), 17.
27. "Choke Rap Helped Inspire Giants to Sweep of Series," *The Sporting News* (August 24, 1962), 3.
28. Joe King, "Juan Gives Frisco Whiff of W.S. Moola," *The Sporting News* (August 24, 1962), 3.
29. George Vecsey, *The Baseball Life of Sandy Koufax* (New York: Scholastic Book Services, 1968), 74.
30. Mays and Sahadi, *Say Hey*, 179.
31. Reichler, *Baseball Encyclopedia Seventh Edition*, 622.
32. Duke Snider and Bill Gilbert, *The Duke of Flatbush* (New York: Zebra Books, 1988), 282.
33. *Ibid.*, 281.
34. Rich Marazzi and Len Fiorito, *Baseball Players of the 1950s: A Biographical Dictionary of All 1,560 Major Leaguers* (Jefferson, North Carolina: McFarland, 2004), 109.
35. Tom C. Brody, "A Giant Shot That Forced a Playoff," *Sports Illustrated* (October 8, 1962), 18–19.
36. *Ibid.*
37. Mel Bowen, "Willie Mays Nonchalant; Other SF Players Jubilant," *Santa Cruz Sentinel* (October 1, 1962), 10.
38. *Ibid.*
39. Gavin Scott, "Troops Fire Over Heads of Rioters," *Santa Cruz Sentinel* (October 1, 1962), 1.
40. Debbie Elliott, "Ole Miss Students Look Back at Integration," npr.org (October 1, 2012), https://www.npr.org/2012/10/01/162083705/ole-miss-students-look-back-at-integration/.
41. Gavin Scott, "Troops Fire Over Heads of Rioters," *Santa Cruz Sentinel* (October 1, 1962), 1.
42. "JFK Said He Had No Choice but to Take Action in Miss.," Associated Press, *Santa Cruz Sentinel* (October 1, 1962), 1.
43. "50–50 For Schirra's Flight," Associated Press, *Santa Cruz Sentinel* (October 1, 1962), 1.

Chapter Three

1. Jack McDonald, "Jocko Shouts 'Foul' Over Giant Sand Bar," *The Sporting News* (October 13, 1962), 7.
2. *Ibid.*
3. Noel Hynd, "Found: Charming 2BR, 1BTH APT, in The Leftfield Stands, Polo Grounds," *Sports Illustrated* (October 20, 1986), 5.
4. Jack McDonald, "Jocko Shouts 'Foul' Over Giant Sand Bar," *The Sporting News* (October 13, 1962), 7.
5. Vecsey, *The Baseball Life of Sandy Koufax*, 79.
6. *The Sporting News* (October 13, 1962), 8.
7. *Ibid.*
8. Charles Maher, "Fairly Happy; Williams, Too," Associated Press, *San Bernardino Sun* (October 3, 1962), A-9.
9. *Ibid.*
10. *The Sporting News* (October 13, 1962), 8.
11. Jack Stevenson, "Dark Says Ump Gave Safe Sign," Associated Press, *San Bernardino Sun* (October 3, 1962), A-9.
12. *Ibid.*
13. Bob Hunter, "Giants Plunge L.A. Fans into Smog of Defeat," *The Sporting News* (October 13, 1962), 8.
14. Jim Becker, "Alston Sees More Runs Today," Associated Press, *San Bernardino Sun* (October 3, 1962), A-9.
15. *Ibid.*, A-10.
16. Mel Bowen, "Dodgers Rally From 5–0 Deficit to Post 8–7 Win," *Santa Cruz Sentinel* (October 3, 1962), 11.
17. Gaylord Perry and Ed Linn, *Me & the Spitter* (New York: Signet Books, 1974), 112–113.
18. Ralph Dighton, "President Phones Spaceman Schirra," *San Bernardino Sun* (October 4, 1962), A-2.
19. Associated Press, "Meredith to Leave Campus for Weekend," *San Bernardino Sun* (October 4, 1962), A-1, A-5.
20. Paul Hirsch, "Ed Roebuck," sabr.org, https://www.sabr.org/bioproj/person/ed-roebuck/.
21. *Ibid.*
22. Mays and Sahadi, *Say Hey*, 189.
23. Leo Durocher and Ed Linn, *Nice Guys Finish Last* (New York: Simon & Schuster, 1975), 19.
24. Rob Neyer, *Rob Neyer's Big Book*

of Baseball Blunders (New York: Fireside Books, 2006), 115.

25. Paul Hirsch, *Ed Roebuck*, https://www.sabr.org/bioproj/person/ed-roebuck/.

26. Peary, *We Played the Game*, 537.

27. Jack Stevenson, "'This Team Kept Bouncing Back,'" *San Bernardino Sun* (October 4, 1962), D-2.

28. Bill Plaschke, "Stan Williams Says He's Gotten Over Blowing a Pennant-Clinching Save in 1962, But He Believes It Made Him an Outcast with Dodgers," *Los Angeles Times* (August 25, 2018).

29. *Ibid*.

30. John Drebinger, "Giants Win Playoff, 6–4, in 9th; Oppose Yanks in Series Today," *New York Times* (October 4, 1962).

31. Snider and Gilbert, *The Duke of Flatbush*, 286.

32. Durocher and Linn, *Nice Guys Finish Last*, 21.

33. "Playoff Pearls," *The Sporting News* (October 13, 1962), 10.

34. Jack McDonald, "50,000 Hail Heroes at 'Frisco Airport," *The Sporting News* (October 13, 1962), 7.

35. Mel Bowen, "Sideline Sidelites," *Santa Cruz Sentinel* (October 4, 1962), 12.

36. Tony Hayes, "He Was a Giant? Carl Boles and the Case of Mistaken Identity," https://www.sportsradioservice2013.wordpress.com/. (April 25, 2020).

37. Jack McDonald, "50,000 Hail Heroes at 'Frisco Airport," *The Sporting News* (October 13, 1962), 7.

38. *Ibid*.

39. Frank Jordan, "A History-Making Ride From 1958 to 2011: San Francisco's World Champion Giants," (March 30, 2011), https://www.mayorfrank.wordpress.com/.

Chapter Four

1. "Dodgers 6–5 Pick Today," *San Bernardino Sun* (October 3, 1962), A-9.

2. Huston Horn, "It's the Yankees vs. the West," *Sports Illustrated* (October 1, 1962), 20–21.

3. "Tough Grind for NL Champs," *The Sporting News* (October 13, 1962), 12.

4. Bob Addie, "Addie's Atoms," *The Sporting News* (October 13, 1962), 14.

5. Nancy Snell Griffith, "Billy O'Dell," *sabr.org*, https://www.sabr.org/bioproj/person/billy-odell/.

6. *Ibid*.

7. "Dark Assures O'Dell He'll 'See Action,'" United Press International, *Monessen (PA) Valley Independent* (December 23, 1961), 12.

8. Peary, *We Played the Game*, 560.

9. Mel Bowen, "Boyer Thrilled by Tie-Breaking HR," *Santa Cruz Sentinel* (October 5, 1962), 7.

10. Joseph Wancho, "Clete Boyer," *sabr.org*, https://www.sabr.org/bioproj/person/clete-boyer/.

11. Bobby Richardson and David Thomas, *Impact Player: A Memoir* (Carol Stream, Illinois: Tyndale House, 2012), 281.

12. Golenbock, *Dynasty*, 502.

13. *Ibid.*, 503.

14. *The Sporting News* (October 27, 1962), 21.

15. *Ibid*.

16. Mel Bowen, "Boyer Thrilled by Tie-Breaking HR," *Santa Cruz Sentinel* (October 5, 1962), 7.

17. *Ibid*.

18. *The Sporting News* (October 27, 1962), 21.

19. "Meredith Has His Breakfast Without Incident at Cafeteria," Associated Press, *Santa Cruz Sentinel* (October 5, 1962), 1.

20. *Ibid*.

Chapter Five

1. *The Sporting News* (October 27, 1962), 22.

2. Warren Corbett, "Jack Sanford," *sabr.org*, https://www.sabr.org/bioproj/person/jack-sanford-2/.

3. Allen Lewis, "Phillies' Sanford Ten Years Making Majors," *The Sporting News* (July 31, 1957), 5–6.

4. Boston Red Sox Roster, *Street & Smith's 1963 Baseball Yearbook* (1963), 79.

5. Allen Lewis, "Phillies' Sanford Ten Years Making Majors," *The Sporting News* (July 31, 1957), 5–6.

6. *Ibid*.

7. Single-Season Leaders and Records for Home Runs, *baseball-reference.com*, https://www.baseball-reference.com/leaders/HR_p_season.shtml/.
8. *The Sporting News* (October 27, 1962), 22.
9. Bob Stevens, "Cepeda, Pagan Given Red Light on Winter Ball Plans," *The Sporting News* (October 6, 1962), 8.
10. Eric Aron, "Alvin Dark," *sabr.org*, https://www.sabr.org/bioproj/person/alvin-dark/.
11. Mays and Sahadi, *Say Hey*, 225.
12. Einstein, *Willie's Time*, 188.
13. Mays and Sahadi, *Say Hey*, 225.
14. Jeff Neuman, "Man Out of Time: The Life of Alvin Dark," *theaposition.com* (November 14, 2014), https://theaposition.com/neumanprose/golf/personalities/903/man-out-of-time-the-life-of-alvin-dark/.
15. *The Sporting News* (October 27, 1962), 22.
16. *Ibid.*
17. Ted Smits, "Yankees Take Setback Calmly; Figure Terry Pitched Well, Too," Associated Press, *Schenectady Gazette* (October 6, 1962), 32.
18. Ted Smits, "Houk Praises Hurling, Eager for Home Games," Associated Press, *San Bernardino Sun* (October 6, 1962), A-15.
19. *The Sporting News* (October 27, 1962), 22.
20. "1962 World Series," *New York Yankees Vintage World Series Films* (A&E Home Video, 2006).
21. Ted Smits, "Houk Praises Hurling, Eager for Home Games," Associated Press, *San Bernardino Sun* (October 6, 1962), A-15.
22. "Giants Pull Even on Classy 3-Hit Blank Job by Sanford," *The Sporting News* (October 27, 1962), 22.
23. *The Sporting News* (October 27, 1962), 22.
24. *Ibid.*
25. *Ibid.*
26. Jim Becker, "Shaky Hands Didn't Spoil Jack Sanford's Big Day," Associated Press, *San Bernardino Sun* (October 6, 1962), A-15.
27. Ted Smits, "Houk Praises Hurling, Eager for Home Games," Associated Press, *San Bernardino Sun* (October 6, 1962), A-15.
28. *The Sporting News* (October 27, 1962), 22.

Chapter Six

1. Philip J. Lowry, *Green Cathedrals: Fifth Edition* (Phoenix: Society for American Baseball Research, 2019), loc. 445 of 679, iBook.
2. Geoffrey C. Ward and Ken Burns, *Baseball: An Illustrated History* (New York: Alfred A. Knopf, 1994), 169.
3. Jack Hand, "Pierce vs. Stafford in New York," Associated Press, *Santa Cruz Sentinel* (October 7, 1962), 13.
4. Jack Stevenson, "Giants at Best Physical Condition in Last Month," Associated Press, *Santa Cruz Sentinel* (October 7, 1962), 13.
5. "Rival Pitchers Become Fathers," Associated Press, *Santa Cruz Sentinel* (October 7, 1962), 13.
6. *Ibid.*
7. Jack Stevenson, "Giants Ponder Hop, Mistake," Associated Press, *San Bernardino Sun* (October 8, 1962), A-12.
8. *The Sporting News* (October 27, 1962), 23.
9. Jerome Holtzman, "Maris Heard Only the Boos," *Chicago Tribune* (December 17, 1985).
10. *Ibid.*
11. *Ibid.*
12. *The Sporting News* (October 27, 1962), 23.
13. Jack Stevenson, "Giants Ponder Hop, Mistake," Associated Press, *San Bernardino Sun* (October 8, 1962), A-12.
14. *Ibid.*
15. "Stafford Almost Fainted When Hit on Shin by Drive," *The Sporting News* (October 27, 1962), 23.
16. *Ibid.*
17. *The Sporting News* (October 27, 1962), 23.
18. *Ibid.*
19. Jack Stevenson, "Giants Ponder Hop, Mistake," Associated Press, *San Bernardino Sun* (October 8, 1962), A-12.
20. Ted Smits, "Stafford Stayed In," Associated Press, *San Bernardino Sun* (October 8, 1962), A-12.
21. *Ibid.*
22. Dan McHale, "Bill Stafford," *sabr.org*, https://www.sabr.org/bioproj/person/bill-stafford/.

23. Dom Forker, *Sweet Seasons: Recollections of the 1955–64 New York Yankees* (Dallas: Taylor, 1990), 147.

Chapter Seven

1. Jan Finkel, "Juan Marichal," *sabr.org*, https://www.sabr.org/bioproj/person/juan-marichal/.
2. *Ibid.*
3. Edward Kiersh, *Where Have You Gone, Vince DiMaggio?* (New York: Bantam Books, 1983), 119.
4. "I shot the cruelest dictator in the Americas," *bbc.com* (May 27, 2011), https://www.bbc.com/news/world-latin-america-13560512/.
5. Kiersh, *Where Have You Gone, Vince DiMaggio*, 119.
6. Jan Finkel, "Juan Marichal," *sabr.org*, https://www.sabr.org/bioproj/person/juan-marichal/.
7. *Ibid.*
8. Ed Attanasio, "The TGG Interview, Jim Davenport," *thisgreatgame.com*, https://www.thisgreatgame.com/jim-davenport/.
9. Jan Finkel, "Juan Marichal," *sabr.org*, https://www.sabr.org/bioproj/person/juan-marichal/.
10. "Weather Data," *Schenectady Gazette* (October 9, 1962), 1.
11. Alan Cohen, "Tom Haller," *sabr.org*, https://www.sabr.org/bioproj/person/tom-haller/.
12. *Ibid.*
13. *Ibid.*
14. Arthur Daley, "Sports of the Times: The Masked Intellectual," *The New York Times* (March 25, 1969).
15. Corey Stolzenbach, "Bobby Bolin," *sabr.org*, https://www.sabr.org/bioproj/person/bobby-bolin/.
16. *The Sporting News* (October 27, 1962), 24.
17. Charles F. Faber, "Don Larsen," *sabr.org*, https://www.sabr.org/bioproj/person/don-larsen/.
18. Earl Nash, "No Windup, Best Windup," *bosoxinjection.com* (December 5, 2013), https://www.bosoxinjection.com/2013/12/05/flamingo-forward/.
19. *The Sporting News* (October 27, 1962), 24.
20. Golenbock, *Dynasty*, 394.
21. Joe Reichler, "Grand Slam Climax to Up-Down Season," Associated Press, *Schenectady Gazette* (October 9, 1962), 20.
22. *The Sporting News* (October 27, 1962), 24.
23. Will Grimsley, "Tom Tresh Thrashes Giants 5–3 as Yankees Seize Lead," Associated Press, *San Bernardino Sun* (October 11, 1962), C5.
24. *The Sporting News* (October 27, 1962), 24.
25. *Ibid.*
26. *Ibid.*
27. Joe Reichler, "Dark, Houk Say Series Will Go Seven Games," Associated Press, *Santa Cruz Sentinel* (October 9, 1962), 11.
28. *Ibid.*
29. Jack Hand, "Haller-Hiller, Giants' Thriller," Associated Press, *Schenectady Gazette* (October 9, 1962), 20.
30. Joe Reichler, "Grand Slam Climax to Up-Down Season," *Schenectady Gazette* (October 9, 1962), 20.
31. Jack Hugerich, "Sanford 'Ready to Pitch' As Frisco Seeks First Lead," *Schenectady Gazette* (October 9, 1962), 20.
32. David E. Skelton, "Chuck Hiller," *sabr.org*, www.sabr.org/bioproj/person/chuck-hiller/.
33. Jim Sandoval and Bill Nowlin, *Can He Play?* (Phoenix: Society for American Baseball Research, 2011), Cy Slapnicka chapter, loc. 76 of 530, iBook.
34. Jack McDonald, "Battler Hiller Winning Fight for Giants' Job," *The Sporting News* (April 5, 1961), 11.
35. "Hiller Borrowed Extra-Light Bat," Associated Press, *San Bernardino Sun* (October 9, 1962), A-16.
36. *Ibid.*
37. Harvey Kuenn, "Giants' Harvey Kuenn Tells of Elation Over 'Old Charlie's' Grand Slam Homer," Associated Press, *Santa Cruz Sentinel* (October 9, 1962), 10.
38. Will Grimsley, "Houk Says It Was His Idea to Remove Ford in the Seventh," Associated Press, *San Bernardino Sun* (October 9, 1962), A15–16.
39. Jack Stevenson, "Hiller Got Pitch," Associated Press, *San Bernardino Sun* (October 9, 1962), A-15–16.
40. Will Grimsley, "Houk Says It Was His Idea to Remove Ford in the Seventh,"

Associated Press, *San Bernardino Sun* (October 9, 1962), A15–16.

41. *The Sporting News* (October 27, 1962), 24.

Chapter Eight

1. John P. Carvalho, *Frick*, *Baseball's Third Commissioner* (Jefferson, North Carolina: McFarland, 2016).
2. *Ibid.*
3. Jerome Holtzman, *No Cheering in the Press Box* (New York: Holt, Rinehart and Winston, 1973), 88.
4. Warren Corbett, "Ford Frick," sabr.org, https://www.sabr.org/bioproj/person/ford-frick/.
5. Chris Lamb, *Conspiracy of Silence* (Lincoln: University of Nebraska Press, 2012), 134.
6. William Marshall, *Baseball's Pivotal Era, 1945–1951* (Lexington: University Press of Kentucky, 1999), 426.
7. Ford C. Frick, *Games, Asterisks and People* (New York: Crown Publishing Group, 1973), 97–98.
8. Warren Corbett, "Ford Frick," sabr.org, https://www.sabr.org/bioproj/person/ford-frick/.
9. Bill Veeck and Ed Linn, *Veeck as in Wreck* (New York: Signet Books, 1962), 385.
10. Warren Corbett, "Ford Frick," sabr.org, https://www.sabr.org/bioproj/person/ford-frick/.
11. Eddie Jones, "Keeping Up with Eddie Jones," *Toledo Blade* (October 9, 1962), 40.
12. *Ibid.*
13. *Ibid.*
14. Arthur Daley, "Sports of the Times," *The New York Times* (October 3, 1971).
15. "Series Still Excites Frick After 41 Years," Associated Press, *Schenectady Gazette* (October 10, 1962), 26.
16. Eddie Jones, "Keeping Up with Eddie Jones," *Toledo Blade* (October 9, 1962), 40.
17. *Ibid.*
18. *Ibid.*
19. Jack Hand, "Sanford, Terry Still Fifth-Game Mound Selections," *Schenectady Gazette* (October 10, 1962), 26.
20. Jack Hand, "Rain Fails to Change Series Strategy," Associated Press, *San Bernardino Sun* (October 10, 1962), A-12, A-14.
21. Will Grimsley, "Terry Doesn't See Any Letdown," Associated Press, *San Bernardino Sun* (October 10, 1962), A-12.
22. "Most Giants Take Delay in Stride," Associated Press, *Schenectady Gazette* (October 10, 1962), 26.
23. *The Sporting News* (October 27, 1962), 25...
24. *Ibid.*
25. *Ibid.*
26. Thomas Van Hyning, *Puerto Rico's Winter League* (Jefferson, North Carolina: McFarland, 2004), 125.
27. Jack McDonald, "Pint-Sized Pagan Fitted for Giant-Sized Pay Boost," *The Sporting News* (October 27, 1962), 6.
28. *Ibid.*
29. *The Sporting News* (October 27, 1962), 25.
30. "We Played Badly Today: Dark," Associated Press, *Schenectady Gazette* (October 11, 1962), 40.
31. Bill James, *The New Bill James Historical Baseball Abstract* (New York: Free Press, 2001), 524.
32. Richardson and Thomas, *Impact Player*, 130.
33. *The Sporting News* (October 27, 1962), 25.
34. Jack Hugerich, "Sanford Down, But Not Beaten After Tough Loss," *Schenectady Gazette* (October 11, 1962), 40.
35. *The New York Times* (October 11, 1962).
36. "Old Mike's Proudest Moment," Associated Press, *Schenectady Gazette* (October 11, 1962), 41.
37. Walter Bingham, "Big Year for the Rookies," *Sports Illustrated* (April 2, 1962), 17.
38. Joseph Wancho, "Tom Tresh," sabr.org, https://www.sabr.org/bioproj/person/tom-tresh/.
39. Philip Bashe, *Dog Days: The New York Yankees' Fall from Grace and Return to Glory, 1964–1976* (New York: Random House, 1994), 95.
40. Joseph Wancho, "Tom Tresh," sabr.org, https://www.sabr.org/bioproj/person/tom-tresh/.
41. Til Ferdenzi, "Mighty Mite Bobby Hypos Yank Attack by Swinging Bigger Stick," *The Sporting News* (October 6, 1962), 14.

42. "The American League Managers' Secret Player Ratings," *Sport* (August 1963).
43. Jack Hugerich, "Sanford Down, But Not Beaten After Tough Loss," *Schenectady Gazette* (October 11, 1962), 40.
44. "Homer Hitting Hero Looking for a Single," Associated Press, *Schenectady Gazette* (October 11, 1962), 40.
45. Jack Hand, "Yanks Whip Giants, 5–3, on Tresh HR," Associated Press, *Schenectady Gazette* (October 11, 1962), 40.
46. "We Played Badly Today: Dark," Associated Press, *Schenectady Gazette* (October 11, 1962), 40.
47. *Ibid.*
48. *Ibid.*
49. "First Win, Second Baby Great Feeling for Terry," *Toledo Blade* (October 11, 1962), 41.
50. Bryan Curtis, "In Memoriam: Sportswriting Iconoclast Stan Isaacs," grantland.com (April 4, 2013), https://www.grantland.com/the-triangle/in-memoriam-sportswriting-iconoclast-stan-isaacs/.
51. *Ibid.*
52. "Homer Hitting Hero Looking for a Single," Associated Press, *Schenectady Gazette* (October 11, 1962), 40.
53. "Old Mike's Proudest Moment," Associated Press, *Schenectady Gazette* (October 11, 1962), 41.
54. *Ibid.*

Chapter Nine

1. "Fifty Years Later: Legacy of Columbus Day Storm Still Stands," oregonstate.edu (October 2, 2012), https://www.today.oregonstate.edu/archives/2012/oct/fifty-years-later-legacy-columbus-day-storm-still-stands/.
2. *Ibid.*
3. Julie Muhlstein, "Columbus Day Storm Revisited in New Book, 'A Deadly Wind,'" *Everett* (WA) *Daily Herald* (October 12, 2018), https://www.heraldnet.com/news/columbus-day-storm-revisited-in-new-book-a-deadly-wind/.
4. *Ibid.*
5. "The Columbus Day Storm 50th Anniversary," *Cliff Mass Weather Blog* (October 10, 2012), https://www.cliffmass.blogspot.com/2012/10/the-columbus-day-storm-50th-anniversary.html/.
6. Jack Hand, "Rain, Gale Winds Force Series Postponement," Associated Press, *Schenectady Gazette* (October 13, 1962), 19.
7. "Storms Lash West," YouTube.com, https://www.youtube.com/watch?v=FbEWC-I3KYo/.
8. "The Ultimate Game: 1962 Game Seven New York Yankees at San Francisco Giants," *Golden Baseball Magazine*, https://www.goldenrankings.com/ultimategame1962.html/.
9. "Rain Swells Potential of Giant Mound Staff," Associated Press, *Schenectady Gazette* (October 13, 1962), 19.
10. Jack Hand, "Ford Will Try to Wrap Up Series for Yankees," Associated Press, *Schenectady Gazette* (October 12, 1962), 28.
11. Forker, *Sweet Seasons*, 146.
12. "Rain Would Help Giants Says Houk, Yank Manager," Associated Press, *Schenectady Gazette* (October 12, 1962), 28.
13. "Hardy Giant Fans Wait All Night," Associated Press, *Schenectady Gazette* (October 13, 1962), 19.
14. Jack Hand, "6th Game Threatened Again by Weather," Associated Press, *Santa Cruz Sentinel* (October 14, 1962), 12.
15. *Ibid.*
16. *Ibid.*
17. Tom Loomis, "Rain Go Away, Our Little Tommy Wants to Play," *Toledo Blade* (October 15, 1962), 20.
18. Golenbock, *Dynasty*, 487.
19. Fred Lieb, "Wets Had High Old Time At 1911 Classic," *The Sporting News* (October 27, 1962), 5, 8.
20. *Ibid.*
21. *Ibid.*
22. Jack Hand, "Rain-Plagued Series Ready to Resume," Associated Press, *Schenectady Gazette* (October 15, 1962), 18.
23. *Ibid.*
24. Ken White, *Getaway Day* (Mustang, Oklahoma: Tate Publishing & Enterprises, 2014).
25. *Ibid.*
26. *Ibid.*
27. *Ibid.*
28. *The Sporting News* (October 27, 1962), 28.

Chapter Ten

1. *The Sporting News* (October 27, 1962), 26.
2. Red Smith, "Series Stalls Frick's Trip," *Calgary Herald* (October 16, 1962), 15.
3. *The Sporting News* (October 27, 1962), 26.
4. *Ibid.*
5. "1962 World Series," *New York Yankees Vintage World Series Films* (A&E Home Video, 2006).
6. *The Sporting News* (October 27, 1962), 26.
7. Joe Reichler, "Billy Pierce Squares Series with Three-Hitter," Associated Press, *Schenectady Gazette* (October 16, 1962), 20.
8. Chris Haft, "Giants Mourn Passing of Davenport," *mlb.com* (February 19, 2016), https://www.mlb.com/news/former-giants-player-jim-davenport-dies-at-82-c164932058/.
9. *Ibid.*
10. *Ibid.*
11. Jim Becker, "Good Pitched Game, We Didn't Hit: Houk," Associated Press, *Schenectady Gazette* (October 16, 1962), 20.
12. *The Sporting News* (October 27, 1962), 28.
13. Jim Becker, "Good Pitched Game, We Didn't Hit: Houk," Associated Press, *Schenectady Gazette* (October 16, 1962), 20.
14. Red Smith, "Series Stalls Frick's Trip," *Calgary Herald* (October 16, 1962), 15.
15. Cecilia Tan, "Elston Howard," SABR Biography Project, https://www.sabr.org/bioproj/person/elston-howard/.
16. *Ibid.*
17. *Ibid.*
18. Golenbock, *Dynasty*, 212.
19. Richardson and Thomas, *Impact Player*, 228.
20. Forker, *Sweet Seasons*, 183.
21. Jack Stevenson, "Cepeda, Pierce Are Giant Heroes," Associated Press, *Schenectady Gazette* (October 16, 1962), 20.
22. Joe Reichler, "Billy Pierce Squares Series with Three-Hitter," Associated Press, *Schenectady Gazette* (October 16, 1962), 20.
23. *Ibid.*
24. *The Sporting News* (October 27, 1962), 26.
25. Jim Becker, "Good Pitched Game, We Didn't Hit: Houk," Associated Press, *Schenectady Gazette* (October 16, 1962), 20.
26. *The Sporting News* (October 27, 1962), 26.
27. Jim Becker, "Good Pitched Game, We Didn't Hit: Houk," Associated Press, *Schenectady Gazette* (October 16, 1962), 20.
28. Jack Stevenson, "Cepeda, Pierce Are Giant Heroes," Associated Press, *Schenectady Gazette* (October 16, 1962), 20.
29. Jim Becker, "Good Pitched Game, We Didn't Hit: Houk," Associated Press, *Schenectady Gazette* (October 16, 1962), 20.
30. Leavy, *The Last Boy*, 210.
31. Mantle, *The Education of a Baseball Player*, 136.
32. Leavy, *The Last Boy*, 247.
33. Red Smith, "Series Stalls Frick's Trip," *Calgary Herald* (October 16, 1962), 15.
34. Jim Bouton and Leonard Schechter, *Ball Four* (New York: World, 1970), 4.
35. *The Sporting News* (October 27, 1962), 26.
36. "Jack Sanford Nervous; Still Has Cold," Associated Press, *Schenectady Gazette* (October 16, 1962), 20.
37. *Ibid.*
38. "World Series Odds 11–10 and Pick 'Em," Associated Press, *Schenectady Gazette* (October 16, 1962), 20.

29. Red Smith, "'Form' Says Nobody Will Win," *The Calgary Herald* (October 13, 1962), 8.
30. *Ibid.*

Chapter Eleven

1. *The Sporting News* (October 27, 1962), 26.
2. *The Sporting News* (October 27, 1962), 27.
3. 1962 10/16 World Series G7 SF Giants vs NY Yankees Candlestick Park, *YouTube*, 2:34:06, posted January 16, 2017,

https://www.youtube.com/watch?v=tMwIgUNLdwU&index=21&list=PLAlDA2cK3weTcC26mfDxP8RCVp5nGmS6q/.
 4. *The Sporting News* (October 27, 1962), 27.
 5. 1962 10/16 World Series G7 SF Giants vs NY Yankees Candlestick Park, *YouTube*, 2:34:06, posted January 16, 2017, https://www.youtube.com/watch?v=tMwIgUNLdwU&index=21&list=PLAlDA2cK3weTcC26mfDxP8RCVp5nGmS6q/.
 6. Mel Bowen, "Terry Thrilled but Title Is Old Hat for Yankees," *Santa Cruz Sentinel* (October 17, 1962), 6.
 7. Golenbock, *Dynasty*, 475.
 8. *Ibid.*, 478.
 9. "Nice Catch," Associated Press photo caption, *Schenectady Gazette* (October 17, 1962), 26.
 10. Jack Stevenson, "Glum Giants Tell Tales of Trouble," Associated Press, *San Bernardino Sun* (October 17, 1962), A-13.
 11. 1962 10/16 World Series G7 SF Giants vs NY Yankees Candlestick Park, *YouTube.com*, 2:34:06, posted January 16, 2017, https://www.youtube.com/watch?v=tMwIgUNLdwU&index=21&list=PLAlDA2cK3weTcC26mfDxP8RCVp5nGmS6q/.
 12. Jerome Holtzman, "Infield in or Back? How Wrong Choice Cost Giants Series," *Baseball Digest* (December/January 1962), 15–28,
 13. *The Sporting News* (October 27, 1962), 27.
 14. "No Regrets—Al," *Toledo Blade* (October 17, 1962), 51.
 15. Kubek and Pluto, *Sixty-One*, 67.
 16. *Ibid.*, 73.
 17. Joe Reichler, "Ralph Terry is Thankful for Second Opportunity," Associated Press, *Schenectady Gazette* (October 17, 1962), 27.
 18. Tullius, *I'd Rather Be a Yankee*, 287.
 19. *The Sporting News* (October 27, 1962), 27.
 20. Mike Mandel, *SF Giants—An Oral History* (Santa Cruz, California: self-published, 1979), 123.
 21. "1962 World Series," *New York Yankees Vintage World Series Films* (A&E Home Video, 2006).
 22. Tom Loomis, "Yanks Win Series on 'Terry-ific' Finish," *Toledo Blade* (October 17, 1962), 51.
 23. Jim Becker, "Ralph Terry Pitches Yankees to 20th World Championship," Associated Press, *Schenectady Gazette* (October 17, 1962), 26.
 24. "Mays' Hit Couldn't Plate Matty," Associated Press, *Schenectady Gazette* (October 7, 1962), 26.
 25. Richardson and Thomas, *Impact Player*, 136.
 26. "All Agree Lockman Acted Wisely in Stopping Alou," *The Sporting News* (October 27, 1962), 27.
 27. "Mays' Hit Couldn't Plate Matty," Associated Press, *Schenectady Gazette* (October 7, 1962), 26.
 28. Mays and Sahadi, *Say Hey*, 195–196.
 29. "All Agree Lockman Acted Wisely in Stopping Alou," *The Sporting News* (October 27, 1962), 27.

Chapter Twelve

 1. Tullius, *I'd Rather Be a Yankee*, 288.
 2. Richardson and Thomas, *Impact Player*, 137.
 3. 1962 10/16 World Series G7 SF Giants vs NY Yankees Candlestick Park, *YouTube.com*, 2:34:06, posted January 16, 2017, https://www.youtube.com/watch?v=tMwIgUNLdwU&index=21&list=PLAlDA2cK3weTcC26mfDxP8RCVp5nGmS6q/.
 4. Tullius, *I'd Rather Be a Yankee*, 288–289.
 5. Richardson and Thomas, *Impact Player*, 136–137.
 6. Forker, *Sweet Seasons*, 25.
 7. Tullius, *I'd Rather Be a Yankee*, 289.
 8. 1962 10/16 World Series G7 SF Giants vs NY Yankees Candlestick Park, *YouTube.com*, 2:34:06, posted January 16, 2017, https:/www.youtube.com/watch?v=tMwIgUNLdwU&index=21&list=PLAlDA2cK3weTcC26mfDxP8RCVp5nGmS6q/.
 9. Richardson and Thomas, *Impact Player*, 138.
 10. Jim Becker, "Ralph Terry Pitches Yankees to 20th World Championship," Associated Press, *Schenectady Gazette* (October 17, 1962), 26.
 11. Tom Loomis, "Yanks Win Series on 'Terry-ific' Finish," *Toledo Blade* (October 17, 1962), 51.

12. Richardson and Thomas, *Impact Player*, 137–138.
13. Til Ferdenzi, "Terry's Hill Pride Preceded Giant Fall," *The Sporting News* (October 27, 1962), 3.
14. "Grandma Sees Ralph Pitch," Associated Press, *Schenectady Gazette* (October 17, 1962), 26.
15. "Terry Wins Sports Car," Associated Press, *Schenectady Gazette* (October 17, 1962), 26.
16. "Mays' Hit Couldn't Plate Matty," Associated Press, *Schenectady Gazette* (October 7, 1962), 26.
17. *The Sporting News* (October 27, 1962), 28.
18. Kiersh, *Where Have You Gone, Vince DiMaggio?* 86.
19. "Mays' Hit Couldn't Plate Matty," Associated Press, *Schenectady Gazette* (October 7, 1962), 26.
20. Jim Becker, "Ralph Terry Pitches Yankees to 20th World Championship," Associated Press, *Schenectady Gazette* (October 17, 1962), 26.
21. Tom Loomis, "Yanks Win Series on 'Terry-ific' Finish," *Toledo Blade* (October 17, 1962), 51.
22. Harry Jupiter, "They're Not Laughing at McCovey Now," *Baseball Digest* (March 1963), 48.
23. Jim Becker, "Ralph Terry Pitches Yankees to 20th World Championship," Associated Press, *Schenectady Gazette* (October 17, 1962), 26.
24. "Yanks Excited, Praise Giants," *Toledo Blade* (October 17, 1962), 51.
25. "No Regrets—Al," *Toledo Blade* (October 17, 1962), 51.
26. "'Best-Pitched Series Game I Ever Saw' Says DiMag," *The Sporting News* (October 27, 1962), 27.
27. "The Greatest Says Yankee Vet," *Toledo Blade* (October 17, 1962), 51.
28. Frank Jordan, "A History-Making Ride From 1958 to 2011: San Francisco's World Champion Giants" (March 30, 2011), https://www.mayorfrank.wordpress.com/.
29. Richardson and Thomas, *Impact Player*, 138–139.
30. *The Sporting News* (October 27, 1962), 28.
31. "Crowd of Zero Welcomes NY," Associated Press, *Santa Cruz Sentinel* (October 17, 1962), 6.
32. David Vincent, "Al Barlick," SABR Biography Project, https://www.sabr.org/bioproj/person/al-barlick/.
33. Timothy Bella, "Willie McCovey, Charlie Brown, and the Moment That Wasn't in the 1962 World Series. Neither Could Forget It." *The Washington Post* (November 1, 2018).
34. Ibid.

Chapter Thirteen

1. Peter Collier and David Horowitz, *The Kennedys: An American Drama* (New York: Warner Books, 1984), 374.
2. Lewis Gulick, "Blockade of Cuba Ordered," Associated Press, *Schenectady Gazette* (October 23, 1962), 1.
3. Collier and Horowitz, *The Kennedys*, 376.
4. Lewis Gulick, "Blockade of Cuba Ordered," Associated Press, *Schenectady Gazette* (October 23, 1962), 1.
5. "The Cuban Missile Crisis, October 1962," history.state.gov, https://www.history.state.gov/milestones/1961-1968/cuban-missile-crisis/.
6. Ibid.
7. Sandy Grady, "The Missing Ingredient," *Baseball Digest* (December/January 1962), 12.
8. Jack McDonald, "Giants Sum Up Series: 'We'll Be Back,'" *The Sporting News* (October 27, 1962), 5–6.
9. Sandy Grady, "The Missing Ingredient," *Baseball Digest* (December/January 1962), 13.
10. Mantle, *The Education of a Baseball Player*, 136.
11. *The Sporting News* (October 27, 1962), 28.
12. Tullius, *I'd Rather Be a Yankee*, 287.
13. "World Series Gate Receipts," baseball-almanac.com, https://www.baseball-almanac.com/ws/wsshares.shtml/.
14. Wade Kapszukiewicz, "Golden Pitches," *Baseball Research Journal* (Spring 2016), 7–8.
15. Ibid.
16. Bruce Brown, "From the Sidelines," *San Bernardino Sun* (October 2, 1962), A-11.

Chapter Fourteen

1. Allen Lewis, "1963 Outlook: Only Players Changed; Flags Will Remain the Same," *Baseball Digest* (April 1963), 18.
2. Forker, *Sweet Seasons*, 24.
3. Golenbock, *Dynasty*, 496.
4. Tom Clavin and Danny Peary, *Roger Maris: Baseball's Reluctant Hero* (New York: Touchstone, 2010), Chapter 28, loc. 292 of 486, Nook.
5. "Maris Pegged Biggest Flop of '62 Season," *The Sporting News* (October 20, 1962), 14.
6. Leavy, *The Last Boy*, 257.
7. "Yogi Berra Quotes," *baseball-almanac.com*, https://www.baseball-almanac.com/quotes/quoberra.shtml/.
8. 1965 Baseball Draft, *baseball-almanac.com*, https://www.baseball-almanac.com/draft/baseball-draft.php?yr=1965/.
9. Bashe, *Dog Days*, 74.
10. *Ibid.*
11. Golenbock, *Dynasty*, 482.
12. Bashe, *Dog Days*, 74.
13. Forker, *Sweet Seasons*, 147.
14. Golenbock, *Dynasty*, 505.
15. Clavin and Peary, *Roger Maris*, Chapter 36, loc. 403 of 486, Nook.
16. Ford and Pepe, *Slick*, 239.
17. Bouton and Schechter, *Ball Four*, 9.
18. *Ibid.*, 398.
19. Cecilia Tan, "Elston Howard," SABR Biography Project, https://www.sabr.org/bioproj/person/elston-howard/.
20. Bashe, *Dog Days*, 94.
21. Leavy, *The Last Boy*, 273.
22. *Ibid.*, 282.
23. Mantle and Gluck, *The Mick*, 240.
24. Leavy, *The Last Boy*, 382.

Chapter Fifteen

1. Ed Prell, "National League Preview," *Street & Smith's 1963 Baseball Yearbook* (1963), 35–36.
2. George Girsch, "Preview—1964 Pennant Races," *Baseball Review* (1964), 19.
3. Enrique Rojas, "Hall of Fame Should Embrace Felipe Alou," *espn.com* (August 22, 2006), https://www.espn.com/mlb/columns/story?id=2556121/.
4. Felipe Alou and Peter Kerasotis, *Alou: My Baseball Journey* (Lincoln: University of Nebraska Press, 2018), ix.
5. Gary Livacari, "The Three Alou Brothers Make History," *baseballhistorycomesalive.com* (September 16, 2016), https://www.baseballhistorycomesalive.com/the-three-alou-brothers-make-history-all-three-in-the-same-outfield/.
6. Einstein, *Willie's Time*, 185.
7. "Giants Fire Dark; Franks Manager," *The Boston Globe* (October 5, 1964), 19.
8. "The TGG Interview: Herman Franks," *thisgreatgame.com* https://www.thisgreatgame.com/herman-franks/.
9. Joe Sargis, "Marichal's Eleventh Pitch," *Baseball Digest* (July 1966), 18–19.
10. Peary, *We Played the Game*, 599.
11. Darren Dunlap, "Recalling Ed Bailey's 'Exciting Life,'" *Knoxville News Sentinel* (March 26, 2007).
12. Alan Cohen, "Tom Haller," SABR Biography Project, https://www.sabr.org/bioproj/person/tom-haller/.
13. *Ibid.*
14. Dale Voiss, "Harvey Kuenn," SABR Biography Project, https://www.sabr.org/bioproj/person/harvey-kuenn/.
15. *Ibid.*
16. *Ibid.*
17. Bill Ryczek, "Revisiting the Cepeda-Sadecki Trade," SABR website, https://www.sabr.org/latest/ryczek-revisiting-the-cepeda-sadecki-trade/.
18. Ron Fimrite, "The Heart of a Giant," *Sports Illustrated Classic* (Fall 1991), 61.
19. Kiersh, *Where Have You Gone, Vince DiMaggio*, 276.
20. William Nack, "From Shame to Fame," *Sports Illustrated* (July 26, 1999), 76.
21. Mays and Sahadi, *Say Hey*, 268–269.
22. James, *The New Bill James Historical Baseball Abstract*, 860.
23. Tom FitzGerald, "A True Classic: Giants Stranded Winning Run in Heartbreaker," *San Francisco Chronicle* (June 22, 2007).
24. Anthony McCarren, "The Liner That Lingers," *New York Daily News* (June 24, 2007).
25. *Ibid.*
26. *Ibid.*
27. Richardson and Thomas, *Impact Player*, 139–140.
28. Kiersh, *Where Have You Gone, Vince DiMaggio*, 86.

29. *Ibid.*
30. Mark Armour, "Willie McCovey," SABR Biography Project, https://www.sabr.org/bioproj/person/willie-mccovey/.

Chapter Sixteen

1. "How a Gun Shot Impacted the Career of New York Yankee Pitcher Marshall Bridges," *baseballhistorian.blogspot.com* (July 9, 2017), https://www.baseballhistorian.blogspot.com/2017/07/how-gun-shot-impacted-career-of-new.html/.
2. Kubek and Pluto, *Sixty-One*, 194.
3. Bill Nowlin, "Rollie Sheldon," SABR Biography Project, https://www.sabr.org/bioproj/person/rollie-sheldon/.
4. Ted Bishop, "Baseball and Golf Helped Ex-Yankees Star Go the Distance," *morningread.com* (December 12, 2017), https://www.morningread.com/news-opinion/feature/2017-12-12/baseball-and-golf-help-ex-yankees-star-go-the-distance/.
5. Forker, *Sweet Seasons*, 26.
6. Berra and Horton, *Yogi: It Ain't Over*, 183–184.
7. Marty Appel, "National Pastime Museum: On deck circle equipment," *appelpr.com* https://www.appelpr.com/?page_id=3371/.
8. Forker, Sweet Seasons, 107.
9. Kubek and Pluto, *Sixty-One*, 198.
10. Thomas Van Hyning, "Jack Reed," SABR Biography Project, https://www.sabr.org/bioproj/person/jack-reed/.
11. "About the Dinner," *The Community of Verboort*, https://www.verboort.org/about-the-dinner/.
12. "San Francisco Giants Feature Report: Bob Garibaldi—Tale of Two Worlds (Series)," *sportsradioservice2013.wordpress.com* (June 1, 2017), https://www.sportsradioservice2013.wordpress.com/2017/06/01/san-francisco-giants-feature-report-bob-garibaldi-tale-of-two-worlds-series/.
13. Golenbock, *Dynasty*, 204.
14. Nancy Snell Griffith, "Billy O'Dell," SABR Biography Project, https://www.sabr.org/bioproj/person/billy-odell/.

Bibliography

Books

Anderson, Dave. *Story of the Yankees*. New York: Black Dog and Leventhal, 2012.

Bashe, Philip. *Dog Days: The New York Yankees' Fall from Grace and Return to Glory, 1964–1976*. New York: Random House, 1994.

Berra, Yogi, and Tom Horton. *Yogi: It Ain't Over*. New York: Harper, 1989.

Bitker, Steve. *The Original San Francisco Giants: The Giants of 1958*. Champaign, Illinois: Sports Publishing, 2011. Nook edition.

Bouton, Jim, and Leonard Schechter. *Ball Four*. New York: World Publishing, 1970.

Brown, Gene. *The Complete Book of Baseball*. New York: New York Times, 1980.

Carter, Craig. *Official World Series Records*. St. Louis: The Sporting News, 1981.

_____. *Take Me Out to the Ballpark, Second Edition*. St. Louis: The Sporting News, 1987.

Clavin, Tom, and Danny Peary. *Roger Maris: Baseball's Reluctant Hero*. New York: Touchstone, 2010.

Collier, Peter, and David Horowitz. *The Kennedys: An American Drama*. New York: Warner, 1984.

Deutsch, Jordan, Richard Cohen, Roland Johnson, and David Neft. *The Scrapbook History of Baseball*. Indianapolis: Bobbs-Merrill, 1975.

Durocher, Leo, and Ed Linn. *Nice Guys Finish Last*. New York: Simon & Schuster, 1975.

Einstein, Charles. *Willie's Time: A Memoir of Another America*. New York: Berkley, 1979.

Enders, Eric. *The Fall Classic: The Definitive History of the World Series*. New York: Sterling, 2007.

Ford, Whitey, and Phil Pepe. *Slick: My Life in and Around Baseball*. New York: Dell, 1987.

Ford, Whitey, Mickey Mantle, and Joseph Durso. *Whitey and Mickey: An Autobiography of the Yankee Years*. New York: Viking, 1977.

Forker, Dom. *Sweet Seasons: Recollections of the 1955–64 New York Yankees*. Dallas: Taylor, 1990.

Golenbock, Peter. *Dynasty: The New York Yankees 1949–1964*. New York: Berkley, 1975.

Houk, Ralph, and Robert Creamer. *Season of Glory: The Amazing Saga of the 1961 New York Yankees*. New York: G.P. Putnam's Sons, 1988.

James, Bill. *The Bill James Guide to Baseball Managers: From 1870 to Today*. New York: Diversion Books, 1997.

_____. *The New Bill James Historical Baseball Abstract*. New York: Free Press, 2001.

Kiersh, Edward. *Where Have You Gone, Vince DiMaggio?* New York: Bantam, 1983.

Kubek, Tony, and Terry Pluto. *Sixty-One: The Team, the Record, the Men*. New York: Macmillan, 1987.

Leavy, Jane. *The Last Boy*. New York: HarperCollins, 2010.

Leventhal, Josh. *Take Me Out to the Ballpark*. New York: Black Dog and Leventhal, 2000.

Lieb, Fred. *Baseball As I Have Known It*. New York: Grosset & Dunlap, 1977.

Lowry, Philip J. *Green Cathedrals*. Phoenix: Society for American Baseball Research, 2019.

Mantle, Mickey. *Mickey Mantle: The Education of a Baseball Player.* New York: Pocket Books, 1967.

____. *The Quality of Courage.* New York: Bantam, 1964.

Mantle, Mickey, and Herb Gluck. *The Mick: An American Hero.* New York: Jove Books, 1985.

Mays, Willie, and Lou Sahadi. *The Autobiography of Willie Mays.* New York: Pocket Books, 1988.

The New York Times Company. *Page One, 1896–1996.* New York: Galahad Books, 1996.

Neyer, Rob. *Rob Neyer's Big Book of Baseball Blunders.* New York: Fireside, 2006.

Okrent, Daniel, and Steve Wulf. *Baseball Anecdotes.* New York: Oxford University Press, 1989.

Peary, Danny. *We Played the Game.* New York: Black Dog and Leventhal, 1994.

Perry, Gaylord, and Bob Sudyk. *Me & the Spitter.* New York: Signet, 1974.

Piersall, Jimmy, and Richard Whittingham. *The Truth Hurts.* Chicago: Contemporary, 1984.

Reichler, Joseph. *The Baseball Encyclopedia: The Complete and Official Record of Major League Baseball, 7th Edition.* New York: Macmillan, 1988.

Richardson, Bobby, and David Thomas. *Impact Player.* Carol Stream, Illinois: Tyndale House, 2012.

Sandoval, Jim, and Bill Nowlin. *Can He Play?* Phoenix: Society for American Baseball Research, 2011. iBook edition.

Schirra, Wally, and Richard N. Billings. *Schirra's Space.* Annapolis, Maryland: Naval Institute Press, 2000.

Shatzkin, Mike. *The Ballplayers: Baseball's Ultimate Biographical Reference.* New York: William Morrow, 1990.

Siwoff, Seymour. *The Elias Book of Baseball Records.* New York: Seymour Siwoff, 2020.

Snider, Duke, and Bill Gilbert. *The Duke of Flatbush.* New York: Kensington, 1988.

Sugar, Bert Randolph, and Ken Samelson. *The Baseball Maniac's Almanac, 5th Edition.* New York: Skyhorse Publishing, 2019.

Thorn, John, Pete Palmer, and Michael Gershman. *Total Baseball, Seventh Edition.* Kingston, New York: Total Sports, 2001.

Tullius, John. *I'd Rather Be a Yankee.* New York: Jove Books, 1986.

Vecsey, George. *The Baseball Life of Sandy Koufax.* New York: Scholastic, 1968.

Veeck, Bill, and Ed Linn. *Veeck as in Wreck.* New York: Signet, 1962.

Ward, Geoffrey C., and Ken Burns. *Baseball: An Illustrated History.* New York: Alfred A. Knopf, 1994.

Westcott, Rich. *Diamond Greats: Profiles and Interviews with 65 of Baseball's History Makers.* Westport, Connecticut: Meckler, 1988.

Zminda, Don. *Go-Go to Glory: The 1959 Chicago White Sox.* Phoenix: Society for American Baseball Research, 2019.

Websites

www.appelpr.com
www.baseball-almanac.com
www.baseball-reference.com
www.baseballhistorian.com
www.baseballhistorycomesalive.com
www.bbc.com
www.bosoxinjection.com
www.cliffmass.blogspot.com
www.espn.com
www.goldenrankings.com
www.grantland.com
www.heraldnet.com
www.historicmodesto.com
www.history.state.gov/milestones
www.mayorfrank.com
www.morningread.com
www.npr.org
www.retrosheet.org
www.sabr.org
www.sfgiants.com
www.space.com
www.sportsradioservice2013.wordpress.com
www.statscrew.com
www.theaposition.com
www.thestormking.com
www.thisgreatgame.com
www.timesonline.com
www.today.oregonstate.edu/archives
www.vault.si.com
www.youtube.com

Periodicals

Baseball Digest
Baseball Research Journal

NBC Baseball magazine, 1962
The New York Yankees, Official 1964 Yankee Yearbook
New York Yankees Yearbook 1962
New York Yankees Yearbook 1964
The Sporting News
Sports Illustrated
Street & Smith's Baseball Yearbook, 1963.

Newspapers

Beaver County (PA) *Times*
Boston Globe
Calgary Herald
Chicago Tribune
Everett (WA) *Daily Herald*
Knoxville News Sentinel
Monessen (PA) *Valley Independent*
New York Daily News
New York Times
San Bernardino Sun
San Francisco Chronicle
Santa Cruz Sentinel
Schenectady Gazette
Toledo Blade

Index

Aaron, Hank 20
Adcock, Joe 20
Alexander, Grover 150
Allen, Bernie 15
Allen, Dick 170
Allen, Phog 13
Allison, Bob 17
Alou, Felipe 24, 28–30, 36, 38–39, 41, 44–45, 52, 59–61, 68, 71–72, 76, 77, 79, 92–93, 95, 100, 115–118, 121, 127–129, 133, 136, 161, 167, 174–175
Alou, Jesus 76, 161, 175
Alou, Matty 24, 28, 43, 59, 61, 71, 76, 81, 84, 92–93, 151, 161, 167, 175; profile 136–137
Alston, Walter 30–31, 36–38, 40, 42–46, 60
Amalfitano, Joe 28, 85
Ann-Margret 16
Arroyo, Luis 11, 15, 18–19, 127, 169–170
Ashe, Victor 164

Bailey, Ed 28, 32, 36, 39, 42–44, 52, 59, 69, 72, 77–78, 81, 100–101, 116, 123, 135–136, 149, 163–164, 174
Barber, Red 66, 155
Barlick, Al 95, 139–140, 144
Bauer, Hank 8, 143
Bavasi, Buzzie 31
Belinsky, Bo 16
Bennett, Tony 50
Berra, Yogi 4, 7–8, 11, 13, 15, 17–19, 58–59, 62, 64, 70, 81, 85, 108, 117–120, 125, 154, 165, 171, 174
Berry, Charlie 62
Blanchard, Johnny 4, 8, 11, 18, 62, 117–118, 125, 129, 132, 144, 156, 171
Blasingame, Don 85
Bochy, Bruce 167
Boles, Carl 47, 136, 175
Bolin, Bob 27–28, 39, 78–80, 173
Bolles, John 22
Borowy, Hank 125
Boudreau, Lou 85

Bouton, Jim 11, 17–18, 124, 127, 144, 154, 157, 170
Bowman, Doc 31
Bowman, Ernie 44–45, 82, 84, 174
Boyer, Clete 11, 14, 62, 70–71, 78–82, 95, 112, 115–117, 121–122, 128–130, 132–133, 136, 140–141, 155–156, 171; profile 53–54
Boyer, Cloyd 171
Boyer, Ken 171
Boyer, Vern 53
Brady, Tom 112
Branca, Ralph 4
Bridges, Marshall 12, 18, 81–82, 84–85, 95, 170
Brock, Lou 20, 164
Broglio, Ernie 32, 164
Brown, Edmund 21
Bruce, Bob 32
Bumgarner, Madison 167
Burdette, Lew 127
Burgess, Smoky 31
Burright, Larry 43, 45

Candlestick Park playing issues 21–23
Cepeda, Orlando 24, 28, 37–39, 42, 45, 52, 59–60, 68, 71, 77, 79, 92, 94, 96, 112, 116, 118, 122, 129
Chance, Dean 16
Chandler, Albert (Happy) 89
Christopher, George 21
Clark, Jack 23
Clemente, Roberto 173
Clevenger, Tex 12, 19, 167, 170
Clooney, George 104
Coates, Jim 11–12, 19, 81, 85, 95, 117–118, 121, 144, 167, 170
Cobb, Ty 31, 35, 89, 151
Colavito, Rocky 98, 175
Conlan, Jocko 35
Conley, Gene 57
Costas, Bob 159
Craft, Harry 33
Croix de Candlestick 23
Crosetti, Frank 13, 169

195

Index

Crystal, Billy 89
Cuban Missile Crisis 146–147

Daley, Bud 11, 18, 96, 129, 134–135, 139, 155, 170
Dalrymple, Clay 75
Dark, Alvin 24, 27–29, 33, 35, 38–40, 43, 46–47, 51, 54, 56, 62, 64–69, 75, 78, 80–81, 83–85, 91, 96–97, 100–101, 106–109, 111, 116, 122, 126, 130–131, 135–137, 143–144, 161–162, 164, 167, 172; profile 59–60
Davenport, Jim 28, 36, 38–39, 42–43, 45, 52–53, 62, 68, 70, 72, 76–77, 79, 81, 92–93, 95, 112, 118–119, 127–128, 130, 133, 135, 149, 161, 163, 167, 174; profile 116–117
Davis, Tommy 38, 42–43, 151
Davis, Willie 151
Dello, Kathie 103
DeMaestri, Joe 8, 115
Dickey, Bill 96, 119
DiMaggio, Joe 7, 13, 67, 123, 126
Ditmar, Art 51, 53
Downing, Al 154
Drysdale, Don 20, 30, 32, 37–38, 45, 151
Duffalo, Jim 27, 85, 111, 127, 173
Duren, Ryne 128
Durocher, Leo 40, 43–46

Edwards, Doc 156
Essick, Bill 13

Fairly, Ron 39, 43
Farrell, Dick (Turk) 32–33
Feeney, Charles (Chub) 22, 28, 110, 160, 165
Feller, Bob 85
Fishel, Bob 11
Ford, Gerald 156
Ford, Whitey 7, 11, 14–15, 50, 52, 54, 69, 75, 77–78, 81, 107, 111, 113, 115–118, 124, 153–154, 156, 165, 170
Fox, Charlie 165
Fraley, Oscar 9
Franks, Herman 162, 164
Frick, Ford 47, 87, 104, 108, 110–111, 114, 127–128; profile 88–90
Fuentes, Tito 162
Fullerton, Hugh 110

Gallo, Bill 112
Garagiola, Joe 58, 127–128
Garibaldi, Bob 111, 173
Gehrig, Lou 67, 144
Giambi, Jason 153
Gibson, Bob 32, 154, 166, 173
Gilbert, Andy 76
Giles, Warren 34
Gilliam, Jim (Junior) 33, 38–39, 42–43, 45
Glenn, John 9

Gomez, Lefty 13
Gomez, Ruben 20, 57
Gonder, Jesse 12
Goodman, Billy 33
Gordon, Joe 13
Griffey, Ken, Jr. 171
Groat, Dick 93

Hadley, Kent 8
Haller, Bill 77, 164
Haller, Frank 77
Haller, Tom 28, 38, 59, 61–62, 79, 85, 93, 95, 100, 112, 123, 129–130, 135, 163–164, 174; profile 77–78
Hamey, Roy 12, 108
Hamilton, Steve 170
Harkness, Tim 43
Hart, Jim Ray 161
Hearst, Patty 23
Hegan, Jim 169
Hegan, Mike 169
Heydler, John 88
Higgins, Mike 19
Hiller, Chuck 28–29, 36, 38, 42, 52, 60–62, 68, 70–71, 78, 82–84, 92–93, 95, 101, 111–112, 115–118, 127–130, 132, 134–136, 149–150, 160, 162, 174; profile 85
Hodges, Gil 123
Hodges, Russ 46
Holtzman, Jerome 130
Honochick, Jim 78, 81, 140
Hornsby, Rogers 9
Houk, Ralph 3–5, 10, 15, 17–18, 47, 50, 53, 58, 64, 71–73, 76, 81–82, 84, 91, 95–96, 98, 101, 107–109, 111, 115, 117–119, 121–125, 128, 130, 132, 134–135, 137–139, 142, 143, 153–155, 169; profile 12–14
Howard, Elston 3, 5, 8, 11, 52–54, 58, 67–68, 71, 82, 93, 116–118, 125–126, 128, 133, 135, 137–140, 149, 171; profile 119–120
Howard, Frank 39, 42–43
Hubbell, Carl 78
Huggins, Miller 67
Hutchinson, Fred 22

Isaacs, Stan 60, 101

Jackson, Al 174
James, Bill 151, 166
James, Charlie 31, 33
James, LeBron 112
Jansen, Larry 27, 172
Jeter, Derek 172
Jordan, Frank 47, 144

Kaat, Jim 17
Kaneda, Shoichi 92
Keane, Johnny 143, 155
Kell, George 4, 127–128, 130, 139–140

Index

Kennedy, John F. 34, 41, 146
Khrushchev, Nikita 26, 146
Killebrew, Harmon 17, 98
King, Clyde 163
Koufax, Sandy 29–30, 32, 36, 42, 49, 151
Kubek, Tony 11, 17–18, 52, 62, 68, 70–71, 77, 79, 85, 92, 94, 96–97, 100, 108, 112, 115–116, 121, 125, 127–128, 130, 134, 140, 144, 149, 153, 155–156, 171; profile 131–132
Kuenn, Harvey 28–29, 33, 36, 41–43, 53–54, 59, 67, 77–78, 82, 85, 112, 118, 121, 136, 149, 164, 174–175

LaBate, Joe 57
Landes, Stan 132
Landis, Kenesaw Mountain 88–90
Lane, Frank 9
Lanier, Hal 161–162
Larsen, Don 8, 28, 43, 67–68, 70, 85, 123, 133–134, 173; profile 80
Law, Vern 53
Leavy, Jane 123, 158
LeMay, Dick 39
Lewis, Joe E. 7
Lieb, Fred 110
Linz, Phil 11, 15, 18, 98, 124, 127, 171
Liston, Sonny 19
Lockman, Whitey 62, 137, 172
Long, Dale 18, 53–54, 58, 115, 117–118, 125, 171
Lopez, Hector 11, 15, 18, 117–118, 121, 123, 125, 129, 132, 167, 172
Louis, Joe 88
Louise, Tina 16

Mantle, Mickey 4, 7–9, 11–15, 17, 19, 52, 55, 60–62, 67–70, 77, 80, 89, 92–93, 95–96, 98, 100, 112, 115, 117, 121–122, 127, 129, 133–135, 143, 147–149, 154, 156, 158–159, 165, 170, 172–173; World Series history 123–124
Marichal, Juan 27, 29, 30, 40–43, 51, 59–60, 62, 77–78, 94, 107, 136, 160, 163, 165–167, 173–174; profile 75–76
Maris, Roger 8, 11, 24, 52, 60–62, 69, 72, 80, 82, 85, 89, 92, 93, 95, 100, 112, 116–118, 121, 123, 129, 135, 137, 139, 142, 147, 149, 153–156, 172; reaction to booing 70, 153; troubles with media 9–10
Marquard, Rube 124
Martin, Billy 128
Martinez, Pedro 161
Martinez, Tino 153
Mass, Cliff 104
Mathewson, Christy 124
Mattingly, Don 171
Mays, Willie 21, 24, 27–30, 32–33, 36, 38–41, 44–45, 47, 52–54, 58, 60, 67–68, 70–71, 78–79, 85, 91–92, 94, 104, 112,
115–118, 123–124, 127–130, 133–134, 136–138, 143, 147–150, 160, 163, 165–167, 174–175; profile 26
Mazeroski, Bill 4, 51, 81, 129, 142
McBride, Ken 16
McCormick, Mike 21, 27–28, 39, 111, 127, 151, 173
McCovey, Willie 24, 28–30, 38, 43–44, 59–61, 63, 68, 70–71, 75, 77, 92–96, 100–101, 117, 123, 127, 129, 133–134, 136–137, 139–140, 142–143, 147, 149–151, 160, 163, 165–168, 174–175
McDougald, Gil 53, 132
McGinnity, Joe (Iron Man) 125
McMillan, Roy 93
Meredith, James 34, 41, 55, 147
Miller, Stu 22–23, 27, 30–31, 33, 38, 100, 130, 158, 173
Mitchell, Dale 81
Modesto team workouts 111–112
Monday, Rick 155
Moon, Wally 38, 42
Moran, Billy 16
Morris, Jack 152
Moses, Wally 169
Murcer, Bobby 23
Mussolini, Benito 171

Nettles, Graig 54
Newhouser, Hal 125
Nieman, Bob 45, 47, 67, 81–82, 127, 175
1960 World Series 4, 14, 51, 53, 67, 81
1962 expansion 7
Nixon, Richard 21

O'Brien, Jack 47
O'Dell, Billy 27, 29, 32, 54, 67, 79, 83–85, 130, 134–135, 163, 173; profile 51–52
Oliver, Gene 33
O'Malley, Walter 31
Orsino, John 39–40, 174

Pagan, Jose 28–29, 32, 37–38, 42, 45, 52, 54, 59–60, 62, 70–71, 78–81, 92, 100–101, 112, 130–133, 135, 149, 160, 162, 174; profile 93–94
Pappas, Milt 164
Pascual, Camilo 17
Patterson, Floyd 19
Patterson, Red 31, 35
Paul, Gabe 12
Peanuts comic strip 145
Pearson, Albie 16
Pendleton, Jim 32
Pepitone, Joe 11, 15, 18, 153, 156
Perranoski, Ron 39, 45
Perry, Gaylord 39–40, 151, 165, 174
Phelon, Bill 110
Pierce, Billy 2, 27, 29, 36, 40, 45, 51, 67–68, 76, 80, 85, 101, 106–107, 113, 115, 117–118,

121–123, 146, 160, 163, 167, 173; history vs. Yankees 69
Piersall, Jimmy 12
Plank, Eddie 124
Plaskett, Elmo 31
Podres, Johnny 32–33, 41–42
Posey, Buster 167
Powell, Boog 154
Power, Vic 17

Radatz, Dick 57
Raitt, John 115
Ramos, Bombo 75
Ramos, Pedro 155
Reed, Jack 17, 118, 167, 172
Reniff, Hal 11, 19
Reynolds, Allie 7
Richardson, Bobby 11, 52, 61–62, 68, 70–71, 77, 79, 84–85, 92, 94–95, 100, 108, 112, 115–116, 120–121, 125, 127–128, 132–133, 135–137, 139–142, 144, 149–150, 156, 159, 167–168, 171; altered batting style 96
Rickey, Branch 76
Rigney, Bill 16, 26
Rivera, Mariano 166
Rizzuto, Phil 7, 119
Robinson, Bill 156
Robinson, Brooks 54, 154
Robinson, Frank 164
Robinson, Jackie 151, 161
Rodgers, Bob 16, 164
Roebuck, Ed 36, 38, 42–44
Rohr, Bill 157
Roseboro, Johnny 42, 44–45, 163
Roselli, Cappy 83
Runnels, Pete 19
Ruth, Babe 9, 50, 59, 67, 70, 88–89, 144, 164, 172

Sadecki, Ray 164–165
Sain, Johnny 128, 135, 169
Sandoval, Pablo 167
Sanford, Jack 27, 29, 32, 37–38, 51, 55, 60–64, 84, 91–98, 100, 106, 108, 125, 127–128, 130, 133, 144, 149, 173–174; profile 56–58
Schirra, Walter (Wally) 34, 41, 48, 147
Schmitt, Orville 47
Schoendienst, Red 123
Schofield, Dick 162
Schulz, Charles M. 145
Schwab, Matty 35, 104, 108, 110, 114–115, 127
Seals Stadium 20–22
Seaver, Tom 166
Shantz, Bobby 120
Sheehy, Pete 144
Sheldon, Roland 11, 15, 129, 156, 170
Sheppard, Bob 91

Sherry, Larry 45
Siebern, Norm 8, 68
Simmons, Curt 32
Sisler, Dave 57
Skowron, Bill (Moose) 8, 14, 52–55, 58, 67–68, 70–71, 78–81, 93, 95, 112, 115, 117–119, 121, 125, 130–133, 135, 140, 144, 153
Slapnicka, Cy 85
Slocum, Frank 114
Smith, Charlie 156
Smith, Jack 39
Smith, Mayo 57, 149
Smith, Red 113, 118, 124
Smith, Wendell 88
Snider, Duke 31, 38, 42–43, 46
Snider, Jimmy (the Greek) 49
Soares, Joe 71
Spahn, Warren 28
Spencer, Daryl 39–40
Stafford, Bill 11, 15, 50, 67–69, 71–72, 107, 129, 134–135, 139, 141, 156, 170; profile 73–74
Stallard, Tracy 9
Steinbrenner, George 155
Stengel, Casey 13–14, 29, 51, 53, 80, 94, 96, 119–120, 129, 132, 149
Stevens, Connie 16
Stoneham, Charles 21
Stoneham, Horace 21–22, 34, 59, 106, 162
Stottlemyre, Mel 154
Sullivan, Frank 57

Taylor, Tony 75
Terry, Ralph 3–5, 11, 15, 19, 50–51, 55, 58–59, 61–62, 64, 68, 81, 84, 92, 94–95, 107–108, 124, 127, 130, 133–137, 139–142, 144, 149–150, 154–155, 167, 170; profile 128–129
Terry, Rose 142
Thomas, Frank 175
Thomas, Lee 16
Thomas, Valmy 57
Thomson, Bobby 4, 40, 46, 172
Throneberry, Marv 8
Topps baseball cards 1, 66, 170
Tresh, Mike 97, 101–102
Tresh, Tom 2, 11, 15, 18, 49, 52, 60–62, 67, 69, 71–72, 77, 80, 84, 92–93, 95–96, 100–102, 112, 116, 121, 124–125, 127–129, 132–135, 143, 149, 153, 157, 172; profile 97–98
Trujillo, Rafael 76
Turley, Bob 17, 170
Turner, Jim 80
Typhoon Freda 103–106

Van Doren, Mamie 16
Veeck, Bill 89
Versalles, Zoilo 15

Wagner, Honus 151
Wagner, Leon 16
Walls, Lee 39, 45
Webb, Del 47, 111
Weiss, George 8
Wertz, Vic 26
Westrum, Wes 46, 172–173
White, Sue Ellen 104
Willey, Carlton 161
Williams, Stan 37, 44–46, 153

Williams, Ted 171, 175
Wills, Maury 31–32, 35, 39–43, 45, 89, 93, 151, 163
Wilson, Earl 57
Winchell, Walter 16
Womack, Dooley 155
Woods, Tiger 112

Yankee Stadium history 66–67

www.ingramcontent.com/pod-product-compliance
Ingram Content Group UK Ltd.
Pitfield, Milton Keynes, MK11 3LW, UK
UKHW042008140426
5217IPUK00015B/1049